"Now it came about in the four hundred and eightieth year after the sons of Israel came out of the land of Egypt, in the fourth year of Solomon's reign over Israel, in the month of Ziv which is the second month, that he began to build the house of the LORD" (1 Kings 6:1).

- Solomon became king in 970 BC and began building the temple in 966 BC.
- The year of the exodus = 1446 BC (966 + 480)

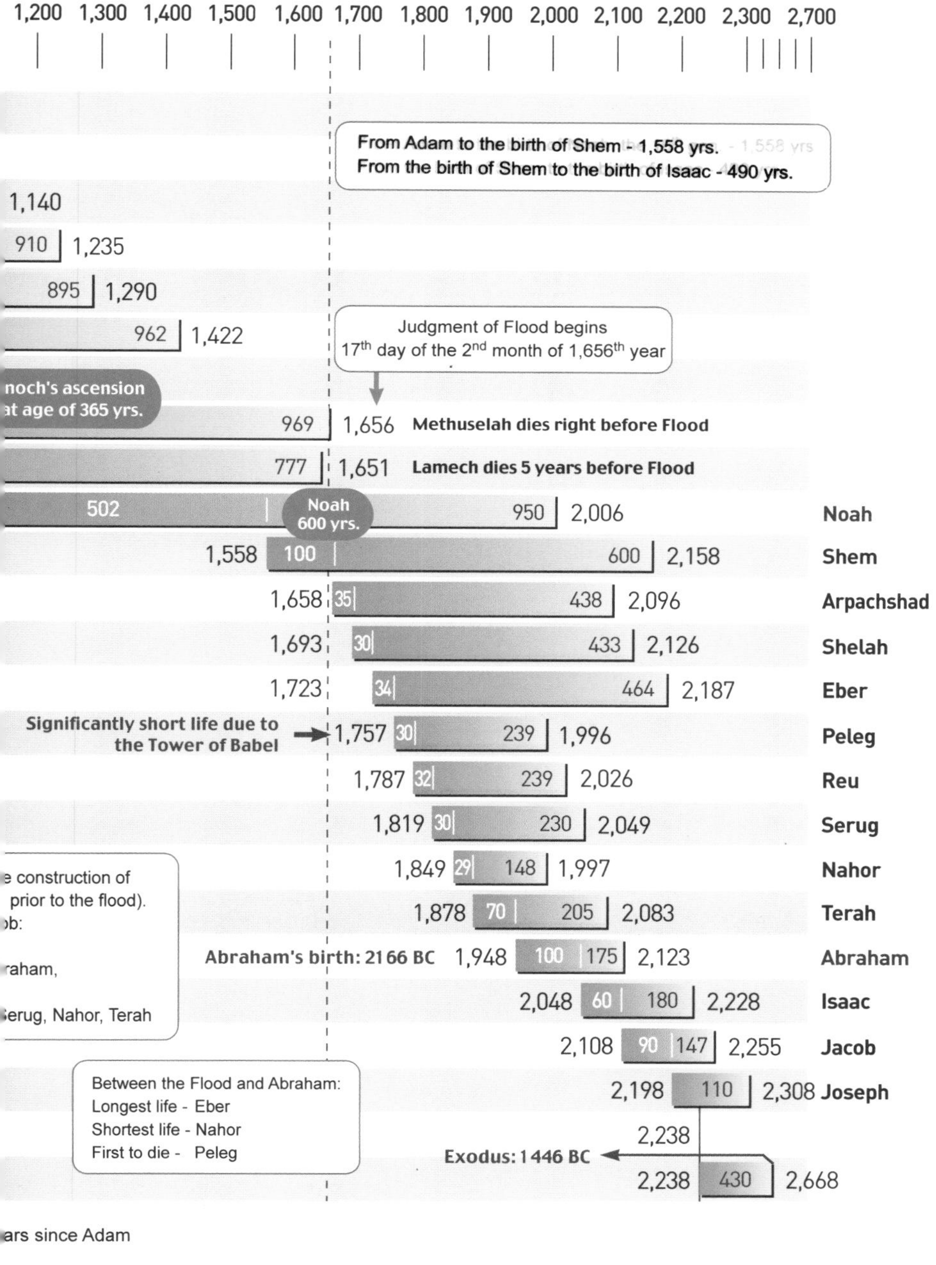

1,200 1,300 1,400 1,500 1,600 1,700 1,800 1,900 2,000 2,100 2,200 2,300 2,700

From Adam to the birth of Shem - 1,558 yrs.
From the birth of Shem to the birth of Isaac - 490 yrs.

1,140

910 1,235

895 1,290

962 1,422

Judgment of Flood begins
17th day of the 2nd month of 1,656th year

noch's ascension
at age of 365 yrs.

969 1,656 **Methuselah dies right before Flood**

777 1,651 **Lamech dies 5 years before Flood**

Born	Age at first son	Lifespan	Died	Name
	502 (Noah 600 yrs.)	950	2,006	**Noah**
1,558	100	600	2,158	**Shem**
1,658	35	438	2,096	**Arpachshad**
1,693	30	433	2,126	**Shelah**
1,723	34	464	2,187	**Eber**
1,757	30	239	1,996	**Peleg**
1,787	32	239	2,026	**Reu**
1,819	30	230	2,049	**Serug**
1,849	29	148	1,997	**Nahor**
1,878	70	205	2,083	**Terah**
1,948	100	175	2,123	**Abraham**
2,048	60	180	2,228	**Isaac**
2,108	90	147	2,255	**Jacob**
2,198		110	2,308	**Joseph**

Significantly short life due to the Tower of Babel → 1,757

Abraham's birth: 2166 BC

e construction of
prior to the flood).
ob:
raham,
erug, Nahor, Terah

Between the Flood and Abraham:
Longest life - Eber
Shortest life - Nahor
First to die - Peleg

2,238
Exodus: 1446 BC ←
2,238 430 2,668

ars since Adam

at death

** The years are based only on biblical accounts and estimations may vary slightly.*

The Genesis Genealogies

The Genesis Genealogies

God's Administration in the History of Redemption

by **Abraham Park, D. Min., D. D.**

PERIPLUS EDITIONS

Published by Periplus Editions (HK) Ltd., with editorial offices at 364 Innovation Drive, North Clarendon, Vermont 05759 USA and 61 Tai Seng Avenue, #02–12, Singapore 534167.

First Korean edition published by Huisun in 2007. www.pyungkang.com

Library of Congress Control Number: 2009926227
ISBN: 978-4-7946-0628-2

Distributed by:
North America, Latin America & Europe
Tuttle Publishing
364 Innovation Drive
North Clarendon, VT 05759-9436 U.S.A.
Tel: 1 (802) 773-8930
Fax: 1 (802) 773-6993
info@tuttlepublishing.com
www.tuttlepublishing.com

Asia Pacific
Berkeley Books Pte. Ltd.
61 Tai Seng Avenue #02-12
Singapore 534167
Tel: (65) 6280-1330
Fax (65) 6280-6290
inquiries@periplus.com.sg
www.periplus.com

Printed in Singapore

12 11 10 09
10 9 8 7 6 5 4 3 2

Contents

Foreword

All too often genealogies are viewed as uninteresting or, even worse, boring. But Dr. Abraham Park's new book, *The Genesis Genealogies: God's Administration in the History of Redemption*, demonstrates the great value and even excitement of an in-depth study of biblical genealogies. A strong foundation is necessary for any enduring structure. And so it is also true that the book of Genesis is a firm foundation for our biblical faith. Genesis not only is the groundwork for understanding our beginnings, but also it is the basis for understanding ourselves as well as our relationship to God and one another. One simply cannot overstate the importance of Genesis as the foundational paradigm for all Christian thinking. Dr. Abraham Park is to be congratulated for his important and worthy contribution to our understanding of this foundational book.

Dr. Park displays a remarkable facility with the Hebrew language. Time and again, his linguistic skills are on display. This indicates not only the seriousness of his research, but also his love for the book of Genesis. He has rightly understood that one cannot fully grasp God's work of salvation unless one digs deeply into the book of beginnings. The old adage that one cannot understand the future without first understanding the past holds true in biblical studies. Dr. Park takes this adage to heart in this remarkable book.

The biblical point of departure for Dr. Park is Deuteronomy 32:7, where the Song of Moses declares, "Remember the days of old, consider the years of all generations...." He carefully considers the ten genealogies of Genesis (of heaven and earth, of Adam, of Noah, of Noah's sons, of Shem, of Terah and Abraham, of Ishmael, of Isaac, of Esau, and of Jacob) and through each of these the history of redemption is clearly expounded. Dr. Park employs these genealogies, which find their ultimate expression in the work of Jesus Christ, to reveal the core of God's work of redemption in history.

There are several distinguishing features of Dr. Park's important book. First, it is a book suffused with Scripture. It is absolutely clear that Dr. Park loves the Bible, and it is obvious that he drinks deeply from the fountain of biblical study. Second, it has a clear evangelistic thrust. At many points the clear implication of his exposition is a warm invitation to embrace Jesus as Lord and Savior. Dr. Park, it would seem, has never lost sight of the Great Commission in Matthew 28:19-20. Third, I was delighted to see that he takes the historicity of the Genesis account seriously. In a day when many modern theologians cast doubt on the historicity of Adam, for example, it is refreshing to see a firm affirmation of historicity. Finally, the text is clearly and well written. The average reader will not get lost in technical jargon, but will indeed see the teaching of Scripture with ease.

This book is a sweeping vista of God's plan of redemption from Genesis down through the ages to its final expression in the person and work of Jesus Christ. Dr. Park's book is a journey worth taking. I heartily recommend this insightful work of Dr. Park for seminaries and colleges. I can assure readers that this book will not disappoint. Read it, study it, pray over it, and then put its wisdom to work in your life and ministry.

Dr. Frank A. James III, Ph.D., D.Phil.
President and Professor of Historical Theology
Reformed Theological Seminary/Orlando

Introduction

In the beginning God created the heavens and the earth.
—Genesis 1:1*

The Book of Genesis is called "The Book of the Beginning" because it is a record of the origin of the universe, the origin of man, the origin of the fall, and the commencement of God's work of salvation. At the same time, Genesis is also the introduction to the entire Bible and the blueprint of the history of salvation (Isa 46:10; 48:3).

The study of the basic foundation of Genesis, the genealogy of the generations (תּוֹלְדוֹת, *tôlēdôth*), holds profound soteriological (salvational) value. The genealogies in Genesis are not merely enumerations of years; they contain God's amazing plan for salvation, which permeates the entire Bible. In-depth study and research into the lives and ideologies of the patriarchs, as well as accounts of significant events, will greatly help our understanding of God's divine administration of redemption.

I took special interest in the years of generations recorded in the Genesis genealogies, and I focused on the Scripture verses "Remember the days of old, consider the years of all generations" (Deut 32:7) and "Stand by the ways and see and ask for the ancient paths, where the good way is, and walk in it" (Jer 6:16). In order to understand the true meaning of the genealogies, I researched for a long period of time, carefully read through the Bible, and referred to various books and resources.

I was able to discover the faith of the patriarchs alive and moving in the Genesis genealogies. Each and every step they took in faith left

* Bible verses quoted in this book are from the New American Standard Bible unless indicated otherwise.

a clear imprint. They lived in eager anticipation of the woman's seed (Gen 3:15); the sound of their charged heartbeats still reverberates today. Tears overwhelmed me and sleep escaped me as I was moved by the grace that led me to understand the hidden meaning of the years of generations.

Grace abounded even more abundantly as I shared my newfound understanding with the beloved members of the Pyung Kang Che-il Church during weekly Wednesday services and special gatherings. I testified of the grace I received from my studies for the first time in 1968 and then in 1983 through a six-month Bible studies at the Wonji-Dong Retreat Center. Since then, I have added to and modified the studies and shared them on different occasions both at home and abroad throughout 2005. The study blessed both me and the congregation with the overflowing inspiration of the Holy Spirit.

I delayed publishing this book because I doubted the need for someone like me to publish a book. However, in 2007 I organized my studies into expository format at the strong urging of my fellow ministers and beloved congregation, in commemoration of the fiftieth "Jubilee" year anniversary of the ministry of God's humble servant. Though this book may be inadequate as fruit presented before God, I took the courage to share it with the world because of the enormous grace that the congregation and I had received. I earnestly hope that even larger waves of grace will sweep across the churches throughout the world through this book.

This book is certainly not a theological or scholarly piece of work. I merely organized what I preached through the enlightenment of the Holy Spirit after repeatedly kneeling in prayer and after reading the Bible through and through. I was greatly blessed by the writings of the forerunners of faith as I referred to them in my research for this book. I borrow the words of the author of Ecclesiastes and confess, "That which has been is that which will be, and that which has been done is that which will be done. So, there is nothing new under the sun" (Eccl 1:9).

The content of this book can hardly be considered complete in describing the infinite Word of God. That is a mystery that cannot be understood entirely even through a lifetime of research and study. I ask that you read this book with a Christlike heart of understanding, forgive any awkward sentences, and give generous tolerance to any unintended mistakes.

When Peter asked, "Lord, how often shall my brother sin against me and I forgive him?" Jesus answered, "I do not say to you, up to seven times, but up to seventy times seven" (Matt 18:21–22). I ask that you overlook my shortcomings with the love and mercy of Christ. If anything has been accomplished through this inadequate servant, I confess that it was not the work of this eighty-year-old sinner, but completely the work of the Lord.

Just as King David confessed, "My times are in Your hand" (Ps 31:15), the life I have lived and the history of the Pyung Kang Che-il Church are wholly in God's sovereign hand of grace. Truly, the mighty strength of God and the power of the Holy Spirit have been present. As I advance beyond the fifty years of ministry made possible only by the grace of God, I feel immensely grateful for the opportunity to leave a trace of this immaterial life in the form of this meaningful book.

Finally, I take this opportunity to express my gratitude to my fellow ministers, elders, leaders, and the congregation of the Pyung Kang Che-il Church, as well as all the helping hands that have made this book possible. In addition, I would like to thank my wife and children for their prayers and support.

I pray that Jesus Christ, the only Savior, who died on the cross for all our sins and rose again on the third day, will always be with His churches around the world. Furthermore, I yearn for the day when the sinful land and all its people are filled with the knowledge of the Lord as the waters cover the sea (Isa 11:9; Hab 2:14; Matt 28:19–20). I lift up all the glory to our only living God. Hallelujah!

朴潤植
Yoonsikpark

October 27, 2007
From the Prayer Room at the Pyung Kang Che-il Retreat Center
Servant of Jesus Christ, Abraham Park

לכל בר דעת דרך המסעות ארבעים שנה במדבר והרוחב והאורך של ארץ הקדושה מנהר מצ
עמלק
מדבר צין הוא קדש
ים המלח
עמרה
הרההר
עתר
מקדה
עיר כרמל
שבט
הצור
ענב
קדש ברנע
מדבר סין
מדבר פארן
מדבר שור
מולדה
אלהולד
באר שבע
שמעון
שבט
בית מרכבות
גת
אשקלון
ארץ פלשתים
ארץ גשן
פתם
צען
אלכסנדרי
לוח המסעות במדבר
אשר על פי ה׳ יסעו ועל פי ה׳ יחנו
א״ רעמסס טו״ רתמה כט״ הרהגדגד
ב״ סכת טז״ רמן פרץ ל״ יטבתה
ג״ אתם יז״ לבנה לא״ עברנה
ד״ פיהחירת יח״ רסה לב״ עציון גבר
ה״ מרה יט״ קהלתה לג״ מדבר צין
ו״ אילם כ״ הרספר לד״ הרההר
ז״ ים סוף כא״ חרדה לה״ צלמנה
ח״ מדבר סין כב״ מקהלת לו״ פונן
ט״ דפקה כג״ תחת לז״ אבת
יוד״ אלוש כד״ תרח לח״ דיבן גד
יא״ רפידם כה״ מתקה לט״ עלמן דבלתים
יב״ מדבר סיני כו״ חשמנה מ״ הרי עברים
יג״ קברות התאוה כז״ מסרות מא״ ערבה מואב
יד״ חצרת כח״ בני יעקן

PART ONE

Consider the Years of All Generations

Remember the days of old,
Consider the years of all generations.
Ask your father, and he will inform you,
Your elders, and they will tell you.
—Deuteronomy 32:7

The Book of Deuteronomy is composed of three farewell sermons—Moses' final words and exhortation to the Israelites at the end of his remarkable 120-year life. He spoke in the Plains of Moab about two months and ten days before their grand entrance into Canaan, on the first day of the eleventh month in the fortieth year of the wilderness journey (Deut 1:3–5). The main audience for these sermons was the Israelites' second generation, who were born in the wilderness after the exodus. All of the first generation had already died before crossing the brook Zered (Deut 2:13–15). Moses preached with the sincere hope that this succeeding generation would become a people of faith and continue to obey the Word of God even after entering Canaan. A suitable title for his first sermon would be "The Account of God's Work of Salvation" (Deut 1:1–4:43); the second sermon, "The Reiteration of the Law" (Deut 4:44–26:19); and the third, "The Future Foretold" (Deut 27–30). The book concludes with Moses' death and the commissioning of Joshua as Israel's new leader (Deut 31–34).

This took place on the first day of the 11th month of the 40th year since the Exodus, thus two months and ten days before the great entry into Canaan (Deut 1:3-5). The main audience was the second generation that was born in the wilderness since all the soldiers had died before crossing brook Zered (Deut 2:13-15). Moses preached with an earnest hope that this second generation in the wilderness would continue to be a generation of faith that obeys the Word of God.

Moses' song in Deuteronomy 32 addresses the somber subject of Israel's betrayal, their fall, and God's subsequent judgment. The fundamental message of this song, however, is God's boundless love and mercy for His chosen people. Calling the Israelites by the affectionate name "Jeshurun" (Deut 32:15),[1] Moses desired to ingrain in their hearts the truth about the God who chose them from before the beginning of time. He is sovereign over all history, He is the source of all blessings, and He governs their future.

In Deuteronomy 32:7, Moses expressed his concern for the dismal events that could unfold after the Israelites enter and settle in the land of Canaan. He warned them forcefully so that they might prevent such events from taking place and gave them three specific commands: "Remember the days of old," "Consider the years of all generations," and "Ask your father." This surely is a demonstration of God's fervent love for His chosen people. In drawing their attention to the walk of faith during the "days of old" and the "years of all generations," Moses hoped that the Israelites who would soon possess the land of Canaan would also continue that walk in faith.

Moses declared that God had chosen the Israelites as His heirs even before creation (Deut 32:8-9; Eph 1:4–5) and that the land of Canaan had been prepared as an inheritance for His people (Deut 32:49). Thus, they were to strictly adhere to the three commands in order to fully inherit this land. Today, these three commands are the basic code of conduct for Christians who are journeying toward the kingdom of heaven, the spiritual Canaan.

---

1. A poetic name for Israel meaning "upright one."

CHAPTER 1

The First Command: Remember the Days of Old

[זְכֹר יְמוֹת עוֹלָם]
Remember how the old days were.

1. The "Days of Old" in Light of God's History of Salvation

The Hebrew term for the "days of old" is יְמוֹת עוֹלָם (*yĕmôt ʿôlām*). It does not simply refer to past history, but rather to a history marked by the fulfillment of God's Word and His promise to save mankind (Deut 4:32; Ps 77:5–6, 11–12; 78:1–8; 143:5; Isa 46:9). The "days of old" encompasses a quite comprehensive period of time; it dates all the way back to the "beginning" and includes the entire time in which God's work of salvation has been in progress. This is evident from the two Hebrew words that compose the expression "days of old": יְמוֹת (*yĕmôt*), the plural form of יוֹם (*yôm*), meaning "day"; and עוֹלָם (*ʿôlām*), meaning "long duration," "antiquity," "eternity," or "everlasting."

For Moses, the "days of old" includes:

1. The fall of Adam and Eve in the Garden of Eden
2. Cain's gruesome murder and the unrighteous deeds of his descendants
3. The overflowing sin and wickedness of Noah's time
4. The construction of the Tower of Babel and man's hubris
5. The covenant of the torch given to Abraham in Genesis 15
6. Israel's 430 years of slavery in Egypt
7. The glorious exodus from Egypt
8. The forty years of trial in the wilderness

God's commitment to the work of salvation has been steadfast despite man's increasing sins after the fall and expulsion from the Garden of Eden until today. Thus, the "days of old" are the days and years of God's work marked by His fervent love and tears. The prophet Jeremiah referred to these days as the "ancient paths" and the "good way" (Jer 6:16).

The "good way" is the path of faith in which the messianic promise was fulfilled. It is a path of suffering that requires people of faith to engage in ongoing battles against evil in order to sustain the good and to overcome any affliction that may come along the way (Heb 11:36). Thankfully, this path promises the blessing of peace in the end (Jer 6:16b). This entire path is compressed into the genealogies in the Book of Genesis. In other words, the traces of the events of old, the good way, God's fervent love, and His tears and zeal have been melted into the genealogies.

2. Remember

In Hebrew, "to remember" is זָכַר (*zākar*). This word means "to remember," "to recall a memory" (Exod 13:3), "to consider" (Job 7:7), "to recollect" (Ps 63:6), "to think in light of the future" (Isa 47:7), and "to remind." In the original Hebrew text, this word *zākar* appears fifteen times in the Book of Deuteronomy (Deut 5:15; 7:18 [2 times]; 8:2, 18; 9:7, 27; 15:15; 16:3, 12; 24:9, 18, 22; 25:17; 32:7). Human beings have the tendency to forget even crucial events after some time has passed or as generations change. The chief cupbearer whose dream Joseph interpreted is an excellent example (Gen 40:23).

The history of the Israelites is, undeniably, full of events too shameful to recall. They spent 430 years slavery in a foreign country (Exod 12:40–41) and wandered in the wilderness for 40 years without having their own land. The 430 years in Egypt were so bitter that the Bible often likens Egypt to an iron furnace (Deut 4:20; 1 Kgs 8:51; Jer 11:4). Through Moses and the other prophets sent throughout the ages, however, God urged the Israelites to remember their detestable years of slavery in Egypt (Exod 13:3, 14; 20:2; Deut 5:6, 15; 6:12; 7:8; 8:14; 13:5, 10; 15:15; 16:12; 24:18; 24:22; Josh 24:17; Judg 6:8; Jer 34:13; Mic 6:4). Moreover, He commanded them to remember how He had allowed them to suffer in the wilderness (Deut 8:2; 9:7); nations that easily forget their times of suffering are doomed to experience greater suffering in the future.

God did not arbitrarily instruct the Israelites to "remember" and leave them without help. God established various memorial days so that the "days of old" would be eternally remembered. He also designated various objects as memorials for His people. The noun form of the verb "to remember" (*zākar*) is זִכָּרוֹן (*zikkārôn*), meaning "memorial" or "reminder."

First, God instituted memorial days to commemorate great historical events. He instituted the Day of Passover and commanded His people to "celebrate it as a permanent ordinance" (Exod 12:14, 17, 24). Accordingly, the Israelites observed Passover by eating unleavened bread and bitter herbs to commemorate God's saving work before the exodus when the angel of death passed over their homes and spared their lives (Exod 12:8; Num 9:11).

> **Exodus 13:16** So it shall serve as a sign on your hand, and as phylacteries on your forehead, for with a powerful hand the LORD brought us out of Egypt.

Besides the Day of Passover, God also commanded the Israelites to observe the Feast of Weeks and the Feast of Tabernacles as reminders of the enormous and wondrous grace of salvation that He poured upon them throughout their history (Exod 34:22–23; Deut 16:16). Furthermore, God commanded them to keep His Sabbaths holy: "You shall surely observe My sabbaths; for this is a sign between Me and you throughout your generations" (Exod 31:13). He also said, "And also I gave them My sabbaths to be a sign between Me and them" (Ezek 20:12, 20).

Second, after He began to intercede in human history, God urged the people to preserve certain objects as memorials. He did this so that they might remember the grace that He had poured out upon them in times of their distress and give thanks to Him. The following are a few examples of memorials mentioned in the Bible. When the Israelites challenged Moses and Aaron's authority, God caused Aaron's rod to bud in order to stop their murmurings. He instructed Moses to place this rod in the Ark of the Covenant to be kept as a sign against the rebels (Num 17:10). God also commanded them to preserve manna—the food with which God had sustained the Israelites in the wilderness—in a jar to be kept in the Ark of the Covenant for their descendants (Exod 16:32–34). Finally, He commanded that the two tablets of the Law be kept in the Ark of the Covenant (Deut 10:2, 5). Consequently, Aaron's budded rod, the jar of manna, and the two covenantal tablets were preserved in the Ark of the Covenant as memorials to remind the people of God's grace throughout the generations (Heb 9:4).

The bronze serpent that Moses made and erected on a pole during the wanderings in the wilderness was also preserved as a memorial (Num 21:4–9; 2 Kgs 18:4). When the Israelites were about to die after being bitten by fiery serpents because of their grumblings against God, He commanded them to look at the serpent made of bronze so that they might be healed and live again. This bronze serpent was the antitype of Jesus Christ, who would be hung on the cross for all eyes to behold (John 3:14–15). At the same time, it was a reminder that God is merciful even in wrath.

After Moses' death, as the Israelites crossed the Jordan River under Joshua's leadership, God commanded them to set up a memorial to commemorate the miracle of the parting waters and the dry land (Josh 3). They were to set up twelve stones in two different places as perpetual memorials of the crossing of the Jordan. God commanded them to take one set of twelve stones from the middle of the Jordan and set them up in Gilgal (Josh 4:8, 20). Then, He commanded them to set up another set of twelve stones in the middle of the Jordan at the place where the priests stood with the Ark of the Covenant (Josh 4:9).

> **Joshua 4:6–7** Let this be a sign among you, so that when your children ask later, saying, "What do these stones mean to you?" [7]then you shall say to them, "Because the waters of the Jordan were cut off before the ark of the covenant of the LORD; when it crossed the Jordan, the waters of the Jordan were cut off." So these stones shall become a memorial to the sons of Israel forever.

The command to "remember the days of old" is a call to discover God's fervent love as well as His grace and guidance throughout the times of suffering, affliction, and trials so that we may come to deeply fathom His amazing plan for redemption.

CHAPTER 2

The Second Command: Consider the Years of All Generations

[בִּינוּ שְׁנוֹת דּוֹר־וָדוֹר]
Think over the years, down the ages.

Moses' second command was to "consider the years of all generations." It is easy to render the significance of this command as being similar to the first command, "remember the days of old," but there is a distinct difference.

1. Years of All Generations

The "years of all generations" and the "days of old" are similar in that both refer to the past, but the "years of all generations" refers to a more defined and specific point in history than does the "days of old." In Hebrew, "years" is שְׁנוֹת (*šĕnôt*), the plural form of שׁנה (*šānâ*). The "days of old" refers to a general time in the past, whereas "years" refer to a significant and meaningful point in time within the "days of old." The word "generations" is composed of the repetition of the Hebrew word דּוֹר (*dôr*), which means "time period" or "generation" and thus refers to each of the generations that appear within the history of salvation. Therefore, the "days of old" refers to the entire history of God's work of salvation, and the "years of all generations" refers to the specific administration of God's redemptive work in each generation within the history of salvation.

The administration of God's redemptive work in each generation presented in the most condensed form is the genealogy. Thus, studying God's work of salvation revealed through the genealogies through the inspiration of the Holy Spirit will lead us to a clearer understanding of His divine administration hidden within each generation.

2. Consider

The word *consider* in the phrase "consider the years of all generations" is בִּין (*bîn*) in Hebrew and means "to discern" or "to have insight." It refers to the act of closely observing or studying the principle of a matter or event in order to gain thorough understanding and insight. Thus, the command to "consider the years of all generations" means not simply to be reminiscent of the past, but rather to gain understanding through research and study. The prophet Isaiah also repeatedly urged the Israelites to "consider."

> **Isaiah 51:1–2** Listen to me, you who pursue saving justice, you who seek Yahweh. Consider the rock from which you were hewn, the quarry from which you were dug. [2]Consider Abraham your father and Sarah who gave you birth. When I called him he was the only one but I blessed him and made him numerous. (New Jerusalem Bible)

This passage is a call to consider the events and experiences of different persons in the years of all generations. Isaiah urged the people to consider the faith of their ancestors Abraham and Sarah and also the history of Israel. He encouraged them not to lose hope even though return from captivity in Babylon might appear impossible in the near future, to reflect upon God's covenant with Abraham, and to think about all of His great works during their years of slavery in Egypt.

CHAPTER 3

The Third Command: Ask Your Father, and He Will Inform You, Your Elders, and They Will Tell You

[שְׁאַל אבִיךָ וְיַגֵּדְךָ זְקֵנֶיךָ וְיֹאמְרוּ לָךְ]
Question your father, let him explain to you, your elders, and let them tell you.

Moses' third command was "Ask your father, and he will inform you, your elders, and they will tell you."

1. Your Father and Elders

The Israelites were to go to their fathers and elders with questions. The Hebrew word for *father* is אב (*ʾāb*) and refers to the male parent, but it also generally means "forefather." In the context of this verse, "father" refers to the patriarchs of all previous generations. *Elder* is זָקֵן (*zāqēn*) in Hebrew and means "elder," "aged," "senior," or "old man." Elders in Israel were not merely old men or aged persons; they were leaders of the people. God commanded Moses to call the elders of Israel together and to consult with them on the plans for the exodus (Exod 3:16, 18).

Thus, the "father" and "elders" in this verse are the patriarchs of faith (e.g., Abraham) and the leaders of the people. They kept God's commands and never strayed outside the boundaries of God's Word and His law. They were profoundly experienced and well trained in God's works by their ancestors through oral tradition.

It is crucial to note that most patriarchs enjoyed astonishing longevity. While there are certain things in life that can be learned relatively quickly, other things can be learned only through experience over an extensive period of time. Thus, the godly patriarchs must have come to understand numerous spiritual truths during their long lives. For them, the Word of God was not just knowledge; it was living wisdom deeply rooted into their lives. Leviticus 19:32 states, "You shall rise up before the grayheaded and honor the aged, and you shall revere your God; I am the LORD." Proverbs 16:31 also states, "A gray head is a crown of glory; it is found in the way of righteousness."

God granted spiritual leadership to the patriarchs who lived godly lives throughout their long years and charged the people to go to them with inquiries. Just as a nation turns to the seniors of society in times of crisis, God commanded His people to seek the advice of their fathers and elders without hesitation if their faith ever wavers as they acclimate themselves to a new society and culture in Canaan.

2. Ask

To ask is שָׁאַל (*šāʾal*) in Hebrew and means "to inquire," "to make a request," or "to beg" and has the connotation of a strong question. The word suggests that the Israelites should proactively seek after their ancestors, ask questions, and plead for answers, just as a starving beggar cries out for food. God is commanding the sons of Israel to take special interest and earnestly desire to learn about all the great works that He has accomplished for them.

In the past, the Israelites and their kings went to God or to His prophets for help when they faced difficult problems (1 Kgs 22:7; 2 Kgs 3:11; 22:13; 2 Chr 18:6). In 1 Kings 22:7, King Jehoshaphat cried out in the middle of battle, "Is there not yet a prophet of the LORD here that we may inquire of him?" King David also looked to God at every moment of his life (1 Sam 23:2; 30:8; 2 Sam 5:19, 23; 1 Chr 14:10). God Himself answered each time that David sincerely inquired of Him. As a result, David tasted the glory of victory in all his battles. On the contrary, Joshua made the grave mistake of not seeking God's counsel before he agreed to a peace covenant with the inhabitants of Gibeon who had come to him in disguise (Josh 9:14–15).

3. He Will Inform You and They Will Tell You

God promised the Israelites that their fathers and elders would answer their questions. He confirmed this in Deuteronomy 32:7: "Ask your father, and he will inform you, your elders, and they will tell you." The fathers will diligently answer those who inquire of them, and the elders will explain in elaborate detail. The Hebrew verb for *inform* is נָגַד (*nāgad*) and is derived from the word that means "to place an object on a high place for all to see." The word *nāgad* is used when God reveals Himself to the people, when He reveals His will in a dream (Gen 41:25), and when the prophets proclaim the Word of God that they have received (Deut 4:13).

The Hebrew word for *tell* is אָמַר (*ʾāmar*), meaning "to speak," "to prove," or "to answer." This means that the leaders not only will tell, but also will explain the matter clearly. The people were to go to the fathers of faith, such as Abraham, for issues concerning faith, and to their leaders or elders for issues concerning their communal or social lives. Although these "fathers" and "elders" have faded into history, they can still answer our questions today. We must inquire of them regarding God's plan for salvation hidden in their respective generations so that we may gain understanding and fulfill God's will in our generation.

4. The Unchanging Word of God

Everything in this world changes constantly, making it almost meaningless to try to distinguish the old from the new. However, the Word of God is eternally unchanging; it is the same yesterday, today, and tomorrow (Heb 1:12; 13:8). It does not corrupt or rust away, for it is living, active, and sharper than any two-edged sword (Heb 4:12). God's Word is a new history in itself. Evil, defects, and profane[1] works emerge in history when we lose the Word of God or have it taken away from us (Deut 32:5).

1. The Hebrew word for *profane* is חָנֵף (*ḥānēp*), meaning "inclining away from righteousness." In Aramaic, the root means "to act falsely toward" or "to act with hypocrisy"; in Akkadian (Amarna letters), "to exercise ruthlessness toward" (Francis Brown, *The New Brown, Driver, Briggs, Gesenius Hebrew and English Lexicon: With an Appendix Containing the Biblical Aramaic* [Peabody, MA: Hendrickson, 1979], 338).

As believers looking forward to Canaan, our land of eternal Sabbath (the kingdom of God, heaven), we must open our ears to Moses' earnest cry to the Israelites before their entry into Canaan and receive it as a message for us today. As we continue to study and delve into the genealogies and contemplate the "days of old" and the "years of all generations," we will discover the great treasures hidden in God's plan for salvation. However, the discovery must not be merely for ourselves; we must pass it on to the godly descendants who will remain on this earth until the day of the Lord's return. This is God's purpose for keeping us on this earth. It is part of His sovereign plan to preserve the covenantal offspring until the end of the world (Gen 45:7). I am sure that those who understand God's will and follow in the footsteps of the godly forefathers mentioned in the days of old and the years of all generations will enter into the Sabbath rest that remains for His people (Heb 4:1–11).

לכל בר דעת דרך המסעות ארבעים שנה במדבר והרוחב והאורך של ארץ הקדושה מנהר מצ
עמלק
מדבר צין הוא קדש
ים המלח
קרהההר
מדבר סיני
שבט
עיר כרמל
מדבר פארן
מדבר שור
שבט
שמעון
באר שבע
ארץ פלשתים
אשקלון
ארץ גשן
פתם
אלכסנדרי
לוח המסעות במדבר
אשר על פי ה׳ יסעו ועל פי ה׳ יחנו
א׳ רעמסס　טו׳ רתמה　כט׳ חר הגדגד
ב׳ סכת　טז׳ רמן פרץ　ל׳ יטבתה
ג׳ אתם　יז׳ לבנה　לא׳ עברנה
ד׳ פיהחירת　יח׳ רסה　לב׳ עציון גבר
ה׳ מרה　יט׳ קהלתה　לג׳ מדבר צין
ו׳ אילם　כ׳ הרספר　לד׳ הר ההר
ז׳ ים סוף　כא׳ חרדה　לה׳ צלמנה
ח׳ מדבר סין　כב׳ מקהלת　לו׳ פונן
ט׳ דפקה　כג׳ תחת　לז׳ אבת
י׳ אלוש　כד׳ תרח　לח׳ דיבן גד
יא׳ רפידים　כה׳ מתקה　לט׳ עלמן דבלתים
יב׳ מדבר סיני　כו׳ חשמנה　מ׳ הרי עברים
יג׳ קברות התאוה　כז׳ מסרות　מא׳ ערבת מואב
יד׳ חצרת　כח׳ בני יעקן

PART TWO

God's Divine Administration

The Bible is not merely an account of the history of the Israelites; it is a magnificent record containing the grand theme of God's work of redemption, starting with the account of creation (Gen 1–2) and concluding with the completion of the new heaven and the new earth (Rev 21–22).

The word *redemption* has a similar meaning to the word *liberation* and refers to salvation, which is freedom from the bondage of sin obtained through a ransom payment. Therefore, redemption entails the premise of a ransom payment for our sins, and the wages of sin is death (Rom 6:23). Jesus is the only one in heaven and on earth who has given up His life as a ransom to redeem us from death (Matt 20:28). In 1 Timothy 2:6 Jesus is described as the one "who gave Himself as a ransom for all, the testimony borne at the proper time." Matthew 20:28 states that Jesus came "to give His life a ransom for many." Ephesians 1:7 says, "In Him we have redemption through His blood, the forgiveness of our trespasses." And 1 Peter 1:18–19 further explains, "knowing that you were not redeemed with perishable things like silver or gold from your futile way of life inherited from your forefathers, but with precious blood, as of a lamb unblemished and spotless, the blood of Christ."

God transferred all the sins of mankind onto Jesus, who was without sin (Heb 4:14–15), and imparted His righteousness as a gift to those who believe in Jesus (Rom 4:25; 8:3–4; 2 Cor 5:21; Eph 2:8; Col 1:20–22; 1 Pet 3:18). God paid the ransom for our lives by sending His Son in the likeness of sinful flesh so that His Son may give up His life in order to fulfill the "requirement of the Law" (Rom 8:3–4). Colossians 1:21–22 states, "And although you were formerly alienated and hostile in mind, engaged in evil deeds, yet He has now reconciled you in His fleshly body through death [v. 20: the blood of His cross], in order to present you before God as holy, blameless and beyond reproach."

Thus, the "history of redemption" refers to the entire course of history in which God saves sinners through the death and resurrection of Jesus Christ. A broader definition of the "history of redemption" is God's divine administration to renew mankind and all creation, thereby recovering the paradise that was lost through the fall of Adam and Eve (Rev 21:5).

The history of this world is founded upon the history of God's work of salvation because God is the origin of all history and sovereign over its development and change (1 Chr 29:11–12; Job 12:23; Dan 4:25; Ps 103:19; Eph 1:11). The history of God's redemptive work is not distinct from the history of this world; God enters history, works with, works through, and works upon the foundations of secular history. Therefore, a careful study of the Bible will give us deeper insight into the truth regarding the past, the present, and the future of this world.

Although we believe in God and have become His children, we easily overlook His greatness. We do not understand the enormity of His heart or the intricateness of His plan. It is my prayer that through this study of God's divine administration for salvation we will gain the insight to discover His greatness and praise His works. Moreover, I pray that each one of us may come to realize where we stand in terms in the progression of God's redemptive work as well as our respective duties and calling.

CHAPTER 4

God's Divine Administration for Redemption

1. The History of Redemption as a Part of God's Divine Administration

The history of mankind is the history of redemption unfolding according to God's plan. It is the history that God the Father devised after the fall, Jesus the Son fulfilled, and the Holy Spirit completed.

(1) What is God's divine administration?

Divine Administration is οἰκονομία (*oikonomia*) in Greek and is used three times in the letter to the Ephesians (Eph 1:9–10; 3:2, 9). It can also be translated as "stewardship" (1 Cor 9:17), "divine administration" (Col 1:25), or "the mystery of His will" (Eph 1:9–10). Also used similarly is the word οἰκονόμος (*oikonomos*), translated as "manager" (Luke 16:2–4; Gal 4:2). Just as a steward manages and administers a house, the Lord of the universe has a divine administration to govern the heavens and the earth for the purpose of saving His chosen people through Jesus Christ and His church (Eph 1:20–23). God's divine administration includes the entire process of managing, allocating, arranging, planning, governing, and ministering the order, movement, and time of all things in the universe (Col 1:25).

God did not just devise His plan and entrust it to be fulfilled by the natural course of history. Instead, He actively intervenes in the specific events of human history so that what He has planned from the beginning of time bears fruit. This is what we call "God's providence." God's providence and His divine administration are part of the larger history of redemption, whose chief focus is the messianic prophecies and their fulfillment.

(2) God's divine administration is fulfilled according to His predestined will.

Predestination refers to the "divine foreordaining" (i.e., God's determined will) of all that will ensue (Eph 1:4–5; 3:11). Our salvation has been predestined from before creation (2 Tim 1:9; Titus 1:2). In Matthew 25:34, the King says to those on His right, "Inherit the kingdom prepared for you from the foundation of the world." God planned and prepared for the salvation of His people through Jesus Christ before the creation of this world (John 1:1–4, 18; 17:5, 24; Prov 8:22–23). For this reason, Ephesians 1:9–10 describes Jesus' coming as the "administration suitable to the fullness of the times," signifying that God's plan for salvation was finally fulfilled through Jesus Christ, the Word who came in the flesh.

The apostle Paul also emphasized that God's divine administration is realized only in Christ (Eph 1:3, 4, 7, 9, 10, 12, 15, 20). However, he was astounded to realize that the notion of the Israelites as the sole "elect people" had collapsed after Jesus' coming and that the scope of God's plan to save had included the Gentiles. He described this as the "administration of the mystery" (Eph 3:9) because it had been kept hidden until then.

Today, God continues to intercede in the history of mankind and brings to fruition portions of His will according to the "administration suitable to the fullness of the times" and the "administration of the mystery." God's work of redemption will proceed without ceasing until His predestined will and plan are all completely fulfilled at the second coming of Jesus Christ.

2. The Focus and Scope of Redemptive History

(1) The focus of redemptive history is the salvation of fallen mankind.

God's grace springs forth from the center of the work of salvation. Redemptive history is characterized not by judgment and wrath, but by the patience, grace, and mercy of God, whose desire is to call more people to salvation (1 Thess 5:9; 1 Tim 2:4; 2 Pet 3:9). There was not a single moment when God relinquished His will to save mankind. He granted unexpected grace every time mankind was at the brink of destruction because of their overflowing sin and wickedness. He desired to preserve the "godly seed" (2 Pet 2:5) and to save the holy "tree stump" for the end (Isa 6:13). In times of total despair He made life to spring up. The greater the sins of mankind, the brighter His grace and mercy shined (Rom 5:20).

(2) The scope of redemption encompasses the redemption of the whole man and the recovery of the entire universe.

The sin of one man, Adam, caused God's wrath and curse to fall not only upon all mankind, but also upon all creation (Rom 5:12, 15, 17, 20). Thus, redemption became necessary for the whole man (i.e., spirit, soul, and body [Rom 8:19–23]) and for the entire universe.

In Romans 8, the apostle Paul spoke of three general types of groaning that resulted from the fall. The first is the groaning of all creation (Rom 8:22). Because the curse fell also upon all creation (Gen 3:17–19), the creation eagerly waits for the glorious day when the sons of God will be restored from the fall (Rom 8:19). This will be the day when the curse upon the creation will be lifted to finally redeem it to its original state.

The second is the groaning of the saints (Rom 8:23). Although they have already become God's children through faith in Jesus Christ, they are still in an imperfect state, still bound by sickness and death of the body. Thus, they eagerly long for the redemption of the body at the second coming of the Lord (1 Cor 15:50–58).

The third is the groaning of the Holy Spirit (Rom 8:26). The Holy Spirit intercedes in prayer for all saints with "groanings too deep for words" in hope that they may soon be redeemed. On that glorious day when God's redemptive work is complete, the groaning will cease, and the entire universe will be fully restored.

(3) Redemption is fulfilled through the atoning work of Jesus Christ.

The history of redemption began with the promise of the "woman's seed" after the fall of Adam and Eve (Gen 3:15). After making this promise, God made garments of skin and covered Adam and his wife (Gen 3:21), foreshadowing how Jesus would come as the sacrificial lamb and shed His blood on the cross to cover the shame of mankind (John 1:29; 1 Cor 5:7; Rev 5:6). This is because the sacrifice of life and the shedding of blood are required to make garments of skin.

The fact that God Himself made the garments and clothed them (Gen 3:21) implies that sinful man is entirely incapable of saving himself (Rom 3:10) and that salvation is possible only through God's sovereign grace.

If the first proclamation of the gospel was made in Genesis 3:15, then the first proclamation of atonement was made in Genesis 3:21. Here, through the account of Adam and Eve, God foretold of His sovereign plan to redeem mankind through the sacrifice of Jesus Christ and the shedding of His precious blood. From this perspective, Genesis 3 contains the origin of the fall, the origin of the gospel that would open up the path to life for mankind, as well as the origin of the gospel of atonement.

3. Christ, the Apex of Redemptive History

The incarnate Jesus Christ stands at the apex of redemptive history because God's divine administration for redemption is revealed and fulfilled through His cross.

(1) The Bible introduces the Messiah progressively.

The Old and New Testaments progressively introduce the Messiah in relation to the events and the flow of each era (John 5:39, 45–47; Heb 1:1–2). Thus, our chief focus when reading the Bible must be on the Messiah and the redemptive history fulfilled by Him—how God saved mankind through Christ and how He will complete the work of salvation.

The messianic promise was first made in Genesis 3:15, which revealed that He would come as the woman's seed. The method of fulfillment of this promise was progressively revealed through Isaiah's prophesy: "A virgin will be with child and bear a son" (Isa 7:14). It was finally fulfilled through the virgin birth of Jesus Christ through the conception of the Holy Spirit (Matt 1:18–25).

(2) Jesus Christ's death on the cross was predestined as part of God's divine administration for redemption.

Jesus' crucifixion was not an incidental or spontaneous event. When the time to bear the cross was imminent, Jesus said, "For indeed, the

Son of Man is going as it has been determined" (Luke 22:22) and "For this purpose I came to this hour" (John 12:27). At the Garden of Gethsemane, Jesus prayed seeking to do the Father's will and not His own (Matt 26:38–42; Luke 22:44; Heb 5:7). Regarding this matter, Paul added that Christ died for our sins "according to the Scriptures" (1 Cor 15:3). Thus, our Savior Jesus Christ came to this earth in accordance with the Scriptures, lived in accordance with the Scriptures, and died on the cross in accordance with the Scriptures. Furthermore, He rose again on the third day after destroying the power of death in accordance with the Scriptures. He remained on the earth forty days after His resurrection and ascended into heaven in accordance with the Scriptures. His second coming will also be fulfilled in accordance with the scriptural prophecies. All these events were predestined as part of God's divine administration for redemption.

(3) Jesus Christ accomplished redemption once and for all through the cross, and its efficacy is everlasting.

Concerning Jesus Christ's redemptive work, the author of Hebrews says, "But through His own blood, He entered the holy place once for all, having obtained eternal redemption" (Heb 9:12).

The crucifixion of Jesus Christ was not a single independent event that occurred two thousand years ago; its power continues to save today, and its efficacy is everlasting. The Old Testament priests had to be continuously replaced when they died. Atonement sacrifices had to be prepared again and again, and the blood of the sacrifice had to be offered repeatedly (Heb 7:20–28). In contrast, Jesus Christ is the everlasting priest (Heb 7:21-24) and the perpetual sacrifice offered once for all (Rom 6:10; Heb 7:26–28; 9:26, 28; 10:10). The Greek word for "once" is ἐφάπαξ (*ephapax*) and means "once for eternity." Jesus' atoning sacrifice on the cross achieved eternal salvation, not a temporal one.

(4) The work of redemption will be completed through the second coming.

The Old Testament testified of Jesus Christ numerous times and in various ways (Heb 1:1). Jesus Christ is the Word who came in the flesh according to the prophecies of the Old Testament. He came at the fullness of time and proclaimed the Word without rest while He was on the earth until His death on the cross (John 5:17; Gal 4:4). He worked with the zeal of the Lord to save sinners who were predestined for salvation from the beginning of time (Isa 9:7; 62:1; 2 Cor 11:2). He demonstrated His boundless love for mankind by shedding His blood on the cross (Rom 5:8; 1 John 4:10), thereby completing the work of redemption. Since then, the Holy Spirit has been working to bestow the virtues of Jesus Christ's work upon all people chosen to receive salvation and to lead them toward salvation. God fulfilled the work of redemption through the first coming, and He will perfect it through the second coming.

When the Lord returns at the second coming, those who died in Christ will be resurrected to a transformed body, and those who are alive will be transfigured to the completion of God's saving work (1 Cor 15:51–54; 1 Thess 4:16–17). After the thousand-year reign, the devil, who had caused the fall of this world, will be thrown into the lake of fire and brimstone. Then, the first heaven and the first earth will pass away, and the new heaven and the new earth will at last be established (Rev 20:1–10; 21:1).

The history of God's work of redemption, which has tirelessly run its course since the fall of Adam, will arrive at its glorious completion through the second coming of the Christ. It is our calling to be used as God's precious vessels until His work of redemption is complete.

CHAPTER 5

God's History of Redemption and the Genealogies

1. The Redemptive Significance of the Genealogies

Man was created in God's likeness, but sinned and fell to the path of death. The history of redemption is the entire history of the salvation of mankind and the restoration of all creation. Thus, the major themes of redemptive history include the creation, the fall, and restoration. All attention is focused on who the Messiah, the seed of the woman, is and how God's people would be saved through Him. These major themes are clearly depicted through each person that appears in the genealogies. The history of redemption is concisely compressed into the names and ages of the persons recorded in the genealogies.

The Bible addresses the broad themes of redemptive history through the various sets of genealogies. For example, Genesis 5 records Adam's genealogy, ten generations from Adam to Noah. Genesis 11 records Shem's genealogy, ten generations from Shem to Abraham. Together, these genealogies reveal the flow from Adam to Abraham, delineating how the Messiah would ultimately come as a descendant of Abraham. The uniqueness of the genealogies in Genesis 5 and Genesis 11 lies in the fact that they include a complete list of each person's birth, age at procreation, and life span even though they lived four thousand to six thousand years ago. The completeness of the genealogies affirms that God's redemptive work did not cease in any generation, but continued throughout history.

Following the genealogies in Genesis, the genealogy of Boaz (Ruth 4:18–22) connects Perez, Judah's son, to King David. This genealogy further confirms that the Messiah will come through the line of Judah, the fourth among Jacob's twelve sons. The genealogy in Matthew 1 summarizes the Old Testament history of redemption. The book opens, "The record of the genealogy of Jesus the Messiah, the son of David, the son of Abraham" (Matt 1:1), and it introduces Jesus as the Messiah, who came through the path delineated in the genealogies of Genesis 5, of Genesis 11, and of Boaz.

Careful study of the Genesis genealogies will lead us to a clearer understanding of God's divine administration for redemption through Jesus Christ. All the descriptions of the persons, their names, and the time of their births and deaths offer insight into the circumstances surrounding each time period. Furthermore, they play important roles in uncovering different aspects of Jesus Christ, who would come through their lineage. In this light, these genealogies are the core of redemptive history, and studying them is a definite shortcut to comprehending God's divine administration.

There are no meaningless sounds in the world, and the biblical genealogies contain countless treasures to be discovered (cf. 1 Cor 14:10). We must not commit the grave mistake of overlooking them as meaningless enumerations of names. With the guidance of the Holy Spirit, we must discover and follow the rich vein of redemptive history that flows through the genealogies.

2. The Structure and Flow of the Genealogies

God's work in redemptive history is carried out in various ways and forms, but it has one clear purpose and direction: to send the promised Messiah (Heb 1:1–2). The Bible is a record of how God carried out this plan, and the genealogies, presented in various formats and structures, record this work in the most concise and condensed form.

(1) The Structure of the genealogies.

First, the genealogies may be listed in either of two linear forms: linear ascending order (listing up from descendants to the ancestors) or linear descending order (listing down from ancestors to descendants). The genealogy in Luke 3 is typical of a genealogy listed in linear ascending order. It traces Jesus Christ's genealogy in ascending order up to Adam. In a linear descending genealogy, the main focus is on the last person on the list. For example, the focus in the genealogy of Genesis 5 is on the tenth generation, Noah. The genealogy in Genesis 11 lists Shem and his descendants down to Abraham (the tenth generation), with the primary focus on Abraham.

Second, genealogies can be categorized as vertical or horizontal. Genealogies in vertical format record the direct line of offspring. Typical of the vertical genealogy format are the genealogy of the line of Cain in Genesis 4 and the genealogy of the line of Seth in Genesis 5. Genealogies in horizontal format simultaneously record the lineages of the different sons of one person. The genealogies of Noah's sons, Ham and Japheth (Gen 10:2–20), of Nahor (Gen 22:20–24), of Keturah (Gen 25:1–6), of Ishmael (Gen 25:12-16), and of Esau (Gen 36:1–43) are examples of horizontal genealogies.

(2) Two distinct flows of genealogies.

Beginning with Cain's act of murder until Herod's conspiracy to kill the infant Jesus, Satan's relentless effort to thwart God's work ran parallel to the progression of redemptive history (Matt 2:1–13). Genesis 4 contains the genealogy of the line of Cain, which attempted to hinder the flow of redemptive history, and Genesis 5 contains the genealogy of the patriarchs in the line of Seth, who were central figures in the history of redemption. Hence, biblical genealogies are divided into two distinct lines: the genealogy of the faithful who lived to fulfill God's will, and the genealogy of the unfaithful whose lives stood against God's will.

The genealogies of the sons of faith are the center stem of the biblical genealogies. The most prominent are the genealogy of Adam in Genesis 5 and the genealogy of Shem in Genesis 11, which show the lineage of faith from Adam to Abraham. Continuing the lineage of faith, the genealogy of Boaz in Ruth 4 lays out the lineage from Judah's son, Perez, down to King David. Finally, the genealogy in Matthew 1 explicitly reveals God's work of redemption through the forty-two generations from Abraham to Jesus Christ.

The Bible also dedicates a considerable amount of writing to the genealogies of the unfaithful. The genealogy of Cain in Genesis 4 is a typical example, along with the genealogies of the sons of Ham (Gen 10:6–20), of Ishmael (Gen 25:12–16), and of Esau (Gen 36:1–43).

The genealogies of the faithful are recorded in vertical format without omitting any generations, from the first patriarch down to the last, until they finally bear fruit with Jesus Christ. In contrast, the genealogies of the unfaithful come to an abrupt end. They opposed God and afflicted His chosen people while becoming founders of lavish new cultures and civilizations. Ultimately, they perished and disappeared from history.

CHAPTER 6

The Genealogies of Genesis

Most of the genealogies in the Bible are concentrated in the Book of Genesis. For this reason, Genesis is also called the "book of genealogies" or the "story of lineages." It is the first of the sixty-six books of the Bible and reveals the origin of mankind as well as God's sovereign work and providence over each godly offspring.

The Book of Genesis covers a span of about 2,300 years of history in fifty chapters, from the creation of Adam until the death of Joseph (see Reference 1: "The Chronology of the Patriarchs"). Because it is impossible to record detailed accounts of God's providence in just fifty chapters, God compressed 2,300 years of history in the form of genealogies. The chief message of the genealogical accounts in Genesis is that God will accomplish His divine administration to save mankind through the godly offspring and that He will fulfill His promise.

1. The Structure of Genesis

Genesis can be organized into two parts: chapters 1–11 (part 1) and chapters 12–50 (part 2).

(1) Part 1 (chapters 1–11).

The theological term for the history outlined in Genesis 1–11 is "primeval history." These chapters cover a span of 2,023 years, which include the creation of heaven and earth, the creation and fall of Adam and Eve, the story of Cain and Abel, the great flood, the Tower of Babel, and the lives of Adam, Noah, and Abraham (see Reference 1: "The Chronology of the Patriarchs").

God continued His work of salvation despite rebellion against His dominion, a rebellion that progressed and climaxed with the attempt to construct the Tower of Babel. In the last part of Genesis 11, Abraham departed from Ur of the Chaldeans and migrated to Haran. God's work depicted in Genesis 1–11 comes to a close with the singling out of Abraham from among all the descendants of Adam to set the stage for a new beginning, starting with Abraham.

(2) Part 2 (chapters 12–50).

Genesis 12–50 covers a span of only about 280 years, a seventh of the first part, but the writing space dedicated to it is five times longer. It includes the narrative of the birth of the chosen people of Israel and focuses on the lives of four patriarchs: Abraham, Isaac, Jacob, and Joseph. It is apparent, therefore, that part 1 of Genesis was shortened because many generations were compressed into the genealogies (Gen 4–5; 10–11).

2. Ten Genealogies in Genesis

There are ten genealogies (תּוֹלְדוֹת: *tôlēdôth*, Hebrew word for "genealogy") in the book of Genesis. The first five belong to part 1 of Genesis (Gen 1-11) and the last five belong to part 2 of Genesis (Gen 12-50).

1 – Genealogy of heaven and earth (2:4–4:26)
Genesis 2:4 This is the account of the heavens and the earth when they were created.

2 – Genealogy of Adam's family (5:1–6:8)
Genesis 5:1 This is the book of the generations of Adam.

3 – Genealogy of Noah's family (6:9–9:29)
Genesis 6:9 These are the records of the generations of Noah.

4 – Genealogy of Noah's sons (10:1–11:9)
Genesis 10:1 Now these are the records of the generations of Shem, Ham, and Japheth, the sons of Noah.

5 – Genealogy of Shem (11:10–26)
Genesis 11:10 These are the records of the generations of Shem.

6 – Genealogy of Terah (Abraham) (11:27–25:11)
Genesis 11:27 Now these are the records of the generations of Terah.

7 – Genealogy of Ishmael (25:12–18)
Genesis 25:12 Now these are the records of the generations of Ishmael, Abraham's son.

8 – Genealogy of Isaac (25:19–35:29)
Genesis 25:19 Now these are the records of the generations of Isaac, Abraham's son.

9 – Genealogy of Esau (36:1–37:1)
Genesis 36:1 Now these are the records of the generations of Esau (that is, Edom).

10 – Genealogy of Jacob (37:2–50:26)
Genesis 37:2 These are the records of the generations of Jacob.

The word *tôlēdôth* appears in the heading of each genealogy and is used either to introduce the genealogy or to transition into a new story. The appearance of the word toledoth clarifies the fact that the passage is not just a mere list of names or a story. Furthermore, this specific format underscores the following important teachings.

First, the Genesis genealogies narrate the history of the fall, judgment, and restoration of man. The genealogy in Genesis 5 introduces Noah as the central figure who would deliver mankind from the catastrophic judgment of the flood after the fall of Adam. The genealogy in Genesis 11 introduces Abraham as the central figure in the work of salvation, singled out by God from among the scattered nations after the attempt to challenge Him through the construction of the Tower of Babel.

Second, the Genesis genealogies channel their focus on Abraham as the chief figure to carry on the redemption work. This is why the division within the ten genealogies in Genesis is centered on Abraham—five before him and five after him.

Third, Genesis 1–11 is considered the introduction to the entire Bible and contains prophecies regarding the beginning and the end of redemptive history. The genealogies do not simply list the lineage of a person or family; they establish the structural framework for redemptive history.

3. Seper Toledoth (Book of the Generations)

While all of the ten genealogies in Genesis begin with the Hebrew word תּוֹלֵדוֹת (*tôlēdôth*), meaning "genealogy," "account," "order of birth," "generations," "descendants," or "biography," Genesis 5:1 uniquely begins the genealogy by pairing the word *tôlēdôth* with another word, סֵפֶר (*sēper*), which means "book": סֵפֶר תּוֹלְדוֹת (*sēper tôlĕdôth*).

Genesis 5:1 This is the book of the generations of Adam.

The "book of the generations" in Genesis 5:1 signifies "a record of family history," "lineage dating back to the ancestors," "a record of people's bloodline," and "an order of academic or philosophical system." The word *sēper* (סֵפֶר, "book") can also be translated as "writing," "letter," or "scroll." Other genealogies are simply *tôlēdôth* (תּוֹלֵדוֹת), but the genealogy in Genesis 5 is *sēper tôlĕdôth* (סֵפֶר תּוֹלְדוֹת).

This difference underscores the fact that Adam's genealogy in Genesis 5 is neither a simple list of names nor an appendix. It contains a significant amount of content, enough to be considered a complete book in itself. From the perspective of God's redemptive history, it holds great covenantal value, similar to a legally binding document or treaty.

The term *sēper tôlĕdôth*, which appears in the genealogy of the first man, Adam (Gen 5:1), appears also (in Greek) in the genealogy of the second man, Jesus Christ, in Matthew 1 (cf. 1 Cor 15:45–47).

Matthew 1:1 The book of the genealogy of Jesus Christ, the son of David, the son of Abraham.

Genesis 5:1 Book of the generations – *sēper tôlĕdôth* (סֵפֶר תּוֹלְדוֹת)

Matthew 1:1 Book of the genealogy – *biblos geneseōs* (βίβλος γενέσεως)

Again, this is not just *tôlēdôth* ("generations"); it is *sēper tôlĕdôth* ("book of generations"). Likewise in Matthew 1, it is not just *genesis* ("genealogy"); it is *biblos geneseōs* ("book of genealogies").

The genealogies of the first man (Gen 5:1) and of the second man (Matt 1:1) both use the modifying word "book": סֵפֶר (*sēper*) in Hebrew, βίβλος (*biblos*) in Greek. The emphasis on "book" implies that the genealogy in Matthew 1, like the genealogy in Genesis 5, contains enough content to be considered a complete book on its own.

It is important to note that only the most crucial information is compressed into the genealogies. The genealogies replace an immeasurable amount of writing necessary to record a detailed narrative of all the great works that each patriarch performed in his generation as he battled against the wickedness of the world (Ps 40:5; 71:15–16; 139:16–18; Heb 11:32).

> **John 21:25** And there are also many other things which Jesus did, which if they were written in detail, I suppose that even the world itself would not contain the books which were written.

What was the common message of these patriarchs (representatives) from each generation? What inspired them to continue their solitary struggle? It was the fulfillment of God's divine administration to save all mankind. For this purpose, the godly descendants of Seth and of Shem continued to faithfully run their respective legs in the course of redemptive history and pass down the baton to the succeeding generations even through the tears, the agony, the loneliness, and the pain of being forsaken by the world.

The genealogies are full of the traces left behind by the godly descendants who fought the good fight until the coming of the promised seed. As we delve deeper into the study of the Genesis genealogies, we will be able to sense the magnitude of God's abundant grace and love. Ultimately, it was His fervent zeal that achieved salvation for mankind through the incarnation of Jesus Christ and His atoning work on the cross.

4. Method of Study for the Genesis Genealogies

The ten genealogies in Genesis are not all recorded in the same format. Some genealogies are recorded twice, and some are written in simple story format. Among them are the genealogy of Seth in Genesis 5 and the genealogy of Shem in Genesis 11. These two are written in the typical genealogy format and include details of the sons' names and ages. In this book, we will study the genealogies according to the line of Cain in Genesis 4, of Seth in Genesis 5, and of Shem in Genesis 11 with a focus on the following factors.

(1) The meaning of the names.

A name distinguishes a person, place, or thing. A person's name not only validates his or her existence, but also connotes that person's character and personality. The greater significance of a name lies, however, in the fact that it not only follows a person throughout life, but also remains on the earth even after death.

The faith of the parents greatly influences the naming of a child. A name does not just describe the child; it reveals the parents' hopes and expectations for the child, and it provides insight into the situation of the times. Thus, by the study of someone's name, it is possible to obtain an extensive amount of information about that person and the times in which he or she was living.

For the godly patriarchs—men of prayer—assigning names to their sons was a solemn matter. The names most likely reflected their understanding of God's will and His desire toward their generation.

Although there may be many children in a family, the child who honors the parents' name is the pride of that family. Similarly, the names of the persons listed in the genealogies of the godly offspring will not fade away, because they contributed greatly to the establishment of God's kingdom. Therefore, it is meaningful to carefully explore the redemptive significance and the origin of the names in Adam's genealogy, especially since God acknowledged them and deemed them worthy to be recorded in the line of Seth.

(2) Life span—birth and death.

Another basic factor in the study of the genealogies is life span—when the patriarchs were born, how long they lived, and when they died. A person's life span reflects the historical circumstances surrounding his or her time. It is, therefore, necessary to examine how religious and social experiences of the different times may have affected life span.

(3) Relationships with preceding and succeeding generations.

It is also crucial to know where each person lived within the historical timeline because it helps us to understand the person's relationship with the preceding and succeeding generations. It also aids in determining which other patriarchs were contemporaries. Ultimately, we can discover the path and method through which God's divine administration for redemption was delivered down from the older generations to the younger generations.

Of special importance is the length of time Adam and Noah—the first and second ancestors of mankind—lived contemporaneously with their direct descendants. This will bring to light many important facts that had once been unknown and will lead us to a better understanding of God's redemptive providence. In summary, understanding the patriarchs' relationship with the preceding and succeeding generations through a close study of their births and life spans will confirm that even the years recorded within these genealogies progressively reveal the Messiah, who would come as the promised seed of the woman (Gen 3:15).

(4) Progressive revelation of the coming of the Messiah.

The Bible progressively reveals Jesus Christ (Luke 24:27, 44; John 5:39, 45–47; Heb 1:1–3). The format of the genealogies and the meaning of the names recorded within contain the hope and anticipation of how the redemptive promise would unfold in each successive generation and eventually be fulfilled through Jesus Christ. Discovering this will greatly broaden our perspective of the flow of redemptive history.

For example, Adam is connected to Noah through Enoch and Methuselah. Noah is connected to Abraham through Shem and Eber. In their respective times, Adam and Noah function as the backbone for the history of redemption.

(5) Additional information about important characters.

There are some parts of the genealogies that deviate from the standard format with the inclusion of additional information for certain persons. These additional details signal important junctions in the flow of the genealogies and also highlight Jesus Christ, the chief figure in redemption history.

For example, additional details were included for the following persons:

- Genealogy of Cain in Genesis 4 – Cain, Lamech (sixth generation)
- Genealogy of Seth in Genesis 5 – Adam, Enoch, Lamech, Noah
- Genealogy of Shem in Genesis 10–11 – Shem, Eber, Peleg, Abram

Out of all the persons enumerated in the genealogies, we must pay special attention to the persons listed above.

(6) Historical placement of the genealogies.

The time period in which a genealogy emerges has great redemptive significance because genealogies often are recorded at a crucial turning point or junction in the history of redemption.

In the biblical genealogies, the most important person often appears at the end and becomes the starting point of a new era. Consequently, persons listed at either the beginning or the end of a genealogy hold great redemptive significance. Good examples are Adam, the first person mentioned in the genealogy of the creation; Noah, the last person (tenth generation) in his genealogy (Gen 5:32); Terah and his son, Abraham, the last persons in the genealogy that follow the generation of Noah (Gen 11:26); and Joseph in the account of Jacob's lineage (Gen 37:2–50:26).

The Genesis genealogies are especially meaningful in that they present a sweeping view of God's unfolding work in the history of redemption. If we study the genealogies with the aforementioned factors in mind, we will discover the intimate connection between God's redemptive work and the genealogies.

The genealogies contain God's divine administration, which has life and actively moves within the genealogies and guides the great flow of redemptive history. They also contain traces of God's revelations that testify of the coming of Jesus Christ, the Messiah (Luke 24:27, 44; John 5:39, 45–47). Further study of the Genesis genealogies will cause Moses' words to resonate clearly: "Remember the days of old, consider the years of all generations" (Deut 32:7).

CHAPTER 7

Years of the Generations in Genesis

1. Perspective on the Inerrancy of the Bible

An increasing number of modern theologians believe that the Bible contains errors. However, the Bible is the Word of the living God and is therefore totally accurate and inerrant. This principle of inerrancy applies to the entire Bible. Consequently, the genealogies in the Bible are also part of the accurate and inerrant Word of God, and the records of the persons that appear in each genealogy, including their lives and years, are all without error.

There are some genealogies with omissions. For instance, there are omissions in the genealogy of Jesus Christ in Matthew 1:8. Three kings—Ahaziah (2 Kgs 8:25), Jehoash (2 Kgs 12:1), and Amaziah (2 Kgs 14:1)—are omitted between Joram and Uzziah. In Matthew 1:11, Jehoiakim is omitted after Josiah (2 Kgs 23:34; 1 Chr 3:16). This is because the genealogy in the Gospel of Matthew was not written for the purpose of preserving a complete historical record or for calculating years. Matthew recorded the names of important persons from each era deemed necessary for the purpose of the genealogy and omitted others that he deemed unnecessary. He composed three groups of fourteen generations and recorded a total of forty-two generations. Matthew 1:17 states, "Therefore all the generations from Abraham to David are fourteen generations; and from David to the deportation to Babylon fourteen generations; and from the deportation to Babylon to the time of Christ fourteen generations."

Therefore, we must not waver in our belief that the biblical genealogies are part of the perfect and inerrant Word of God. Not all genealogies were written for the purpose of recording and calculating the years; certain generations were intentionally omitted in order to communicate God's specific will.

2. Years of the Generations in Genesis 5 and Genesis 11

The genealogies in Genesis 5 and Genesis 11 together contain twenty generations of patriarchs. The genealogy of the line of Seth, which covers the generations from Adam to Abraham, contains no chronological gaps.

In his study of the Genesis genealogies, Old Testament scholar and creation scientist Henry M. Morris based his calculations of the ten generations from Adam to Noah on the years of birth and death. He argues that there are no gaps in these genealogies:

> There is no reason to think there are any "gaps" in this record, or that the years are anything other than normal years (except for the quizzical possibility that the original year was 360 days long, instead of the present 365¼). The record is perfectly natural and straightforward and is obviously intended to give both the necessary genealogical data to denote the promised lineage and also the only reliable chronological framework we have for the antediluvian period of history.[1]

Old Testament theologian Travis R. Freeman also believes that the genealogies in Genesis 5 and Genesis 11 flow without gaps or disconnections. Freeman states:

> Some modern theologians believe not only that Genesis 5 and 11 contain the names of actual historical figures, but that those names form a continuous (without generational omissions) linear genealogy from Adam to Abraham. While they readily acknowledge fluidity as a fairly common occurrence in ancient genealogies, they reason that the occurrence of fluidity in some genealogies does not prove fluidity in all genealogies. They see the genealogies of Genesis 5 and 11 as two of the many exceptions to the fluidity rule.[2]

In his analysis of early biblical genealogies, Samuel R. Külling begins by acknowledging that many biblical genealogies, such as those in Ezra 7 and Matthew 1, contain gaps. He believes, however, that biblical genealogies come in more than one genre. He places the genealogies of Genesis 5 and Genesis 11 with the chronological genealogies because of the many numerical notations therein, especially the fathers' ages at procreation, and claims that there are no gaps in the two genealogies.

---

1. Henry M. Morris, *The Genesis Record: A Scientific and Devotional Commentary on the Book of Beginnings* (Grand Rapids: Baker, 1976), 154.
2. Travis R. Freeman, "A New Look at the Genesis 5 and 11 Fluidity Problem," *Andrews University Seminary Studies* 42, no. 2 (2004): 266.

He emphasizes that the purpose of the passages in Genesis stating Abraham's age at Isaac's birth and Isaac's age at Jacob's birth was to create an accurate chronology.[3]

What, then, is the basis for the belief that the chronological records of the genealogies in Genesis 5 and Genesis 11 are inerrant? There are three arguments.

First, the genealogies in Genesis 5 and Genesis 11 accurately narrate the time of birth, age at procreation, and life span for all twenty generations of patriarchs. Such precise notations of years cannot be found in other genealogies and thus impart additional credibility to these records. The narrative of the twenty generations of patriarchs is an actual historical and chronological record. If the purpose were not to record actual accounts, there would be no reason for such a detailed narrative.

Second, the order of the twenty patriarchs in Genesis 5 and Genesis 11 does not contradict any other genealogy in the Bible. The order of names in the genealogies in Genesis 5 and Genesis 11 is perfectly consistent with the order of names in the genealogies in 1 Chronicles 1:1–4, 24–27.

(1 Chr 1:1) Adam, Seth, Enosh
(1 Chr 1:2) Kenan, Mahalalel, Jared
(1 Chr 1:3) Enoch, Methuselah, Lamech
(1 Chr 1:4) Noah, Shem, Ham, and Japheth
(1 Chr 1:24) Shem, Arpachshad, Shelah
(1 Chr 1:25) Eber, Peleg, Reu
(1 Chr 1:26) Serug, Nahor, Terah
(1 Chr 1:27) Abram (Abraham)

Moreover, the genealogies in Genesis 5 and Genesis 11 are in agreement with the genealogy of Jesus Christ in Luke 3. In Luke 3:34–38, however, there is a difference in the case of one person. Cainan is listed between Arphaxad (Arpachshad) and Shelah in Luke 3, but not in Genesis 11. The appearance of Cainan, however, does not affect the calculation of years (see Reference 5: "Perspective on Cainan").

3. Samuel R. Külling, *Are the Genealogies in Genesis 5 and 11 Historical and Complete, That Is, without Gaps?* (Riehen: Immanuel-Verlag, 1996), 30–31.

Unless there is definite proof that there is a gap in the chronological order of the years, it is far more accurate to base calculations on the Hebrew text than on noncanonical records that could be incomplete or inaccurate.

Third, the genealogy in Matthew 1 and the genealogies in Genesis 5 and Genesis 11 are separate genealogies recorded for different purposes. While it is true that the genealogy in Matthew has omissions compared to other historical records in the Bible, this is because the purpose of the genealogy was not to narrate a historical bloodline. By the inspiration of the Holy Spirit, Matthew was calling attention to the fruition of God's plan for redemption.

The genealogy in Matthew contains three groups of fourteen generations of persons who played critical roles in shedding light on God's work of redemption until it reached its zenith with the coming of Jesus Christ (Matt 1:17). It is not an exhaustive list of all the generations in biblical history. Matthew also began the genealogy of Jesus Christ with Abraham so that the Jewish audience might understand that Jesus is their Messiah and accept Him. In light of this, the genealogy in Matthew placed its focus on the continuity of faith rather than on the narration of the births and lives of every descendant. It was written from the redemption perspective.

Therefore, skepticism on the historicity and accuracy of the genealogies in Genesis 5 and Genesis 11 based on the genealogy in Matthew 1 is unfounded. If we use the records in Genesis 5 and Genesis 11 for our calculations, we will once again realize the astounding inerrancy of the Bible and the profoundness of the spiritual world.

3. A Point of Reference for Calculating the Years

Although there are many genealogies in the Bible, not every genealogy records the years of birth or death; thus, reference points are necessary. Selecting precisely recorded dates as reference points and using them to perform calculations forward and backward in time will help to build a complete chronological timeline. One such biblical reference point is the year of the exodus.

(1) The year of the exodus is 1446 BC.

The year of the exodus is an important reference point for calculating the generations of the patriarchs who lived prior to the exodus. The first record that assists in calculating the year of the exodus is found in the records of the kings. According to 1 Kings 6:1,

> Now it came about in the four hundred and eightieth year after the sons of Israel came out of the land of Egypt, in the fourth year of Solomon's reign over Israel, in the month of Ziv which is the second month, that he began to build the house of the LORD.

Furthermore, 2 Chronicles 3:1–2 confirms the specific date: the second day in the second month.

> Then Solomon began to build the house of the LORD in Jerusalem on Mount Moriah, where the LORD had appeared to his father David, at the place that David had prepared, on the threshing floor of Ornan the Jebusite. [2]And he began to build on the second day in the second month of the fourth year of his reign.

It is commonly known that Solomon succeeded the throne in 970 BC and began construction work for the temple in 966 BC, the fourth year of his reign. Thus, calculations show that the year of the exodus was 1446 BC (966 + 480 = 1,446). While there are theologians who believe that the exodus occurred in thirteenth century BC, the vast majority of conservative theologians agree that it is more biblical to view the time of the exodus as 1446 BC.

(2) The Israelites were in Egypt for 430 years.

It is clearly recorded in the Book of Exodus:

> **Exodus 12:40–41** Now the time that the sons of Israel lived in Egypt was four hundred and thirty years. [41]And it came about at the end of four hundred and thirty years, to the very day, that all the hosts of the LORD went out from the land of Egypt.

So if the year of the exodus was 1446 BC, then the year that the Israelites entered Egypt was 1876 BC (1,446 + 430 = 1,876).

(3) The time period between Abraham's birth and Israel's migration to Egypt was 290 years.

Abraham had Isaac at the age of one hundred (Gen 21:5). Isaac had Jacob at the age of sixty (Gen 25:26). Jacob migrated to Egypt at the age of 130 (Gen 47:9). Thus, 290 years passed between Abraham's birth and Jacob's migration to Egypt (100 + 60 + 130 = 290). By adding 1,446 (the year of the exodus), 430 years in Egypt, and 290 years between Abraham's birth and Israel's migration into Egypt, we obtain the year of Abraham's birth: 2166 BC (1,446 + 430 + 290 = 2,166).[4]

Hence, unspecified dates of events and births can be accurately calculated by using reference points in the Bible. By building a chronological timeline for the twenty generations of patriarchs from Adam to Abraham, we are able to calculate the year of birth for the last person (Abraham). If we trace the years using the year of Abraham's birth as a reference point, we can also accurately calculate the years in which the twenty generations of patriarchs lived.

From this point, we will continue to examine God's divine administration for redemption as revealed through the genealogies in Genesis 4–5; 10–11.

4. Eui Won Kim, *Heaven, Earth, and the Toledoth of the Patriarchs* (Seoul: Presbyterian General Assembly Education Department, 2004), 233–34.

לכל בר דעת דרך המסעות ארבעים שנה במדבר והרוחב והאורך של ארץ הקדוש
עמלק
מדבר צין הוא קדש
ים המלח
הר ההר
מדבר סיני
מדבר פארן
מדבר שור
ארץ פלשתים
עיר כרמל
שבט
שבט
שמעון
באר שבע
ארץ גשן
פתם
לוח המסעות במדבר
אשר על פי ה׳ יסעו ועל פי ה׳ יחנו
א״ רעמסס טו״ רתמה כט״ הרהגדגד
ב״ סכת טז״ רמן פרץ ל״ יטבתה
ג״ אתם יז״ לבנה לא״ עברנה
ד״ פיהחירת יח״ רסה לב״ עציון גבר
ה״ מרה יט״ קהלתה לג״ מדבר צין
ו״ אילם כ״ הרספר לד״ הרההר
ז״ ים סוף כא״ חרדה לה״ צלמנה
ח״ מדבר סין כב״ מקהלת לו״ פונן
ט״ דפקה כג״ תחת לז״ אבת
יוד״ אלוש כד״ תרח לח״ דיבן גד
יא״ רפידם כה״ מתקה לט״ עלמן דבלתים
יב״ מדבר סיני כו״ חשמנה מ״ הרי עברים
יג״ קברות התאוה כז״ מסרות מא״ ערבת מואב
יד״ חצרת כח״ בני יעקן

PART THREE

The Genealogy According to the Line of Cain

If Genesis 3 is the account of man's original sin, then Genesis 4 is a record of subsequent sins committed after the original sin. The impact of the original sin committed by Adam was not limited just to him; its influence spread to all of his descendants. The results of sin inherited from Adam first became apparent in Cain, but this sinfulness was also not limited to Cain. Sin prospered and grew increasingly strong in the people who were unable to restrain its powers through the Word of God. Sinfulness and wickedness became a common trait apparent in all of the descendants in the line of Cain. The cycle of sin and violence that began with Cain's act of murder advanced in the succeeding generations and reached its culmination during the generation of Lamech.

The genealogy according to the line of Cain is a "genealogy apart from God"; any mention of God's name and His works is conspicuously absent.

In this chapter, we will study the genealogy of the line of Cain recorded in Genesis 4 and examine the lives of his descendants. We will learn about how unbelief continued to reappear in their lives as they followed after Cain's sinfulness and trace the spiritual root of that unbelief.

CHAPTER 8

The Descendants of Cain

1. Cain (קַיִן): gotten one, received

Adam and Eve had relations and gave birth to their first son, Cain, by the grace of God (Gen 4:1). He brought great joy to them because he was the first son born to them after they received the promise of the woman's seed in Genesis 3:15.

> **Genesis 4:1** Now the man had relations with his wife Eve, and she conceived and gave birth to Cain, and she said, "I have gotten a manchild with the help of the LORD."

Eve expressed her joy after giving birth to Cain, saying, "I have gotten a manchild with the help of the LORD." The name *Cain* was Eve's confession of faith after receiving the first fruit of mankind. She believed that she had received this son with "the help of the LORD," by His absolute grace and guidance. It is evident that Adam and Eve had great expectations for their first son. They named him with the hope that the lost paradise would be reconstructed through him.

In connection with the birth of her first son, Eve called God by a new name, *Jehovah* (or *Yahweh*), meaning the "Lord of redemption." This is an expression of her faith in the promise of the woman's seed in Genesis 3:15 and her hope for salvation.

Eve's gratefulness and praises to God are also apparent in the name *Cain*. The name itself is her prayer of thanksgiving for the grace that saved her from pain and danger during her first childbirth after the curse had fallen on them (Gen 3:16). Her confession indicates that she had repented and lived with faith in God's promise after banishment from the Garden of Eden. This is also evident from the fact that Cain and Abel made offerings to God even after many years had passed. Their parents must have nurtured their faith in God. So, if Cain was born to Adam and Eve by the grace of God, and if he had been raised in faith, what caused him to kill his brother?

(1) Why Cain became a murderer.

The problem began when Cain and Abel made offerings to God. God had regard for Abel and his offering, but for Cain and his offering He had no regard. What was the difference between the two men?

First, Cain had lost his faith.

Hebrews 11:4 states, "By faith Abel offered to God a better sacrifice than Cain, through which he obtained the testimony that he was righteous, God testifying about his gifts, and through faith, though he is dead, he still speaks." The superiority of Abel's offering made in faith was manifested in his offering of the "firstlings" of the flock. Because Abel possessed faith in God, he willingly presented the best of what he had. God has always consecrated the first of the fruits and the first son (firstborn) as His own. However, there is no mention of "first" with regard to Cain's offering (Gen 4:3–5).

> **Exodus 23:19** You shall bring the choice first fruits of your soil into the house of the LORD your God. You are not to boil a kid in the milk of its mother.
>
> **Proverbs 3:9** Honor the LORD from your wealth, and from the first of all your produce.
>
> **Ezekiel 48:14** Moreover, they shall not sell or exchange any of it, or alienate this choice portion of land; for it is holy to the LORD.

Thus, God had no regard for faithless Cain or his offering; though Cain had believed in God at one point, he had lost his faith by the time he made his offering to God.

> **Proverbs 15:8** The sacrifice of the wicked is an abomination to the LORD, but the prayer of the upright is His delight.
>
> **Romans 12:1** I urge you therefore, brethren, by the mercies of God, to present your bodies a living and holy sacrifice, acceptable to God, which is your spiritual service of worship.

Second, Cain missed the opportunity to repent.

After God rejected his offering, Cain should have realized that it was because he had lost his faith. He should have asked Abel to mediate on his behalf in making another offering to God. Cain's response, however, was an unexpected one. He became very angry before the Lord, and his countenance fell. Becoming angry before God is nothing less than the manifestation of darkness.

> **Genesis 4:5–6** But for Cain and for his offering He had no regard. So Cain became very angry and his countenance fell. [6]Then the Lord said to Cain, "Why are you angry? And why has your countenance fallen?"

God saw that sin had its desires in Cain and warned him to overcome it (Gen 4:7). Cain, however, did not heed to this divine warning and missed the opportunity to turn back and repent. Sin, thus, had its way with him so that he ultimately struck and killed Abel, becoming the first murderer and committing the first fratricide. Nonetheless, in His mercy God sought out Cain once again and offered him a final chance to repent. He asked Cain, "Where is Abel your brother?" (Gen 4:9). This is similar to how God had questioned Adam by asking, "Where are you?" (Gen 3:9) after he ate the fruit of the tree of the knowledge of good and evil and hid from God. God already knew everything. Just as He had known exactly where Adam was hiding when He questioned him, He also knew what had happened to Abel.

God questioned Cain hoping to rouse him to repentance. Perhaps he would confess, "God, I killed Abel. I have sinned. Please forgive me." God advised Cain and poured His love upon him until the very end out of the desire to preserve him, but Cain rejected all the opportunities to repent. Instead of humbling himself, Cain boldly and impudently opposed God:

> **Genesis 4:9** Then the LORD said to Cain, "Where is Abel your brother?" And he said, "I do not know. Am I my brother's keeper?"

Third, Cain belonged to the wrong side.

What was the primary reason for Cain's failure to protect his faith? The Bible points out that it was because he belonged to the wrong side. 1 John 3:8–9 states that Cain was "of the devil" and that he was not born of God. Cain did not have "His seed." 1 John 3:12 reiterates that Cain slew his brother because Cain was "of the evil one."

By killing his brother, Cain became the first person to blatantly violate the commandment to love one's brother. This is why the apostle

John explained that Cain is of the devil's seed (offspring) that belongs to the evil one, and that he committed murder, because he essentially did not have God's seed (1 John 3:8–9).[1]

Cain ended up belonging to the evil one because he accepted the thoughts of the devil (John 13:2). Cain was born by the grace of God after Adam had relations with Eve. Initially, Cain was a man of faith because of his parents' influence, as is evident from the fact that he made offerings to God. However, Satan secretly sowed into Cain the thoughts of the devil and the thoughts of darkness (Matt 13:25–30).

> **Matthew 13:25–28** But while men were sleeping, his enemy came and sowed tares also among the wheat, and went away. [26]But when the wheat sprang up and bore grain, then the tares became evident also. [27]And the slaves of the landowner came and said to him, "Sir, did you not sow good seed in your field? How then does it have tares?" [28]And he said to them, "An enemy has done this!" And the slaves said to him, "Do you want us, then, to go and gather them up?"

This is similar to how Satan sowed disbelief into the hearts of the Israelites at the first coming of Jesus Christ. Jesus exposed the true identity of those who claimed to be children of Abraham, saying, "You are of your father the devil" (John 8:44). Although they called themselves children of Abraham, they did not perform the deeds of their father Abraham (John 8:39).

The same people who were born in the land of Israel and boasted of their pure lineage rejected Jesus and crucified him. This shows that their father was not Abraham, but the devil. They were not sons of God's kingdom, but sons of the evil one (Matt 13:38). Hence, John the Baptist vehemently rebuked, "You brood of vipers, . . . do not begin to say to yourselves, 'We have Abraham for our father'" (Matt 3:7-9; Luke 3:7–8). This was a sharp rebuke against people who boasted of their "elect" status. They pretended to be holy, but their hearts were filled with evil intentions. The unrepentant Pharisees and Sadducees asserted that they were children of Abraham, but in truth they were children of the serpent through whom Satan had deceived and corrupted Adam and Eve in the Garden of Eden.[2]

---

1. Matthew Henry, *Matthew Henry's Commentary* (Peabody, MA: Hendrickson, 1991), 5:20, 141, 275, 806; 6:868–69.

2. "***You brood of vipers:*** This is similar to the Lord's rebuke toward the Pharisees (Matt

Jesus called the apostle Peter "Satan" when he stood against the will of God, even though Peter had been one of His foremost disciples (Matt 16:23). During the age of the early church, Ananias made an offering, perhaps a large one, but his heart was full of lies and deception. Peter, being full of the Holy Spirit, said of him, "Satan filled [his] heart" (Acts 5:3). False prophets in sheep's clothing may appear righteous and holy, but they are ravenous wolves, full of deceit and lies (Matt 7:15).

May this Word be a mirror for us so that we may examine ourselves and see if we also possess the traits of Satan: habitual deceptiveness.

(2) Cain, a model of the evil one.

Through the parable of the weeds in Matthew 13:24–30, Jesus explained how people become children of darkness from moment to moment without realizing it, and how they become enslaved by Satan just as Cain had been. The main point of the parable is that the master had sown only good seeds, but the enemy came and sowed tares among the wheat and went away (Matt 13:25). Jesus repeated this parable to His disciples and explained to them that the one who sows the good seed is the Son of Man (Matt 13:37), and the enemy who sows the tares is "the evil one" (Matt 13:28, 39). Regarding Judas Iscariot, the Bible states, "... the devil having already put into the heart of Judas Iscariot, the son of Simon, to betray Him" (Luke 22:3; John 13:2, 27). This is an example of Satan sowing tares. Jesus further explained that the good seeds represent the "sons of the kingdom," and the tares represent the "sons of the evil one" (Matt 13:38).

Judas heard Jesus' messages about the kingdom of heaven along with the rest of the disciples. Yet, he became a son of the evil one, not

---

23:23). . . . Though they were confident that they were Abraham's children, he was telling them that they are actually children of the serpent, the messenger of Satan who tempted Adam in Eden" (Sang Kun Lee, *The Lee's Commentary on the Gospel of Matthew* [Seoul: Presbyterian General Assembly Education Department, 1966], 33).

"I speak the things which I have seen with My Father; therefore you also do the things which you heard from your father: The Jews did what they heard from their father (i.e. the devil)" (Yune Sun Park, *A Commentary on John* [Seoul: Yung Eum Sa, 1966], 63).

"You are of your father the devil: What he had twice said more obscurely, he now expresses more fully, that they are *the devil's children*. . . . He calls them *children of the devil*, not only because they imitate him, but because they are led by his instigation to fight against Christ" (John Calvin, *Commentaries on the Gospel according to John [1–11]*, trans. William Pringle [Grand Rapids: Baker, 1989], 44).

a son of heaven. Likewise, Cain belonged to Satan and possessed his traits because he had been more receptive to Satan's thoughts than to the Word of God.

The good seed signifies the Word of God (Luke 8:11). Peter compares the Word of God to a "seed which is . . . imperishable" (1 Pet 1:23). The Word of God is the "good seed," and the sons of the kingdom who receive this seed are also the "good seed" (Matt 13:38; John 6:63). Those who receive the Word of God become sons of the kingdom of heaven, but those who reject the Word of God and accept the thoughts of the devil become sons of the evil one.

The serpent deceived Eve with its craftiness in the Garden of Eden and caused her to fall (2 Cor 11:3). What is the identity of this craftiness? According to 2 Corinthians 11:4, it is a different gospel, another Jesus, and a different spirit. Cain belonged to Satan because he had received the devil's seed, a different gospel, another Jesus, and a different spirit.

Furthermore, Cain was like the ones described in Romans 8:5–9. He lived according to the flesh with his mind set on the things of the flesh and was, therefore, hostile toward God. He became a "son of the devil" and was led by the spirit of the devil (Rom 8:12–14). For certain Cain was a son born to Adam and Eve. From his offering to God, it is certain that he had believed in God at first. However, Satan planted the thoughts of darkness in him (lies and murder [John 8:44]). This is why he killed his brother, and his fruit was his title as the first murderer. Cain forsook the God he had first believed in; he abandoned God and became an "offspring of evildoers" who do not see it as fitting to acknowledge God any longer (Isa 1:4; Rom 1:28).

Matthew 7:16 states, "You will know them [trees] by their fruits." Cain's fruit proved what kind of tree he was from. John 8:44 explains that the sons of the devil follow the desires of the devil, who is a murderer and a liar.

> **John 8:44** You are of your father the devil, and you want to do the desires of your father. He was a murderer from the beginning, and does not stand in the truth, because there is no truth in him. Whenever he speaks a lie, he speaks from his own nature; for he is a liar, and the father of lies.

As a result, Cain turned out contrary to Eve's confession and expectations in Genesis 4:1, which she had made in joy and hope after giving birth to him.

(3) Desires of sin dwelling in Cain.

The identity of the evil seed that dwelt in Cain is vividly described by Paul, the great apostle of the early church, in Romans 7:20: "But if I am doing the very thing I do not wish, I am no longer the one doing it, but sin which dwells in me." Romans 7:20 identifies the seed of darkness that was in Cain as "sin." Sin always involves the whole person, both the inner and the outer person. In Romans 7, Paul repeatedly exposed sin as the cause of the tragic conflict within him. This is similar to God's rebuke to Cain: "If you do well, will not your countenance be lifted up? And if you do not do well, sin is crouching at the door; and its desire is for you, but you must master it" (Gen 4:7).

The Bible warns that there is woe for those who walk in the "way of Cain" (Jude 11). In order to escape that woe, Christians today must learn to master sin. The parable of the tares teaches us that no one, including the chosen believer, is exempt from becoming Satan's target. The tares are sown in the night, and the results become evident only when they bear fruit.

Therefore, it is important for believers to stay alert and awake at all times so that tares may not be sown in the field of the good seed, the seed of God's Word (Prov 4:23; 16:32). Otherwise, even believers can acquire Satan's traits and become his perpetrators regardless of how much faith they may have built up over the years.

The Bible says that man is enslaved by what overcomes him (John 8:34; Rom 6:16; Titus 3:3; 2 Pet 2:19). Believers must become God's servants and bear fruit resulting in sanctification (Rom 6:22). They must become a people for His own possession, zealous for good deeds (Eph 2:10; Titus 2:14).

(4) Cain settled in the land of Nod.

Even after committing sin, Cain shamelessly objected to God's punishment, claiming that it was more than he could bear (Gen 4:13–14). His words reveal no trace of repentance or grief over what he has done. His attitude was a direct contrast to that of the repentant psalmist who cried, "Do not cast me away from Thy presence, and do not take Thy Holy Spirit from me" (Ps 51:11).

What was the curse that fell upon Cain the murderer? The first was this: "When you cultivate the ground, it shall no longer yield its strength to you" (Gen 4:12). This curse was much graver than the one that fell upon Adam (Gen 3:17–18), because the land was to totally reject Cain. Adam had to toil to eat the produce of the earth, but for Cain it would not produce any fruit at all. Regardless of his labor, there would be no harvest. The second curse was that Cain would be cast away from the earth (Gen 4:12). His life as a wanderer had begun, and from this point, there would be no place to rest in peace.

Accordingly, sin keeps us from God. In fact, sin cuts off all of our relationships. When our relationship with God becomes distant, our relationship with all creation will also become distant. Furthermore, the relationships that we have built within our communities will also fail so that we eventually feel isolated and alienated.

After the sons of Cain turned their backs to God, they settled in the land of Nod to the east of Eden (Gen 4:16). The name *Nod* (נוֹד) means "wandering," "vagrant," or "fugitive." This describes the state of mankind after departure from God: restless wandering without a definite goal or purpose in life. This is a direct contrast to Eden, the land of joy. No sinner, regardless of who he or she is, can escape the curse upon this earth. The only way to break the yoke of this curse and enjoy wealth and prosperity is to believe in Jesus Christ.

Cain built a city as he settled in the land of Nod (Gen 4:17). The Hebrew word used here is *ʿîr* (עִיר), meaning "city" or "town." This construction of the first city (city-state) reveals the underlying desire to dilute the curse of God that cast Adam and Eve out of Eden. Moreover, it manifests the desire to gain independence from God's intervention by building a high city through the unified efforts of men. The construction of cities by men who have forsaken God comes to a climax with the construction of the Tower of Babel in Genesis 11.

Restless wandering began the moment man forsook God to live independently of His care in their man-built cities. Their dwelling place was a land in which they could gather nothing but dust despite their effort and struggle; it was truly the land of *Nod*. After building the city, Cain named it *Enoch* after his son—evidence that he desired for his descendants to inherit his seedbed of sin and wickedness (Gen 4:17).

2. Enoch (חֲנוֹךְ): dedication,[3] initiated,[4] teacher[5]

Cain's son, Enoch, shares the same name with Enoch, the sixth generation in the line of Seth. However, Enoch from the line of Seth was a godly man who reached the highest peak of faith, whereas Enoch from the line of Cain was an ungodly and corrupt man. Enoch was the first son born to Cain after he departed from God (Gen 4:16–17) and was thus the first fruit of humanism. It can be inferred that Cain named his son *Enoch*, meaning "dedication," with a hope that he might be dedicated to the success of his humanistic lineage.

The birth of Enoch is described in greater detail than any other person in the line of Cain.

> **Genesis 4:16–17** Then Cain went out from the presence of the LORD, and settled in the land of Nod, east of Eden. [17]And Cain had relations with his wife and she conceived, and gave birth to Enoch; and he built a city, and called the name of the city Enoch, after the name of his son.

The following significant points can be construed from the meanings of the name *Enoch* ("dedication," "initiation," "teacher"):

1. Cain built a city and named it "Enoch" after his son. The name *Enoch* was *dedicated* to the purpose of flaunting the citadel (city-state) of humanism built by those who had forsaken God.
2. Those who departed from God overthrew all the good and beautiful things that they had once enjoyed while they were with God. They *initiated* a movement to live according to the human will and not the divine will.
3. Enoch became a *teacher* (*beginning, source, ancestor*) who instructed in the ways of rebellion, disbelief, and the betrayal of God.

The name *Enoch* probably became very well known after Cain's city was named after him. Enoch the person probably was famous throughout the land as well, but his name will not be remembered by God, because he had nothing to do with God.

---

3. Gordon J. Wenham, *Genesis 1–15*, Word Biblical Commentary 1 (Waco, TX: Word, 1987), 111; Chul Won Suh, *The Book of Genesis* (Seoul: Grisim, 2001), 238.

4. H. D. M. Spence and Joseph Exell, eds., *The Pulpit Commentary*, vol. 1, *Genesis, Exodus* (Peabody, MA: Hendrickson, 2004), 87; *The Oxford Bible Interpreter.* Edited by Disciples Publishing House (Seoul: Bible Study Material Publisher, 1989), 1:337.

5. *The Oxford Bible Interpreter*, 1:371.

Enoch had a name that he was alive, but he was already dead in God's eyes (Rev 3:1). His name had no significance in the spiritual world. Conversely, the names of the precious saints, though they may appear insignificant in this world, will be written in the book of life and will not be erased (Rev 3:5). Jesus died on the cross to fulfill the will of the Father, and as a result, God awarded Him with "the name which is above every name" (Phil 2:9). To all those who follow in Jesus' steps, God will also grant the honor of having their names written in the book of life, never to be blotted out (Phil 4:3).

Cain and his son Enoch started off without God. Cain named the first son born to him after his independence from God *Enoch*, meaning "dedication," "initiation (start)," and "teacher." Then, he named the city that they built for themselves "Enoch." Cain and Enoch's humanistic pursuits devoid of God were truly grand. They probably aspired to build for themselves a magnificent city, a godless paradise on earth reminiscent of the Garden of Eden.

However, what was the ultimate destiny of lives that began without God? They became fathers of great massacres, violence, and wickedness. Paradise on earth seemed so close to being established, but contrary to the grand start, their city turned into a city of sinfulness, murder, injustice, and corruption.

There are also many times when we begin things in our lives without God. We do not always include Him in the plans that we make for the major events in our lives, such as a successful business, a happy marriage, or retirement. God is the beginning of all things. From start to finish, He will guide us when we pray to Him, seek answers from the Bible, and turn to His people for advice. He will take responsibility for us until our final goals are achieved.

3. Irad (עִירָד): runner, fleet,[6] boastful[7]

Irad was Enoch's son. He was a braggart, as the meaning of his name indicates. Presumably, he was the kind of person who fled from God's presence, committing all kinds of sins and saying, "Where is God? God

6. Spence and Exell, *Genesis*, 88.
7. Disciples Publishing House, *Oxford Bible Interpreter*, 1:339.

cannot see what I am doing!" He probably had no fear or hesitation about committing the grave sin of denying God's existence. The Bible calls this kind of person the most foolish of all.

> **Psalm 10:4** The wicked, in the haughtiness of his countenance, does not seek Him. All his thoughts are, "There is no God."
>
> **Psalm 14:1** The fool has said in his heart, "There is no God." They are corrupt, they have committed abominable deeds; there is no one who does good.

God not only sees our actions, He also searches the depths of our hearts to discover the hidden motivation behind those actions (Ps 94:9; Prov 5:21; Jer 17:10). He sees not only the present, but also the past and the future (Ps 139:1–3). We cannot deceive God and nothing can be hidden from Him for He has seven eyes (Zech 3:9; 4:10; Rev 5:6). He is omnipresent; He is everywhere in the entire universe and watches over all things under the light of seven days (Isa 30:26). His eyes are like fire, moving to and fro throughout the earth so that no one can flee from them (2 Chr 16:9). Proverbs 15:3 says that His eyes watch "the evil and the good." Psalm 33 says, "The LORD looks from heaven; He sees all the sons of men." It continues, "From His dwelling place He looks out on all the inhabitants of the earth," and concludes that He understands all their works (Ps 33:13–15). Job 34:21–22 states, "For His eyes are upon the ways of a man, and He sees all his steps. There is no darkness or deep shadow where the workers of iniquity may hide themselves." Regardless of how deep a person hides or how far a person runs within the God-created time and space, God can command all heaven and earth to stand together and stand exactly in the hiding place (Isa 48:13).

Although none of the Israelites knew that Achan had stolen the mantle, the gold, and the silver, God knew and exposed his sin (Josh 7:1–26). No one knew that Michal looked down from her window at King David as he was leaping and dancing and despised him in her heart (2 Sam 6:16). God, however, saw and knew this. As a result, she remained childless until the day she died (2 Sam 6:23).

No one other than his wife knew that Ananias held back some of the proceeds from the sale of their property. God revealed his evil intention to Peter, and after Peter rebuked Ananias for his evil deed, Ananias fell and died on the very same day (Acts 5:1–11). Truly, those who try to keep things from God, those who try to deceive Him with lies, and those who try to run away from Him are foolish!

"Boastful," one of the meanings of the name *Irad*, describes the act of making something appear greater than what it actually is. It refers to the exaggeration of one's current wealth, appearance, power, or honor in order to impress others and satisfy oneself. When Nebuchadnezzar, king of Babylon, surveyed the grandeur of his kingdom and boasted of his power and glory, a voice came from heaven even before he finished speaking. Immediately, King Nebuchadnezzar degenerated to the level of animals in accordance with the prophecy of the voice (Dan 4:28–37).

God declared that the kingdom of Judah would come to ruin because King Hezekiah did not speak of God's grace but only boasted of his own strength and power to Berodach-baladan, the king of Babylon (2 Kgs 20:16–19; Isa 39:6–7).

When God is not present in people's hearts, they try to fill the void by adorning themselves with power, honor, and fame. They use the power of money, knowledge, and authority to oppress the weak and the poor. For this reason, the Bible advises not to "boast in your arrogance," for "all such boasting is evil" (Jas 4:16). The only boasting that we should do is of Jesus Christ (Gal 6:14).

4. Mehujael (מְחוּיָאֵל): blotted out by God[8]

Mehujael, the name of Irad's son, means "blotted out clean by God" (Gen 4:18). The name *Mehujael* is a combination of the root words מחה (*māḥâ*), meaning "to blot" or "to wipe out," and אֵל (*ʾēl*), meaning "God." Consequently, the name can be interpreted as "the one whom God wiped out" or "the one whose name God blotted out." This is a truly frightful curse. A name attests to a person's existence, and blotting it out voids that person's existence altogether. This is truly the harshest judgment.

What kind of life did Mehujael live that he should receive such a cursed name? Although the Bible makes no mention of his deeds or his

8. Wenham, *Genesis 1–15*, 112; Spence and Exell, *Genesis*, 88.

character, we can make inferences about his life based on other uses of the Hebrew word *māḥâ* in the Bible.

The word *māḥâ*, the root of *mehu*, was used to describe the act of using a sponge or fabric to absorb and wipe away ink spots from a scroll. The act of wiping away an individual's name, an individual's achievements, or even an entire nation just as an ink spot is wiped away from a scroll is associated with fearful judgment of obliterating one's existence. Consequently, this word was mainly used in connection with the punishment and judgment of criminals. The word *māḥâ* is used to mean "to blot out" in Genesis 6:7, "And the LORD said, 'I will blot out man whom I have created from the face of the land,'" and in Genesis 7:23, "Thus He blotted out every living thing that was upon the face of the land." This word is used many times throughout the Bible with two different renderings.

First, *māḥâ* signifies the complete destruction of a city or tribe that has sinned before God. Here, the word literally means "to remove" and "to make extinct." In the verse "I will wipe Jerusalem as one wipes a dish" (2 Kgs 21:13), the word "wipe" (*māḥâ*) connotes God's judgment upon the city.

In a discussion regarding the way to save the tribe of Benjamin, "that a tribe may not be blotted out from Israel" (Judg 21:17), *māḥâ* is rendered as "to blot out" or "to make disappear." The word is used in connection with judgment upon a city or tribe resulting in destruction so utterly complete that it will be wiped out even from people's memories.

Second, the word is used to refer to the blotting out of a person's name or the memory of that person's existence. A good example is the account of the Amalekites. In Exodus 17:14, God said, "I will utterly blot out the memory of Amalek from under heaven," and in Deuteronomy 9:14, "Let Me alone, that I may destroy them and blot out their name from under heaven." Here, *māḥâ* signifies the act of blotting out from a person's memory. The Amalekites had attacked the faint and weary stragglers at the end of the Israelites' wilderness procession (Deut 25:18; 1 Sam 15:2). God remembered what they had done and commanded the sons of Israel to blot out the name of Amalek from their memory.

These two examples demonstrate how the word *māḥâ* was used to describe God's judgment upon nations, tribes, cities, and individuals that stood against His will and committed sin. We can infer from the name *Mehujael* that he lived his life similarly to the Amalekites who endlessly challenged God and afflicted His people and to the people before the flood who were wicked and violent in their purpose.

5. Methushael (מְתוּשָׁאֵל): man of Sheol or man of God[9]

Methushael, the name of Mehujael's son (Gen 4:18), has two suggested meanings that contradict one another.

First, *Methushael* can be rendered as a compound word (name) made up of מַת (*mat*), which means "man," and שְׁאוֹל (*šĕʾôl*), which means "Sheol" or "hell," thus giving the meaning "man of hell." In the Old Testament, Sheol usually refers to the grave, hell, or the world of the dead. This implies that Methushael did not walk with God, but that he lived his life seeking to satisfy his worldly greed and personal desires and ultimately fell into Sheol, the world of the dead.

Second, *Methushael* can be rendered as a compound word made up of *mat*, God's name *ʾēl*, and *ša* (*sa*), meaning "of," thus giving the meaning "man of God."

It can be presumed that Mehujael gave his son a name that means "man of God." Knowing that his own name means "to blot out" and that everything he had achieved in his life had disappeared altogether in fulfillment of the meaning of his name, he probably wished a different life for his son. He probably hoped that his son would become a man of God, guided by His hand into a life of peace and blessings.

Unfortunately, judging from the fact that Lamech, Methushael's son, became a more wicked murderer than Cain (Gen 4:23–24), Methushael must have lived as a man of hell and not as a man of God.

Like the two meanings of the name *Methushael*, all human beings walk one of the two paths of life. Some live as people of God and follow His will; they are used for His glory, to perform His great and honorable work. What a glorious honor it is for helpless human beings to be called "people of God," to belong to Him, and to be used by Him!

9. Wenham, *Genesis 1–15*, 112; Spence and Exell, *Genesis*, 88.

Moses (Deut 33:1), Samuel (1 Sam 9:8), Elijah (1 Kgs 17:18), Elisha (2 Kgs 4:7; 5:8), King David (Neh 12:24), and other unnamed prophets (1 Sam 2:27; 1 Kgs 13:1) were called "men of God." Paul also called Timothy "man of God" (1 Tim 6:11).

Others live their lives enslaved by Satan and confined in darkness as children of hell. Jude 11–13 describe the lives of people such as Cain, Balaam, and Korah, who stood against God, as "wandering stars, for whom the black darkness has been reserved forever." The "black darkness" refers to hell.

There are always two opposing paths lying before all people. Moses spoke the words of God, saying, "See, I have set before you today life and prosperity, and death and adversity" (Deut 30:15). He continues, "I have set before you life and death, the blessing and the curse," and then he instructs the people, "So choose life in order that you may live, you and your descendants" (Deut 30:19). We must choose life. We must love God and obey His Word (Deut 30:20). Then our lives will take shape as lives of people of God, and the meaning "man of Sheol" will not apply to us.

6. Lamech (לֶמֶךְ): a strong youth,[10] the conqueror[11]

The Bible furnishes most details for the account of Lamech, the last of Cain's six descendants (Gen 4:19–24). Sin advanced down the line of Cain after the fall and reached its peak with the last generation, Lamech, who yielded the fruit of darkness and wickedness in abundance.

The Hebrew derivation of the name *Lamech* (or *Lamek*) is uncertain. In Arabic, it means "strong youth" or "oppressor." Theologian John P. Lange interprets it as "strong youth."[12] The meaning of the name suggests arrogance and boasting of one's own strength.

Those who are incomparably stronger and more powerful freely practice violence against the weak and try to overpower and control them. Furthermore, they become intoxicated with their own heroism and drift far away from God.

10. Wenham, *Genesis 1–15*, 112; Spence and Exell, *Genesis*, 88.

11. Henry M. Morris, *The Genesis Record: A Scientific and Devotional Commentary on the Book of Beginnings* (Grand Rapids: Baker, 1976), 155.

12. John P. Lange, *Commentary on the Holy Scriptures: Critical, Doctrinal and Homiletical—Genesis*, trans. and ed. Philip Schaff (Grand Rapids: Zondervan, 1893), 261.

(1) Lamech defiled God's ordained principle of holy matrimony, turning it into a fleshly and hedonistic practice.

Lamech was a lustful man who took for himself two wives and became the first polygamist. Genesis 4:19 states, "And Lamech took to himself two wives." The table below shows the sons who were born to Lamech through the two women.

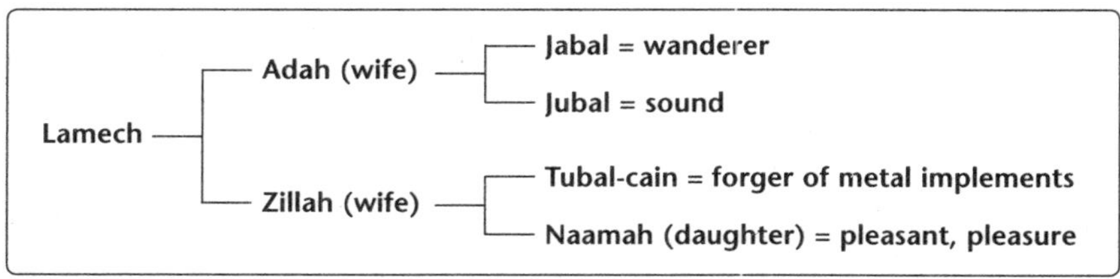

① Adah was Lamech's first wife.

The name *Adah* means "adorn," "decorate," or "glow," suggesting outward attractiveness and seductiveness rather than inner beauty. Presumably, she was a superficial woman who delighted in her own beauty. She probably invested a great deal of time in adorning herself with fancy clothing, cosmetics, and jewelry in order to seduce men.

② Zillah was Lamech's second wife.

The name *Zillah* means "shade" or "shadow"[13] (perhaps alluding to shady places of sin). It also means "protection" (perhaps alluding to her desire to be protected by any man). The name can also mean "to tinkle," an allusion to the sweet sound of the female voice.[14] She probably was a lewd woman who whispered flattery into her husband's ears and encouraged him to perform greater evil.

Even after committing murder, Lamech returned home without any sense of guilt and boasted of his strength before his wives. With the weapon still in his hand, he sang a song about his gruesome deed.

> **Genesis 4:23–24** And Lamech said to his wives, "Adah and Zillah, listen to my voice, you wives of Lamech, give heed to my speech, for I have killed a man for wounding me; and a boy for striking me; [24]if Cain is avenged sevenfold, then Lamech seventy-sevenfold."

---

13. Spence and Exell, *Genesis*, 88.
14. Wenham, *Genesis 1–15*, 112; Spence and Exell, *Genesis*, 88.

Rather than admonishing their husband for his evil deeds, Lamech's wives probably praised and applauded him as he told stories about how he killed with his sword. Zillah probably sang along with her husband, luring him with the "tinkling" sounds of her voice. Both wives probably spent all their time and energy adorning themselves to please him.

(2) Lamech misused the name of God and indulged in the act of retaliation without feeling any guilt.

Lamech sang in his poem, "If Cain is avenged [by God] sevenfold, then Lamech seventy-sevenfold" (Gen 4:24). He sang that God would avenge him as He had avenged Cain, but in actuality Lamech avenged himself. The Bible states, however, that vengeance belongs to God (Deut 32:35; Rom 12:19; Heb 10:30).

In addition, Lamech turned God's special favor and mercy toward Cain into the divine protection for murderers. He turned the law of compassion into a law of retribution. In Cain's case, God prevented others from taking revenge against him, but Lamech took revenge into his own hands. This was an infringement upon God's sovereign authority.

In Lamech's poem about his killing, he misused the name of God Almighty and openly declared that he would take vengeance and kill anyone without mercy. This surely was a flagrant display of man's arrogance and a blasphemous outburst against God.

(3) Lamech disdained the value of life and humanity.

Lamech boasted that he had killed a man for "wounding" him and a boy for "striking" him (Gen 4:23).

"To wound" is פָּצַע (*pāṣaʿ*) in Hebrew, and it refers to a light bruise, not a life-threatening injury. Lamech refused to restrain his anger even for a small offense—a slight bruise. Instead, he mercilessly killed a young boy, displaying his strength and power before others. His actions, unfortunately, reflected the developing spirit of his age: the exaltation of oneself and the degradation of human life even though human life should have been held in high esteem because it holds the image of God.

(4) Lamech passed down to his children a civilization founded upon strife and murder.

For the descendants of Cain, the purpose of education was far removed from any desire for restoration in the fields of intellectuality, humanity, or spirituality. They developed their civilization for the purpose of expanding the influence of humanism, and their opposition to God grew stronger with the passage of time.

① Lamech had Jabal and Jubal through Adah, his first wife.

> **Genesis 4:20–21** And Adah gave birth to Jabal; he was the father of those who dwell in tents and have livestock. [21]And his brother's name was Jubal; he was the father of all those who play the lyre and pipe.

The name *Jabal* means "to lead," "to carry," or "to flow" (searching for wet places).[15] He became the father of those who "dwell in tents and have livestock." The word *livestock* here is מִקְנֶה (*miqneh*), and it refers to flocks or herds of animals used for mercantile purposes. Jabal was the first nomad to migrate from place to place dwelling in tents and may have been the first livestock trader. He was not, however, the first to raise herds; Abel was also a "keeper of flocks" (Gen 4:2).

The name *Jubal* means "sound" or "music." He became the father of all who played the lyre and pipe. Unfortunately, their instruments were not used to praise and worship God. Their music produced sounds of debauchery and licentiousness. The Hebrew word for "pipe," עוּגָב (*ʿûgāb*), is derived from the verb עָגַב (*ʿāgab*), which means "to fall into sensual love." Thus, it is certain that Jubal's music was designed not for praising God, but rather for sensual pleasure and entertainment.

② Lamech had Tubal-cain and Naamah through Zillah, his second wife.

> **Genesis 4:22** As for Zillah, she also gave birth to Tubal-cain, the forger of all implements of bronze and iron; and the sister of Tubal-cain was Naamah.

Tubal-cain became a forger of all kinds of sharp implements and tools of bronze and iron. He was a blacksmith. The name *Tubal-cain*

15. Spence and Exell, *Genesis*, 88.

(תּוּבַל קַיִן) is a compound word made up of תּוּבַל (*tûbal*) and קַיִן (*qayîn*). *Tubal* derives its meaning from Arabic roots: "to overflow," "to multiply" (breed), or "to run." Combined with *Cain*, the name reveals Lamech's desire for the future prosperity of the Cainite descendants. The attachment of the name *Cain* (the father of this sinful lineage) in the name of Tubal-cain suggests that the sinfulness flowing through the lineage was most prominent during his time. Tubal-cain smelted and sharpened implements of metal. These implements were used not as farming or peacemaking tools, but as killing weapons by his father, Lamech.

Lamech's daughter, Naamah, was born of his second wife Zillah (Gen 4:22) and was Tubal-cain's sister. Her name means "pleasant," "sweet," or "beauty (exceptional)." Naamah must have been a seductive woman who was adept in arousing sexual desires in men. Traditionally, women's names are excluded from the list of descendants. Naamah's name was recorded in this genealogy probably because she was extraordinary in her sensual beauty, pleasure, and lust, not because she was godly in any way.

(5) Lamech deified (heroized) himself.

The metal implements aided Lamech's massacre campaign and led to the birth of "heroes" during his time. Naturally, a great band of servile followers formed, eventually building enormous strength and challenging God. This was the evil product of the advancement of human civilization.

The development of human civilization was geared toward humanism, hedonism, and sexual corruption. The underlying philosophy was that the development of individual power should allow them to become supernatural beings similar to God. This is an example of Satan at work, tempting people to always disregard God, rebel against Him, and try to gain independence from Him.

Lamech had reached a point where he no longer feared God's wrath. Adam's sin was in disobeying God's command. Cain's sin was in rejecting the Word and manifesting his wickedness through murder. Lamech's sin was in normalizing the act of murder and heightening the spirit of revenge. The readiness to shed blood, which first manifested in Cain, reappeared in an intensified form in Lamech. The ungodliness of the Cainite lineage had reached its peak with Lamech.

CHAPTER 9

The Descendants of Sin in the Line of Cain

The genealogy of Cain reached its apex with Lamech as civilization flourished and developed, but it came to a sudden halt with no further accounts of Cain's descendants after Lamech. On the other hand, the genealogy of Seth continued down to Noah, Abraham, David, and ultimately, to the Messiah.

This is not to say that all the descendants of Cain perished during Lamech's time. Cain's lineage undoubtedly continued through Lamech's three sons, probably forming a great nation. The Bible, however, discontinues the genealogy of Cain as a warning to readers that a civilization without God and life without God will come to a sudden halt even at their peaks regardless of how developed and flourished a civilization may be.

The Bible testifies that Cain's fleshy genealogy does not stop with Lamech. Rather, Cain's sinfulness will continue down through the lives of different persons until the end time. The genealogies that continue down through Nimrod (a descendant of Ham who led the people to build the Tower of Babel), Ishmael, and Esau are prominent examples.

1. The Descendants of Nimrod (נִמְרוֹד) and the Construction of the Tower of Babel

The descendants of Cain in Genesis 4 were pioneers of human civilization. Lamech's three sons became fathers of those who engaged in livestock trading, played musical instruments, and made metal implements. Nimrod became a mighty hunter and a mighty warrior on the earth comparable to Cain and Lamech (Gen 10:8–9).

(1) Nimrod, the mighty one on earth.

Genesis 10 describes Nimrod as the first mighty one on the earth, a mighty hunter before the Lord, and the father of Babel. It mentions the genealogy of Ham and continues down to Nimrod but pauses to offer a detailed account of his works to highlight his significance.

First, Nimrod was a "mighty one." "Mighty one" is defined in the Hebrew lexicon as "hero," "vigorous man," or "influential man." It is also interpreted as "one who is distinguished in valiance, ability, and wisdom to the extent of achieving a great work." Although Nimrod was called a mighty one on the earth, he was not a hero in God's sight, because he was brave in challenging God and skillful at standing against His will. He possessed singular ability and wisdom for plundering souls through deception.

"Mighty one" is גִּבּוֹר (*gibbôr*) in Hebrew and generally means "one who rules with violence" or "a tyrant." Nimrod was a tyrant who oppressed people and opposed God. He conquered tribes through violence and challenged God by instigating people to build the Tower of Babel.

Second, Nimrod was a "mighty hunter." This description speaks of his work and relationship with God. "Mighty hunter" implies that he was a distinctively more skillful hunter than others. The region in which Nimrod dwelt was a fertile land inhabited by numerous beasts of the field (Exod 23:29–30; Deut 7:22). Henry Morris comments, "The reference to Nimrod's hunting prowess suggests that wild beasts were thought to be a real source of danger at the time and that Nimrod acquired his heroic reputation by protecting the population against these beasts."[1] It was by this means that Nimrod apparently gained servile followers and rose to the position of a heroic leader in his time. His power increased as the number of his followers multiplied, and he used this power to deify himself. He sat in God's place and opposed Him. He flaunted his ability to entice and reign over people's souls. Nimrod was the archetype of the antichrist, robbing the souls of mankind and turning them away from God:

---

1. Henry M. Morris, *The Genesis Record: A Scientific and Devotional Commentary on the Book of Beginnings* (Grand Rapids: Baker, 1976), 252.

> **Genesis 10:8–9** Cush was also the ancestor of Nimrod, who was the first heroic warrior on earth. [9]Since he was the greatest hunter in the world, his name became proverbial. People would say, "This man is like Nimrod, the greatest hunter in the world." (New Living Translation)

Third, Nimrod became the founder of Babel (Gen 10:10; 11:4), the atheistic city-state that challenged God's will, through the support of his followers. Similar in character to the Cainite descendants, the nation of Babel exalted the names of men rather than the name of God. Nimrod led the people to the plains of Shinar for the purpose of building the Tower of Babel so that he might achieve his great ambition.

(2) Constructing the Tower of Babel.

Under Nimrod's leadership, the people's desire to build the Tower of Babel originated from their ambition to establish a self-sufficient civilization independent from God. The Bible speaks of three purposes for the construction of the Tower of Babel.

The first purpose was to build for themselves a city and a tower whose top would reach into heaven (Gen 11:4). This tower was a *ziggurat*, a structure in the form of a terraced pyramid of successively receding stories. At the center of the ziggurat were steps to the top, where a small temple or shrine was built. In the ancient world, building a high religious structure to reach the heavens was in pursuit of unity, combining human strength to build a great empire. The desire to build a safe and strong nation independent of God was manifested in the construction of the Tower of Babel.

This incident occurred not too long after the catastrophic flood that destroyed the entire world. Thus, the construction of the Tower of Babel was an expression of their discontentment with God's judgment. They disregarded God's covenant of the bow—the promise that He would never again judge the world with water (universal flood [Gen 9:8–17])—and attempted to prepare for God's judgment. How foolish and arrogant it is for men to reject God's protection and seek their own through the means of human strength and power! This act is reminiscent of how Cain had disregarded God's sign of protection and built a city for his protection, naming it after his own son Enoch (Gen 4:15–17). The root of this kind of evil is the power of the dark and evil devil.

The situation is similar today not only in the secular world, but also within the church. There are forces of darkness that seek unity of human strength by emphasizing one heart and one will rather than focusing on the Word of God. Unity outside of the Word of God and gatherings that do not acknowledge faith in God will only lead to conflicts, hurt feelings, a sense of futility, and regrets. Furthermore, unified powers apart from God and gatherings for the purpose of human comfort and convenience not only are lawless, unrighteous, and wicked, but also are in opposition to God's plan for redemption.

The second purpose for building the Tower of Babel was to make for themselves a name (Gen 11:4). Like the descendants of Cain, they sought after their own honor and exaltation rather than the glory of God's name. They used the power of science and civilization to challenge God's authority and reached the peak of humanistic arrogance: the desire to become like God (Isa 14:12–14). God, however, destroyed their haughty plans by confusing their language and scattering them abroad over the face of the whole earth (Gen 11:7–8).

Adam and Eve were deceived by the serpent's words in the Garden of Eden: "For God knows that in the day you eat from it your eyes will be opened, and you will be like God, knowing good and evil" (Gen 3:5). They ate from the tree of the knowledge of good and evil in their proud desire to become like God and were expelled from Eden (Gen 3:23–24). James 4:6 tells us, "God is opposed to the proud."

The third purpose for building the Tower of Babel was to avoid being scattered abroad over the face of the whole earth (Gen 11:4). This was an act of defiance against God's command upon creation. After God created man, the first command He gave to Adam was "Be fruitful and multiply, and fill the earth, and subdue it" (Gen 1:28). God also gave the same blessing to Noah and his sons after the flood: "Be fruitful and multiply, and fill the earth" (Gen 9:1, 7). This command reveals God's intent to spread His children throughout the whole world so that they may prosper and turn the entire world into a kingdom of God's people. Nimrod, however, gathered his followers to build the Tower of Babel in order to prevent people from being scattered abroad over the face of the whole earth. All this was evil in the eyes of God, and He destroyed all their intentions.

> **Genesis 11:8–9** The LORD scattered them abroad from there over the face of the whole earth; and they stopped building the city. [9]Therefore its name was called Babel, because there the LORD confused the language of the whole earth, and from there the LORD scattered them abroad over the face of the whole earth.

God used the confusion of languages as a means to halt the construction of the tower and to scatter the people. Language is more than mere sounds that come from the mouth. Unity in language signifies oneness in philosophy and lifestyle. Therefore, the confusion of languages not only leads to differences in philosophy, but also causes chaos in all aspects of life. It brought the construction to an immediate end, demonstrating that man's achievements can come to a sudden halt even after careful planning, great investment, and detailed coordination. The prophet Isaiah declared God's Word to such foolish people: "Surely My hand founded the earth, and My right hand spread out the heavens; when I call to them, they stand together" (Isa 48:13). In 1 Samuel 2:6–10, Hannah, who was barren, gave birth to Samuel by the grace of God. After the birth of Samuel, she realized that all things are part of God's sovereign providence and praised Him, saying, "Those who contend with the LORD will be shattered; against them He will thunder in the heavens" (1 Sam 2:10).

This world is quick to unite for the purpose of carrying out evil schemes, powerful in its driving force, and ambitious in its dreams. We must examine our lives to see if our plans, our ways, and our goals are human-centered like the plans of those who built the Tower of Babel. In His sovereign providence God called us for His good purpose. Paul encourages, "Therefore, walk in a manner worthy of the calling with which you have been called" (Eph 4:1). Those who are called according to His purpose will work together for good to fulfill what God has planned (Rom 8:28). The times are calling for people of faith who will conduct themselves in "a manner worthy of the gospel of Christ" so they may be pleasing to God (Phil 1:27).

2. Ishmael (יִשְׁמָעֵאל) and Esau (עֵשָׂו)

The history of the wicked civilization of the descendants of Cain ended after Lamech but manifested itself again with the attempt to build the Tower of Babel. It was unsuccessful because God scattered the people, but the history of the line of Cain did not stop there. It continued again through Ishmael, Abraham's son.

(1) Ishmael, a wild donkey of a man.

The Bible states that Abraham's son Ishmael, born of Hagar the maid, would live the life of a "wild donkey." The angel of the Lord spoke of Ishmael in Genesis 16:12, "And he will be a wild donkey of a man, his hand will be against everyone, and everyone's hand will be against him; and he will live to the east of all his brothers." This suggests that the children of Ishmael and of Abraham's promised son Isaac will be in competition and confrontation.

His dwelling place will be "to the east." The literal translation of "to the east" is "before the face of." According to the Revised Standard Version translation, he will dwell "over against" his kinsmen. Hence, the statement that he will live "to the east" of all his brothers implies that he would become an offspring of sin and wickedness like Nimrod and stand against God and afflict His people. Just as Nimrod became a mighty hunter and reigned over people who opposed God, Ishmael became like a wild donkey that violently afflicted God's people.

From the verse "His hand will be against everyone, and everyone's hand will be against him" we can infer that he was the kind of person who stirred up dissension and instigated unnecessary fights wherever he went. He continuously raised his hands to strike God's people and to challenge God's will. Ishmael's entire life was filled with hostility and animosity toward others. In the end, if "everyone" turns against him, how pitiful would his life become (Jer 17:6)?

Ishmael had already begun to be against others from a young age when he mocked his brother Isaac (Gen 21:9). Furthermore, he associated himself with Nimrod when he took a wife from the land of Egypt (Gen 21:21). In Genesis 10:6, Cush, Mizraim, Put, and Canaan were born to Ham, Noah's son. Mizraim became the father of the Egyptians. Cush became a father of Nimrod. Thus, by marrying an Egyptian, Ishmael drew closer to Nimrod's lineage.

(2) Esau, father of the Edomite tribe.

Esau, the father of the Edomites, was one of Isaac's twin sons. He lost his place in God's covenantal blessings because he took the privileges of his birthright lightly and sold it to Jacob his brother (Gen 25:29–34; Heb 12:16–17). Esau took wives for himself, including Adah the daughter of Elon the Hittite, Oholibamah the daughter of Anah from Canaan, and Basemath the daughter of Ishmael (Gen 36:2–3). Through these marriages he simultaneously linked himself with the line of Canaan the son of Ham and the line of Ishmael. Thus, the ungodly descendants of Cain not only shared a common philosophy and lifestyle, but also became a part of each other's bloodline through marriage. They united in the effort to stand against God's will and to continue on the path of disbelief.

One of the most notable persons among the descendants of Esau was Amalek (Gen 36:12). Amalek was born to Eliphaz, Esau's son, through his concubine Timna. It was the descendants of Amalek who would attack the children of Abraham in Rephidim later in history as they journeyed through the wilderness during their exodus from Egypt. Their attack on the chosen people incited God's great anger. As a result, He vowed to wage war against Amalek from generation to generation (Exod 17:16) and commanded Israel to blot out the memory of Amalek from under heaven (Deut 25:17–19). The Amalekites, however, continued to afflict the people of Israel, even by allying themselves with neighboring countries to attack Israel (Obad 1, 2, 10, 18).

There was also a time when Israel came close to being destroyed because of Haman the son of Hammedatha the Agagite (Esth 3:1–15). However, they were miraculously saved from destruction through Queen Esther's sacrificial faith. The Bible introduces Haman as an Agagite, revealing that he was a descendant of Esau (Esth 3:1, 10; 8:5; 9:24). In 1 Samuel 15:8, Agag is described as "the king of the Amalekites"—evidence that Agag was an Amalekite and thus a descendant of Esau. Therefore, Haman was also a descendant of Esau.

All who afflict the people of God's covenant and hinder His work of redemption the way Nimrod, Ishmael, and Esau had done are followers of the way of Cain (Jude 11). Their deeds of darkness will not cease until the day that the work of redemption is complete. Cain's disbelief was inherited by Nimrod and the people of Babel and continued through Ishmael and Esau. In the Book of Revelation, these descendants of Cain are altogether called "Babylon" (Rev 17:5; 18:2).

Babylon refers to those who could not protect their faith and have been tempted to become partakers of the abominable deeds and of the great harlot of the world. They depend on the civilization that they have built and stand against the will of God. In the end, these people will be split into three parts and will fall (Rev 16:19). The genealogies of the unfaithful teach an important lesson: plans that begin without God and plans that oppose Him will collapse even at the height of their success. The genealogy of Cain was suddenly cut off during Lamech's generation, and the construction of the Tower of Babel came to an abrupt halt. The Bible testifies that the great city Babylon that will appear in the end time will also be "fallen, fallen" in the end (Rev 14:8; 18:2).

This was God's sovereign providence and His way of working toward achieving salvation for His chosen people. The line of Cain became a force that attempted to interfere with God's work of redemption and will continue to resist until the end (1 John 3:12). Although the sinfulness of the line of Cain was great, God's sovereign will was even greater and more fervent. His divine administration for salvation will carry on until the day that Satan's head is crushed and made a footstool for God's feet (Ps 110:1; Luke 20:43; Acts 2:35; Heb 1:13; 10:13).

Even as the tides of sin and wickedness swell over the earth, God's work of redemption will continue on as the great and undaunted waterway of life that resuscitates the dying ocean. Our current world, completely decorated with all kinds of sin, is evidence that the final segment of the history of redemption is quickly approaching. It is time to prepare the spiritual oil for the lamp (Matt 25:1–13; 24:44). It is now time to wake up from slumber (Luke 21:36; Rom 13:11). The final fulfillment of God's work of redemption is closer now than at any other time. It is important for all to diligently prepare in faith and to invest all efforts in achieving godliness and living lives with no regrets (2 Cor 13:5; 1 Tim 4:7–8; 2 Pet 1:5–8).

לכל בר דעת דרך המסעות ארבעים שנה במדבר והרוחב והאורך של ארץ הקדושה מנהר מצ
ים המלח
מדבר צין הוא קדש
עמלק
הר ההר
עיר כרמל
שבט
מדבר סיני
קדש ברנע
מדבר פארן
מדבר שור
באר שבע
שמעון
שבט
ארץ פלשתים
אשקלון
אלכסנדרי
פתם
ארץ גשן
לוח המסעות במדבר
אשר על פי ה׳ יסעו ועל פי ה׳ יחנו
א״ רעמסס טו״ רתמה לט״ הרהגדגד
ב״ סכת טז״ רמן פרץ ל״ יטבתה
ג״ אתם יז״ לבנה לא״ עברנה
ד״ פיהחירת יח״ רסה לב״ עציון גבר
ה״ מרה יט״ קהלתה לג״ מדבר צין
ו״ אילם כ״ הרספר לד״ הרההר
ז״ ים סוף כא״ חרדה לה״ צלמנה
ח״ מדבר סין כב״ מקהלת לו״ פונן
ט״ דפקה כג״ תחת לז״ אבת
יוד״ אלוש כד״ תרח לח״ דיבן גד
יא״ רפידם כה״ מתקה לט״ עלמן דבלתים
יב״ מדבר סיני כו״ חשמנה מ״ הרי עברים
יג״ קברות התאוה כז״ מסרות מא״ ערבות מואב
יד״ חצרת כח״ בני יעקן

PART FOUR

The Genealogy According to the Line of Seth

Genesis 4 sums up the genealogy of those who have forsaken God, and Genesis 5 introduces a new genealogy of faith that begins with Seth. The emergence of the line of Seth in a world stained by Cain's unbelief and cruel act of murder meant renewed hope and a new beginning for all mankind. There are twenty generations in the genealogy of Seth: ten generations from Adam to Noah and another ten immediately following Noah, from Shem to Abraham.

First, God's divine administration for the coming of the Messiah flows through this genealogy.

Second, this genealogy introduces Noah (the tenth generation from Adam) and Abraham (the tenth generation from Shem). These two central figures in the history of redemption are the presages of the Savior who would come to save mankind from judgment.

Third, this genealogy presents a model of proper faith for believers who place their hope in the second coming. The God who worked through these twenty patriarchs is also working through us today.

This chapter will introduce the twenty patriarchs through a study of their names, the historical background of their times, and a description of their lives of worship and godly faith. In addition, we will examine how God's plan for the redemption of mankind continuously flows through the core of this genealogy.

CHAPTER 10

The Genealogy from Adam to Noah

The cycle consisting of the fall of man, judgment, and restoration is repeated twice in the genealogy from Adam to Noah. The first cycle began with Adam's sin and banishment from the Garden of Eden and Cain's act of murder and Abel's death, and it concluded with recovery from sin and judgment through Seth. In the second cycle, God judged the world overflowing with sins committed by the sons of God and the daughters of men with the flood, but He esteemed Noah and established him as the second ancestor of mankind to begin a new history.

Lamech, from the line of Cain, was an important figure whose deeds were recorded in greater detail than others in his line. Likewise, Enoch (the seventh generation from Adam) was the focus of attention from the line of Seth. Enoch lived 308 years contemporaneously with Adam and believed in Adam's testimony of the Word of God. As a result, he became the first man to walk with God and to overcome death, man's inevitable fate.

In the genealogy from Adam to Noah there are no additional narratives for the lives of Kenan, Mahalalel, Jared, and Methuselah. Their longevity, nonetheless, testifies of their godly lives of faith. Countless number of passages in the Old and New Testaments emphasize that longevity is God's special blessing bestowed upon those who live godly lives (Deut 4:40; 5:16; 6:2; 11:9; 12:25, 28; 22:7; Exod 20:12; 1 Kgs 3:14; Ps 21:4; 55:23, 91:16; Prov 3:1–2, 7-8, 16; 4:20–23; 9:11; 10:27; 16:31; Eccl 7:17; 8:13; Eph 6:1–3). Proverbs 3:1–2 states, "My son, do not forget my teaching, but let your heart keep my commandments; for length of days and years of life, and peace they will add to you." The lives of the wicked, however, will be reduced to half (Ps 55:23).

All the patriarchs from Adam to Noah enjoyed astonishing longevity. Excluding Enoch, who was taken up to heaven without seeing death at the age of 365, the years of the other nine patriarchs in the order of longevity were as follows: Methuselah (969), Jared (962), Noah (950), Adam (930), Seth (912), Kenan (910), Enosh (905), Mahalalel (895), and Lamech (777). Seven patriarchs lived over nine hundred years—longevity impossible to achieve today. Despite the inevitability of death resulting from sin, longevity was a special privilege awarded to the godly offspring and the greatest blessing for men on earth. Eui Won Kim observes that the blessing of longevity was God's special blessing given to the descendants of Seth, but not to the descendants of Cain.[1] Yune Sun Park also notes that there is a close relationship between godliness and longevity. He interprets longevity as the result of God's plan, and also as the result of special reverence for God in each generation.[2]

We will now proceed to examine the unique structure of the genealogy recorded in Genesis 5—the lives of the ten patriarchs and the spiritual meaning hidden in their names—in order to understand God's sovereign plan and providence.

1. Eui Won Kim, *Heaven, Earth, and the Toledoth of the Patriarchs* (Seoul: Presbyterian General Assembly Education Department, 2004), 157.

2. Yune Sun Park, *A Commentary on Genesis*, vol. 1 (Seoul: Yung Eum Sa, 1991), 123.

1. First Generation: Adam

אדם (*ʾādām*): man, mankind, human

> **Adam became the father of Seth at the age of 130. He lived 800 more years and had other children. He died at the age of 930 (Gen 5:3–5; 1 Chr 1:1).**
>
> **His name is recorded in the genealogy of Jesus in Luke 3:38 as** Ἀδάμ **(*Adam*).**

The name *Adam* comes from the Assyrian root *adamu*, meaning "to make" or "to create." Man can never be the creator; he is only the creation and the creature. Adam was formed from the dust (Gen 2:7; 3:19, 23). "Dust" is עפר (*ʿāpār*) in Hebrew, meaning "dust" or "ashes," not "mud" or "dirt." Without the breath of God, the essence of man is only dust (Gen 18:27; Job 4:19; 33:6; Ps 103:14; Eccl 3:20; Isa 64:8; 1 Cor 15:47).

(1) Adam lived until Lamech, his ninth generation, was fifty-six years old. After the fall, Adam and Eve probably testified about their blessed lives before the fall, their fellowship with God, and the conditions in Eden. All the generations from Seth (second generation) to Lamech (ninth generation) probably received a full account from Adam about the eternal world before the fall, their spiritual experiences, Satan's deception, the consequences of disobedience, and the promise of salvation.

Adam received the assured gospel regarding the woman's seed (Gen 3:15) and probably preached this gospel to his descendants with tireless diligence, because it was the only ray of hope for him and for all mankind. More than anyone else, Adam believed that the woman's seed would come according to the promise that he received. This is evident in the name he gave to his wife after they received the promise in Genesis 3:15: *Eve* ("life" [Gen 3:20]). Through this name, Adam declared that Eve would become the mother of all the living. This was the first confession of faith in the promise of the seed and the expression of hope in the day when life conquers death. His conviction probably strengthened each time he called out her name.

The garments of skin with which God had clothed Adam and Eve before banishing them from Eden (Gen 3:21) were the assurance of His covenant in Genesis 3:15, which for Adam was more precious than life itself. The garments made of skin imply that sacrifice is the basic principle of salvation. It also reveals how the redemption of mankind would be accomplished. This is a foreshadowing of Jesus Christ's sacrifice on the cross, for the sacrifice of life is required to make garments of skin.

Throughout his life, Adam cherished the garments of skin because they were his confirmation of the covenant. He firmly believed that the day would come when the promised seed will bruise the head of the serpent. This probably is the faith that he taught and passed down to his descendants.

(2) Adam testified of the glorious experiences in the Garden of Eden.

① Adam probably taught his descendants that the Garden of Eden was a world without shame, for they were naked but were not ashamed.

> **Genesis 2:25** And the man and his wife were both naked and were not ashamed.

After the fall, however, as soon as their eyes were opened to sin, they saw their nakedness and used fig leaves as makeshift clothing and hid themselves (Gen 3:7). In Genesis 3:10, Adam says, "I heard the sound of Thee in the garden, and I was afraid because I was naked; so I hid myself." Their sense of shame brought fear and led them to hide from God's face.

Adam not only vividly experienced this shame and fear, but also clearly understood the causes. He probably engraved into the hearts of his descendants descriptions of the shameless world of Eden. With God's glory, peace, and love overflowing, there was no fault, guilt, or condemnation. How could Adam forget such a world?

② Adam probably told them about the days when he heard the voice of God and conversed with Him as He walked through the garden (Gen 2:15–16; 3:9, 10, 11, 17).

The Garden of Eden was a garden of happiness and blessings because it was where they heard God's tender voice and conversed with Him

(Ps 36:8). After they sinned, however, the same tender voice caused fear and anguish. When God asked, "Adam, where are you?" he could not answer, "Here I am," as he had previously done. Instead, he hid among the trees from the face of God, and ultimately he was banished from Eden (Gen 3:23). It is likely that Adam testified of God to his descendants without ceasing and with zealous longing for the restoration of Eden, where he had once enjoyed indescribable joy and happiness through fellowship with God.

③ Adam probably told them about how he named all creation with the wisdom God bestowed upon him.

> **Genesis 2:19** And out of the ground the LORD God formed every beast of the field and every bird of the sky, and brought them to the man to see what he would call them; and whatever the man called a living creature, that was its name.

Created in God's own image, Adam possessed great wisdom and creativity. It is simply impossible to name thousands and millions of different creatures and living things with human wisdom; it is possible only when God's Spirit is working within. This wisdom is like the wisdom that God bestowed on Solomon, who "spoke of trees, from the cedar that is in Lebanon even to the hyssop that grows on the wall . . . also of animals and birds and creeping things and fish" (1 Kgs 4:32–34).

Adam must have genuinely enjoyed his sovereign power over all creation as he named them. This wisdom, however, vanished along with his authority and power over God's creation when he sinned. He was degraded to a being who could hardly sustain himself. Adam probably shared these experiences with his descendants as well.

(3) Adam died at the age of 930, fifty-seven years before Enoch was taken up to heaven

Calculation:

987 years after Adam (Enoch's transfiguration)
– 930 years (Adam's age at death)
= 57 years

Adam lived contemporaneously with Enoch for 308 years, but he was not able to witness Enoch's ascension because he died 57 years before Enoch was taken up. Enoch did not walk with God during the first 65 years of his life before his son, Methuselah, was born. He started walking with God at the age of 65 after Methuselah was born and continued to walk with Him for 300 years until the age of 365 (Gen 5:21–24). Thus, Adam witnessed Enoch's walk with God for 243 years. Adam presumably exerted great influence on Enoch's life through his testimonies about life before and after his sin and banishment from Eden.

Adam lived 930 years and died. Genesis 5:5 states, "So all the days that Adam lived were nine hundred and thirty years, and he died." The Hebrew word for "die" is מוּת (*mût*), and it refers to natural death. This is the Bible's first reference to natural death since the account of the murder of Abel. The word מוּת (*mût*) is first recorded in the Bible in Genesis 2:17. In this verse, God sternly warns Adam, saying, "But from the tree of the knowledge of good and evil you shall not eat, for in the day that you eat from it you shall surely die." This warning became reality through Adam's death.

The fact that God destroyed the life of Adam, into whom He Himself had breathed the breath of life, demonstrates the extent of His wrath toward sin. Adam's death was truly tragic because it marks the beginning of death, which all his descendants ultimately would inherit (Rom 5:12).

Life, however, was propagated through Adam's descendants even after his death. This is expressed through the phrases "he begot," "he had," "he became the father of," and "after he became the father of," which in Hebrew is יָלַד (*yālad*). This word appears twenty-eight times in Genesis 5. God's long journey toward the redemption of life began when sin brought the curse of death upon all men. God did not abandon man after his tragic failure and fall; rather, He transformed death into life through His abounding grace and love.

2. Second Generation: Seth

שֵׁת (*šēt*): substitute,[3] granted,[4] appointed one,[5] foundation or grounds[6]

Seth was born 130 years after Adam. He became the father of Enosh at the age of 105. He lived 807 more years and had other children. He died at the age of 912 (1,042 years after Adam [Gen 5:6–8; 1 Chr 1:1]). He lived 800 years contemporaneously with Adam and witnessed Enoch's ascension at the age of 857.

His name is recorded in the genealogy of Jesus in Luke 3:38 as Σήθ (*Sēth*).

Adam's second son was Abel (Gen 4:2). In Hebrew, *Abel* is הֶבֶל (*hebel*) and means "vain," "emptiness," and "breath (vapor)." This is a foreboding of the abrupt end that his life would encounter. It is parents' natural inclination to give good names to their children, but Adam named his second son *Abel*, hinting at his realization of the vanity and futility of man's existence as a result of sin.

Adam and Eve's first son, Cain, belonged to the evil one; he killed his brother, Abel, and broke their hope in the new life. Furthermore, Cain departed from God's presence and left Adam and Eve grieving (Gen 4:16). Cain abandoned the path of faith not long after he killed Abel, so they had essentially lost both sons at once. When Jacob heard that his most beloved son, Joseph, had died, he mourned for him for a long time, refusing to be comforted by his other children. He lamented, "Surely I will go down to Sheol in mourning for my son"

3. Gordon J. Wenham, *Genesis 1–15*, Word Biblical Commentary 1 (Waco, TX: Word, 1987), 115; *The Grand Bible Commentary: With Comprehensive and Synthetic Exegetical Study Methods*. Edited by Disciples Publishing House. 16 vols (Seoul: Bible Study Material Publisher, 1991), 385.

4. Robert Alter, The Five Books of Moses: *A Translation with Commentary* (New York: W. W. Norton, 2004), 33; Kim, *Heaven, Earth, and the Toledoth of the Patriarchs*, 153.

5. Henry M. Morris, *The Genesis Record: A Scientific and Devotional Commentary on the Book of Beginnings* (Grand Rapids: Baker, 1976), 155; Yune Sun Park, *Commentary on Genesis*, 119.

6. William L. Holladay, *A Concise Hebrew and Aramaic Lexicon of the Old Testament: Based upon the Lexical Work of Ludwig Koehler and Walter Baumgartner* (Grand Rapids: Eerdmans, 1988), 385.

(Gen 37:34–35). Jacob's great sorrow is similar to the grief that Adam and Eve experienced after losing both sons.

As immense sorrow and despair enveloped Adam's family, God brought comfort and hope by promising "another seed" in the place of Abel. Seth, the son born to Adam at the age of 130, was truly an expression of God's abounding grace and a gift of overflowing hope and comfort.

The name *Seth* is derived from שִׁית (*šit*), which means "to put" and "to set." Abel's life was true to the meaning of his name. Unable to fill his years, he disappeared like a fog without ever receiving the chance to become deeply rooted. Thus, the hope was for God's work to be reestablished and deeply rooted through Seth.

(1) Seth was a son in Adam's image and likeness.

Adam had a son in his own image and likeness.

> **Genesis 5:3** When Adam had lived one hundred and thirty years, he became the father of a son in his own likeness, according to his image, and named him Seth.

This is the declaration that God's image was being passed down through the line of Seth. Seth, not Cain, was the son bearing the image of his father, Adam, and God's promise was given to the line of Seth, not to the line of Cain. This demonstrates that the life of God given to Adam and the image of God, though in imperfect form because of sin, were inherited by Seth. The dignity and the value of human beings, which distinguish them from beasts, are based on the fact that they are created in God's own image (Gen 9:6; Jas 3:9). Though it may not have been in a perfect form, the image of God continued to be passed on through fallen mankind.

(2) Seth was "another seed" that God granted (Gen 4:25).

As the descendants of Cain continued to corrupt the world through murder and deception, Adam realized that God had granted him "another seed" as a part of His redemptive purpose. In response, he gave thanks to God and named his son *Seth*. It is apparent from this name that Adam desired and firmly believed that the path of the promised Savior would be opened up through the line of Seth.

After being plagued by chaos, painful tears, and sorrow, Adam's family was now being reestablished through Seth. This is clearly an indication of God's determination to bring forth the woman's seed, even if it required granting "another seed." His providence for salvation continued on and on until Jesus Christ was born through Mary. Jesus was not of the seed of Joseph; He was "another seed" conceived by the Holy Spirit (Matt 1:18–20). Truly, God's plan is too great for man to comprehend and too immense to measure.

(3) Seth's name contained the hope of securing the path for the coming of the Messiah.

Besides the meaning "another seed," Seth's name also means "to place" and "foundation." In terms of redemptive history, this expresses the hope that Seth, who inherited the image of God, would firmly establish the path for the promised Messiah.

A true church established upon the Word of Jesus Christ, the rock, will neither collapse nor be overcome by the power of darkness (Matt 16:18, 7:24–27). The churches of the end time will also stand firmly upon the foundation of Jesus Christ who came from the line of Seth.

(4) Seth witnessed Adam's death and later Enoch's ascension.

Chronologically, Seth died 112 years after Adam and 55 years after he witnessed Enoch's ascension. Noah (Adam's tenth generation), the archetype of the Savior, was born 14 years after Seth's death.

Calculation: Year of Seth's death (1,042 years after Adam)
– Year of Adam's death (930)
= 112 years

Year of Seth's death (1,042 years after Adam)
– Year of Enoch's ascension (987)
= 55 years

Year of Noah's birth (1,056 years after Adam)
– Year of Seth's death (1,042)
= 14 years

3. Third Generation: Enosh

אֱנוֹשׁ (*ʾĕnôš*): man, mortal frailty[7]

Enosh was born to Seth at the age of 105 (Gen 5:6; 1 Chr 1:1), which was 235 years after Adam. Enosh became the father of Kenan at the age of 90. He lived 815 more years and had other children. He died at the age of 905 (1,140 years after Adam [Gen 5:9–11]). He lived 695 years contemporaneously with Adam and 84 years with Noah. He witnessed Enoch's ascension at the age of 752.

His name is recorded in the genealogy of Jesus in Luke 3:38 as Ἐνώς (*Enōs*).

The name *Enosh* is derived from אָנַשׁ (*ʾănash*), which means "incurable" and "very sick." *Enosh*, like *Adam*, can be used either as a proper name or as a common noun for "man."[8] The name communicates man's total helplessness and predetermined frailty. It likens the state of sinful man to the condition of one groaning in sickness and affliction from an incurable illness (Jer 15:18; Mic 1:9). Enosh's father, Seth, recognized that man, without seeking God, was too frail to overcome the temptations of sin that violently swept over the world. The name *Enosh* was a confession of faith from the mouth of Seth who began to call upon the name of God. Through the name *Enosh*, we can better understand the developing spirit of the times.

(1) People began to call on the name of the Lord (Jehovah) during Enosh's time.

The Bible states that around the time Seth named his son *Enosh*, men began to call upon the name of the Lord (Jehovah).

> **Genesis 4:26** And to Seth, to him also a son was born; and he called his name Enosh. Then men began to call upon the name of the LORD.

7. Morris, *The Genesis Record*, 155, Park, *Commentary on Genesis*, 119.
8. Wenham, *Genesis 1–15*, 115.

The phrase "call upon the name of the LORD" underscores the fact that people began to develop a personal relationship with God. Even in human relationships, addressing someone by name rather than by title is typical of closer and more familiar relationships. The Bible connects the significant act of men calling upon the name of the Lord directly to the matter of salvation.

> **Acts 2:21** And it shall be, that everyone who calls on the name of the Lord shall be saved.
>
> **Romans 10:13** For "Whoever will call upon the name of the Lord will be saved."

The fact that men began to call upon the name of the Lord implies that a proactive relationship between God and men had begun. The word "call" (קרא, *qārā'*) used here also means "to proclaim" and "to cry out." It signifies that the name of Jehovah had been proclaimed even in the far regions. It is thus possible to conjecture that the practice of true worship was well established during Enosh's time, becoming the foundation upon which the gospel began to be preached to many people.

(2) Proper worship and development of faith in God began during Enosh's time.

The statement in Genesis 4:26 that men began to call upon the name of the Lord indicates that formal worship had begun. The New Living Translation of Genesis 4:26 renders it as an act of worship: "When Seth grew up, he had a son and named him Enosh. At that time people first began to worship the LORD by name." This worship, however, is not the first offering of sacrifices in the 235 years after the fall of Adam. Seeing that Cain and Abel offered sacrifices to God, we can understand that the people had begun offering sacrifices long before. Thus, the phrase "men began to call upon the name of the LORD" refers to formal worship services of holiness and faith. Theologians concur that the fundamental philosophy and attitude of worship that calls for the presence of God was established during the time of Enosh. It was an expression of people's desire to surrender their will in order to fully commit to God's sovereign rule. At the same time, it was a dire cry to God for deliverance from a pervasively sinful world.

Whereas the descendants of Cain were arrogant and relied on their own strength in all aspects of life, the godly descendants of Seth stood humbly before God confessing their need for Him and established a life of worship and fellowship with Him.

(3) Enosh represents mankind, which is frail and unable to attain salvation on its own.

When we acknowledge that we are frail beings (like the meaning of *Enosh*) unable to escape death, we can properly present ourselves as a living and holy sacrifice acceptable to God. This is true spiritual worship (Rom 12:1). Furthermore, we receive the gift of salvation when we call upon the name of the Lord with a heart of true worship (Acts 2:21; Rom 10:13).

The apostle Paul cried out, "Wretched man that I am!" (Rom 7:24). Realizing that he was a weak being (like Enosh) who cannot overcome death by his own strength, he confessed, "For the law of the Spirit of life in Christ Jesus has set you free from the law of sin and of death" (Rom 8:1-2). Furthermore, Paul heard the voice of God telling him, "My grace is sufficient for you, for power is perfected in weakness," and he rejoiced in his own weakness, saying, "Most gladly, therefore, I will rather boast about my weaknesses" (2 Cor 12:9). He was able to make this confession because he came to understand the profound truth that the power of Christ dwells in those who call upon the name of the Lord in their weakness.

As the meaning of the name *Enosh* ("weakly man") points out, human beings are weak, powerless before sin, and easily susceptible to temptation; they are destined to die in sin. Hence, people who lived during Enosh's time wholeheartedly confessed that they were helpless beings overpowered by the burden of sin and death. They devoted their hearts and souls to worshiping God and calling upon His name. There is an earnest call today for people who sincerely anticipate God's eternal reign to confess that they are like Enosh (i.e., weak) and to revive true worship.

4. Fourth Generation: Kenan

קֵינָן (*qēnān*): a child, one begotten,[9] possession[10]

Kenan was the son born to Enosh at the age of 90 (1 Chr 1:1–2). He was born 325 years after Adam. He became the father of Mahalalel at the age of 70. He lived 840 more years and had other children. He died at the age of 910 (1,235 years after Adam [Gen 5:12–14]). He lived 605 years contemporaneously with Adam and 179 years with Noah. He witnessed Enoch's ascension at the age of 662.

His name is recorded in the genealogy of Jesus in Luke 3:37 as Καϊνάν **(*Kainan*).**

Kenan is קֵינָן (*qēnān*) in Hebrew and shares the same root as קֵן (*qēn*), which means "nest" and קִנֵּן (*qinnēn*), which means "to make a nest." The descendants of Seth realized their weakness and powerlessness and began a movement to revive their faith by calling upon the name of the Lord in true repentance. However, Kenan's name suggests that it was during his time that the people finally built a nest of faith.

(1) *Kenan* means "unexpectedly found mercy."

Kenan probably was an unexpected gift from God, a son of great joy born through His providence. This is the foreshadowing of salvation through Jesus Christ, God's great gift of mercy. Why is Jesus Christ an unexpected gift for mankind?

First, the love and grace of salvation are unexpected gifts in that they are too great, too high, and too deep for man to fathom. However, it is a gift that is granted to anyone and a great joy to those who receive it.

Second, it is unexpected because salvation is granted without merit; it is granted entirely by grace and not due to any virtue or acquaintanceship. It is truly a gift of joy, a gift of glory, and the greatest possible gift that mankind could ever receive.

---

9. H. D. M. Spence and Joseph Exell, eds., *The Pulpit Commentary*, vol. 1, *Genesis*, *Exodus* (Peabody, MA: Hendrickson, 2004), 95, Chul Won Suh, *The Book of Genesis* (Seoul: Grisim, 2001), 232.

10. Spence and Exell, *Genesis*, 95; The *Oxford Bible Interpreter* (Seoul: Bible Study Material Publisher, 2002), 1:368.

> **Ephesians 2:8–9** For by grace you have been saved through faith; and that not of yourselves, it is the gift of God; [9]not as a result of works, that no one should boast.

Mary's conception of Jesus Christ through the Holy Spirit is also an unexpected gift. The conception of Jesus Christ was the foremost and greatest blessing for Mary.

> **Luke 1:28–30** And coming in, he said to her, "Hail, favored one! The Lord is with you." [29]But she was greatly troubled at this statement, and kept pondering what kind of salutation this might be. [30]And the angel said to her, "Do not be afraid, Mary; for you have found favor with God."

The unexpected news about Jesus Christ's birth was "good news of a great joy" to the shepherds who were tending their sheep at night (Luke 2:10).

Jesus came in the fullness of time (Gal 4:4); He is the gospel and an unexpected gift to all hopeless sinners (John 1:14, 16; 3:16; Rom 5:15; 2 Cor 9:15).

(2) *Kenan* means "vast possession."

It appears that Enosh hoped to enlarge the borders of faith and further recover the lost sovereignty of Eden through his unexpectedly begotten son Kenan. The meaning of Kenan's name, "vast possession," hints at the hope of recovering the lost work of creation (Matt 4:9; Luke 4:5–7), the lost dominion over the creation, and the lost sovereignty (Gen 1:28; 2:15, 19). From the perspective of redemptive history, the name *Kenan* foreshadows Jesus, the Lord of creation, who would bring the good news to the earth, save all mankind, and completely restore all creation.

It is possible to conjecture from their confessions that the descendants of Seth had expanded their spiritual territory through greater faith in the awesome God, the Lord and creator of the vast universe.

Today, we must obey the commands to "subdue the earth" (Gen 1:28) and to "make disciples of all the nations" (Matt 28:18-20) by conquering this world with the gospel and turning it into God's vast possession.

5. Fifth Generation: Mahalalel

מַהֲלַלְאֵל (*mahălalēl*): praise of God,[11] God be praised, glory to God

Mahalalel was the son born to Kenan at the age of 70 (Gen 5:12; 1 Chr 1:2). He was born 395 years after Adam. He became the father of Jared at the age of 65. He lived 830 more years and had other children. He died at the age of 895 (1,290 years after Adam [Gen 5:15–17]). Mahalalel lived 535 years contemporaneously with Adam and 234 years with Noah. He witnessed Enoch's ascension at the age of 592.

His name is recorded in the genealogy of Jesus in Luke 3:37 as Μαλελεήλ (*Maleleēl*).

Mahalalel is a compound word made up of a Hebrew noun that means "praise" (מַהֲלָל, *māhălāl*), which originates from the verb "to praise" (הָלַל, *hālal*), and the name of God אֵל (*ʾēl*). Together, it means "praise to God" or "praise of God."

To praise is to sing of God's wonderful virtues using lyrics and music. It is the greatest form of exaltation for the wonders of nature and the greatness of people. Only God, who governs all history, is worthy to receive true praise and worship (Rev 5:12; 19:1–5).

Praising God is emphasized through this name, suggesting that the people of that time had grown close to God through spiritual revival and growth in faith. The act of formal worship that started in the time of Enosh evolved into a nest of holy believers in the time of Kenan. Congregational worship in the time of Mahalalel developed further into worship filled with praises in which God may dwell and be glorified (Ps 22:3).

(1) Only God is worthy to be praised (Rev 5:12).

It is the creatures' rightful duty to praise God for who He is (Ps 79:13; 105:1–4; Isa 43:7, 21; Eph 1:6, 12, 14). Singing praises is exalting God through music. The psalmist sings, "Let everything that has breath

11. Spence and Exell, *Genesis*, 95.

praise the LORD. Praise the LORD!" (Ps 150:6). Here, the phrase "praise the LORD" is a rendering of the Hebrew expression "Hallelujah." Augustine called a song with the praise of God a hymn. Further, he defines a true hymn as the act of "singing to the praise of God."[12] Like the meaning of the name *Mahalalel*, we must also glorify God by living our lives to the praise of God.

(2) Praise is a force that unleashes God's power.

The sound of powerful praises brought down the wall of Jericho (Josh 6:16–20), drove out the evil spirit in Saul (1 Sam 16:23), and caused a violent earthquake that opened the prison gates and unfastened the chains (Acts 16:25–26). Battles were always victorious when people singing God's praises marched before the army (2 Chr 20:20–23). These amazing works were possible because God is enthroned upon praises (Ps 22:3).

After King Solomon completed the construction, God's presence was upon the temple when a choir clothed in fine linen praised the Lord with cymbals, harps, and lyres, along with 120 priests blowing trumpets (2 Chr 5:12). God manifested His presence when they praised Him in unison with singing and music (2 Chr 5:13). The cloud of God's glory filled the temple so that the priests could not minister because of it (2 Chr 5:14). Thus, praise is the holy aroma that draws God closer and displays His powerful and amazing works unimaginable for man.

(3) Praise is an inspired confession of grace received.

The godly descendants of Seth engaged in fierce, ongoing, spiritual battles against sin and wickedness and saw that God's help resulted in victory (Deut 1:30; 20:4; Josh 10:14, 42; 23:1; Neh 4:20). Kenan must have named his son *Mahalalel* as a confession of the grace that he had received in order to glorify God and to testify before many people that God is alive. Those who have experienced God's grace cannot help but sing praises and testify of His grace (John 1:41; Acts 9:22; 18:5, 28).

The name *Judah*, one of the twelve tribes of Israel, means "praise the LORD" (Gen 29:35). The tribe of Judah stood at the forefront of every battle and always returned victorious (Judg 1:1–10; 20:18). From the

12. Augustine, *Expositions on the Psalms*.

perspective of redemption history, Mahalalel is the archetype of the Messiah, who was to come from the tribe of Judah to save all mankind through the cross, obtain victory through the resurrection, and be enthroned in praises (Ps 78:68–70; Heb 7:14; Rev 5:5). Truly, only the Lord Jesus deserves our worship of praise, for He came and granted salvation to sinful mankind, helplessly frail and deserving of death.

6. Sixth Generation: Jared

יֶרֶד (*yered*): descent or descendant,[13] to go or come down (from a higher place)[14]

Jared was the son born to Mahalalel at the age of 65 (Gen 5:15; 1 Chr 1:2). He was born 460 years after Adam. He became the father of Enoch at the age of 162. He lived 800 more years and had other children. He died at the age of 962 (1,422 years after Adam [Gen 5:18–20]). He lived 470 years contemporaneously with Adam and 366 years with Noah. He witnessed Enoch's ascension at the age of 527.

His name is recorded in the genealogy of Jesus in Luke 3:37 as Ἰάρεδ (*Iared*).

The name *Jared* originates from the Hebrew word יָרַד (*yārad*), which means "to carry down," "to transport," or "to put down."

This is an indication that the spiritual movement to praise God had not been limited to a few, but rather was widespread among the people at that time. It also suggests that the practice of worship had been successfully passed down through the generations. The name *Jared* contains the earnest hope that God, who is worthy to be praised upon the foundation of faith laid by Enosh, Kenan, and Mahalalel, would come down to the earth and save them. There was simply no way for mankind, who cannot even break free from the cycle of sickness and death associated with this world, to restore the lost paradise. They realized that they could not neutralize the serpent's lethal venom by their own strength.

Their sincere longing for the woman's seed (Gen 3:15) is also evident from the alternative meaning of the name *Jared*: "descendant." As the fulfillment of this hope, Jesus Christ, the Word made flesh, came into this world and dwelt among the people (John 1:14).

13. Spence and Exell, *Genesis*, 95; Suh, *Book of Genesis*, 235.
14. Wenham, *Genesis 1–15*, 127; Spence and Exell, *Genesis*, 95.

(1) Jared lived longer than the preceding patriarchs.

Jared lived 962 years and thus lived the longest among the patriarchs from Adam to Jared. He lived thirty-two years longer than Adam. Only Methuselah, Jared's grandson, outlived him by seven years and set the record for longevity with 969 years. Thus, Jared lived the second-longest life in primeval history. Longevity was the special privilege and the greatest blessing on this earth that the godly descendants received from God.

In regards to Jared, Chul Won Suh observes in his exegesis of Genesis, "He received this blessing because he was godly. He had entrusted everything to God and educated his children well so that they were righteous and evil did not thrive among them."[15]

Those who perhaps do not share the same beliefs on God's blessing of longevity assert a negative interpretation of the name's origin. They believe that the meaning "to go down" or "to descend" suggests that Jared had fallen into sin. Their argument, however, is unconvincing in light of the fact that Jared was blessed with the longest life among the first five generations in the line of Seth and the second-longest in primeval history.

(2) Jesus Christ humbled Himself and came down in the lowest and humblest form (Phil 2:6–8).

Similar to the meaning of the name *Jared*, Jesus rejected the glory of His throne in heaven and came down to this lowly world (John 3:13; 6:41). He was born in a stable, where the smell of animal excrement radiated throughout. He grew up in a poor carpenter's family and was looked down upon even by His own brothers (John 7:5). Religious leaders had contempt for Him because He did not receive proper education (John 7:15). He came unto His own people but had to spend thirty-three years of His life in sorrow because His own people did not receive Him (John 1:11).

Nevertheless, Jesus completely obeyed the command of the Father who sent Him (John 8:42; 16:28). Throughout His life, He sought to glorify the Father (John 7:18), praying in tears and working to fulfill the will of the Father (Luke 22:42). He did only what was pleasing

15. Suh, *Book of Genesis*, 237.

to the Father (John 8:29). He spoke what the Father taught Him and acted according to what the Father showed Him (John 5:19; 7:16; 8:28, 38; 12:49). He considered the Father's command as eternal life (John 12:50) and was obedient even to the point of death on the cross (Phil 2:8). This is why God was always with Jesus—"Immanuel" (John 8:29).

Let us examine ourselves to see if we are bearing the fruit of obedience to the Father's will and sincerely repent so that we may also meet with God, Immanuel.

(3) Enoch was Jared's fruit of faith.

As the meaning of his name suggests, Jared lowered himself before God and always lived with humility. This is also apparent in the name of his son Enoch. *Enoch* means "dedicated" or "offered," hinting that Jared had wanted to completely dedicate his son to God. Jared's hope in faith was later fulfilled when Enoch reached the pinnacle of godly faith by overcoming death and being taken up to heaven. Enoch was truly Jared's fruit of faith.

Jared's devotion and faith in God also shined through in the name *Enoch*. One could not possibly name his child "dedicated" before God if he himself were not dedicated in faith. As Hannah had offered Samuel to God's temple (1 Sam 1:22), and as Abraham had offered Isaac to God on a mount in Moriah (Gen 22:2), Jared also offered his son to God because he realized that his son ultimately belonged to Him even though he was God's gift (Ps 127:3). He acknowledged that the ownership of his son belonged totally to God, and he wished for his son to be used according to His will.

Jared had accurately sensed the corruption of his time. In his desire to set the standard for righteousness and truth, he consecrated his son apart from the sinful world by willingly offering him to God so that he might live as a public figure dedicated to the nation and to the times. Jared was mature in faith; he sought after God instead of shifting blame for the social decay of the times.

7. Seventh Generation: Enoch

חֲנוֹךְ (*ḥănôk*): dedicated (offered),[16] begin or initiated,[17] teacher

> **Enoch was the son born to Jared at the age of 162 (Gen 5:18; 1 Chr 1:2–3). He was born 622 years after Adam. He became the father of Methuselah at the age of 65 and walked with God for 300 years, had other children, and ascended up to heaven without seeing death at the age of 365 (987 years after Adam [Gen 5:21–24; Heb 11:5–6; Jude 14–15]). He lived 308 years contemporaneously with Adam. Noah was born 69 years after Enoch's ascension, so the two men did not meet.**
>
> **1,056 years after Adam (Noah's birth)**
> **– 987 years after Adam (Enoch's ascension)**
> **= 69 years**
>
> **His name is recorded in the genealogy of Jesus in Luke 3:37 as** Ἑνώχ **(*Henōch*).**

In Hebrew, the name *Enoch* is חֲנוֹךְ (*ḥănôk*). It is the noun form of the verb meaning "to offer," and the most common rendering is "offered" and "dedicated one." The root of this name is חָנַךְ (*ḥānak*), which means "to inspire" or "to teach." Thus, the noun form would be rendered as "teacher." It appears that Jared named his son "dedicated (offered)" out of the desire to fully dedicate this son to God as the first fruit of his godly life. Enoch presumably lived out God's teachings in his life and deeply inspired many people. As presaged by the meaning of his name, Enoch was the archetype of Jesus Christ, the Lamb who was fully dedicated before God to die on the cross as an atoning sacrifice for the sins of mankind (John 1:29; 1 Cor 5:7).

Until Enoch, every genealogy concluded with the inevitable phrase "and he died," as though it were natural. The phrase "and he died" appears eight times in Genesis 5 (Gen 5:5, 8, 11, 14, 17, 20, 27, 31). However, there was one person whom death could not govern: Enoch. He was like the morning star shining brightly in the dark night sky. He walked

16. Spence and Exell, *Genesis*, 95.
17. Ibid.

with God and attained eternal life without seeing death; his life and ascension demonstrated the height of godly life. The break in the reign of death was the greatest and foremost of all blessings, unseen until then.

There is only one record of Enoch's deed on this earth (Jude 14–15). He prophesied about God's judgment against "ungodly deeds" and "ungodly speech" prevalent during his time. Enoch lived up to his father's expectations by dedicating his life to God as a true prophet of his age.

(1) Enoch was a teacher who taught an important lesson to all mankind.

Besides the meaning "dedicated" or "offered," Enoch's name also means "successor," "beginning," and "teacher." The following conclusions can be drawn regarding Enoch's ministry from the perspective of redemptive history:

① Enoch received God's trust by walking with Him and pleasing Him (Heb 11:5).

② Enoch was the first to teach mankind that whoever walks with God in faith will obtain eternal life (Gen 5:21–24). He taught that there was a way to reach heaven without seeing death: transfiguration and ascension into heaven.

(2) Enoch walked with God and was taken up by God.

God did not take Enoch after he died. In Hebrew, *to take* is לָקַח (*lāqaḥ*), and its usage here connotes the act of "snatching (taking) away" from death to a place different from this world (the kingdom of God). This signifies that God had transfigured Enoch into spiritual form and took him up to heaven without allowing him to experience death (Heb 11:5). Elijah was the other person in the Bible who had been transfigured. He was taken up to heaven by a whirlwind, and the word לָקַח (*lāqaḥ*) was also used in his case (2 Kgs 2:10–11). The word לָקַח (*lāqaḥ*) teaches us that death, an impassable obstacle for man, kneels before the power of God Almighty.

What enabled Enoch to be transfigured into a heavenly form? Genesis 5:24 explains that Enoch was taken because he walked with God. The Hebrew word for *to walk* in Genesis 5:24 is יִתְהַלֵּךְ (*yithallēk*), the reflexive form of the verb הָלַךְ (*hālak*), and means "to subject oneself and follow." According to this meaning, walking with God means more than just traveling together with Him; it refers to taking each step in accordance with His will without harboring different thoughts. Ultimately, walking with God is to become one with God, so that the two may appear as one.

There was no change of heart for Enoch during his three-hundred-year walk with God. He willingly and joyfully followed God and embraced His will in his heart; this is what pleased God and compelled Him to grant Enoch the glory of ascension up to heaven without seeing death (Heb 11:5). We, too, can be liberated from the reign of death over our lives if we hold God's hand and wholly walk with Him.

Before we ask the question "Would it be possible for me to be transfigured now without seeing death?" we must ask ourselves, "Am I truly walking with God?" The Hebrew word הָלַךְ (*hālak*) for *to walk* also appears in Deuteronomy 30:16 and is associated with life, meaning that walking with God contains the secret to being transferred from death to life. The Bible promises that reconciliation and close fellowship with God overcomes sin, liberates us from death, and grants us eternal life.

(3) Enoch lived contemporaneously with Adam for 308 years and ascended into heaven fifty-seven years after Adam died at the age of 930.

Calculation:

987 years after Adam (year of Enoch's ascension)
– 930 (Adam's age at death)
= 57 years

Enoch's ascension was a special event that shed light back to God's greatest gift: eternal life. Enoch's transfiguration attested to the prospect of eternal life and at the same time sowed conviction in life's victory over death. This is great encouragement and hope for the righteous who thirst for the good news of eternal life while living under the shadows of sin and death.

After receiving his sentence from God, Adam also received the firm promise that Eden would be restored by the seed of the woman (Gen 3:15). He witnessed to his descendants through accounts of the blessed world of Eden and emphasized to them that the most significant issue that mankind needs to resolve is the issue of death. Furthermore, he probably testified in detail about the world before and after sin. Adam's desire, born in faith, finally materialized and yielded fruit through

Enoch. There were godly descendants after Adam who believed in God, but only Enoch yielded fruit through his transfiguration. This was because Enoch had reverence for the Word of God, which he received through Adam during the 308 years. Among Adam's numerous descendants, only Enoch followed the Word fully. As a result, he walked with God for three hundred years until God took him because there was no reason to further keep him on the earth.

Enoch was not excluded from the curse of death brought on by the fall; he was to die just as Adam had died fifty-seven years earlier. However, God granted him the special privilege of directly entering into eternal life by overcoming death. His example was testimony to the final reward for those who maintain godliness while the ungodliness of their environment is at its peak.

(4) There were seven witnesses to Enoch's deeds, transfiguration, and ascension.

All the patriarchs of primeval history were alive at the time of Enoch's ascension except Adam, who died fifty-seven years earlier, and Noah, who was born sixty-nine years later.[18] These seven patriarchs were Seth, Enosh, Kenan, Mahalalel, Jared, Methuselah, and Lamech.

When Enoch was taken up to heaven, Seth was 857 years old, Enosh 752, Kenan 662, Mahalalel 592, Enoch's father Jared, 527, Methuselah 300, and Lamech 113. They witnessed Enoch boldly preaching the Word of God, his judgment against the ungodly world (Jude 14–15), his flawless walk with God, his godliness while raising a family, and his ascension. His ascension confirmed Adam's teachings about the Garden of Eden and that the world of eternal life without death is real.

(5) The birth of Enoch's son, Methuselah, was a sign of the judgment by flood.

When Enoch gave birth to Methuselah, he received a revelation from God regarding judgment upon the pervasively wicked world through the flood.

① Enoch gave birth to a son at the age of 65 and began to walk with God. He named this son *Methuselah* ("when he dies, judgment").

18. Matthew Henry, *Matthew Henry's Commentary* (Peabody, MA: Hendrickson, 1991), 1:40.

② Methuselah lived 969 years, which coincides precisely with the year of the flood (Gen 5:27-32; 7:6; 11:10).

Calculation:

Methuselah was 187 years old when he gave birth to Lamech;
Lamech was 182 years old when he gave birth to Noah;
the flood occurred when Noah was 600 years old:
187 + 182 + 600 = 969

Therefore, Methuselah's birth was God's revelation and sign of the judgment by flood.

(6) Enoch demonstrated the eternal life that Adam possessed before the fall.

Enoch was the proper form of Adam. The eternal life that he received after walking with God showed the world what Adam would have possessed had he not sinned. Enoch's walk with God—the secret to his transfiguration—revealed the kind of life that God wanted and expected from Adam when He created him. God wanted Adam to be of one heart and will with Him; He wanted Adam to eat and live before Him. Adam, however, disregarded God's command and listened to Eve's words. In his arrogance, he made the decision to eat the fruit of the knowledge of good and evil without asking God. As a result, Adam drifted far away, prompting God to remind him of his place and state by asking, "Where are you?" (Gen 3:9).

Close examination of the ten generations between Adam and Noah reveals that although Enoch was the seventh generation from Adam, none of Adam's direct descendants had died before Enoch's ascension. Adam was the only person to die prior to Enoch's ascension. After Adam's death, the second patriarch among the ten generations from Adam to Noah to conclude his life on earth ascended up to heaven instead of passing through the gates of death (see Reference 1: "The Chronology of the Patriarchs").

Enoch's ascension teaches all mankind an important lesson. Through the death of the first man, Adam, God clearly demonstrated that the wages of sin is death (Rom 6:23); however, following Adam's death, through Enoch, God revealed the way to overcome the power of death. This is the hope for all: mankind can sufficiently overcome death if they restore fellowship with God and walk with Him the way Enoch had done. Enoch's ascension is a revelation to all generations to come that only faith has the power to overcome death.

About 2,200 years after Enoch, the prophet Elijah also was taken up to heaven without seeing death (2 Kgs 2:10–11). Enoch prophesied in the time between Adam and Abraham, while Elijah prophesied in the time between Abraham and Christ.

(7) Enoch foreshadows three events in the history of redemption.

① Enoch's walk with God pleased Him. This foreshadowed how Jesus Christ's life would please God (John 8:29). Additionally, Enoch's ascension was the foreshadowing of Jesus Christ's triumph over the powers of Satan, the eternal destruction of death, and the assurance of salvation for mankind through His resurrection and ascension.

② Enoch was the presage of the precious truth that although all mankind are under condemnation through Adam, by the grace of God, there is life for all men through His only begotten Son, Jesus Christ (Rom 5:18–21; 1 Cor 15:22).

③ Enoch was the presage of the glorious transfiguration of the saints at the second coming of Jesus Christ, when suffering and rebellion reach their culmination (Matt 24:40; John 8:51; 11:25–26; 1 Cor 15:50–54; 1 Thess 4:16–17; Phil 3:21). Matthew Henry states, "Enoch's translation was . . . an evidence to faith of the reality of a future state, and of the possibility of the body's existing in glory in that state."[19]

Enoch's life became the foremost testimony of eternal life as he leapt over the great obstacle of death, which stood between God and man. This was the special grace and blessing that Enoch received as a result of his faith in the Word of God preached through Adam and of his walk with God in obedience to the Word. It is our sincere hope that we also receive the Word of God and believe in it without doubting so that we might also defeat the power of death and be transfigured into a spiritual body at the second coming of Jesus Christ.

---

19. Ibid., 1:41.

1 Corinthians 15:51–54 Behold, I tell you a mystery; we shall not all sleep, but we shall all be changed, [52]in a moment, in the twinkling of an eye, at the last trumpet; for the trumpet will sound, and the dead will be raised imperishable, and we shall be changed. [53]For this perishable must put on the imperishable, and this mortal must put on immortality. [54]But when this perishable will have put on the imperishable, and this mortal will have put on immortality, then will come about the saying that is written, "Death is swallowed up in victory."

8. Eighth Generation: Methuselah

מְתוּשֶׁלַח (*mĕtûšelaḥ*): when he dies, judgment,[20] man of dart

Methuselah was the son born to Enoch at the age of 65 (Gen 5:21; 1 Chr 1:3). He was born 687 years after Adam. He became the father of Lamech at the age of 187. He lived 782 more years and had other children. He died at the age of 969 (1,656 years after Adam). Amazingly, the year of his death and the year of the flood coincide (Gen 5:25–27). He lived contemporaneously with Adam for 243 years, with Enoch 300 years, and with Noah 600 years.

His name is recorded in the genealogy of Jesus in Luke 3:37 as Μαθουσαλά (*Mathousala*).

Methuselah was the son of Enoch, who was taken up to heaven without seeing death. The name *Methuselah* has a derived meaning: "when he dies, the world will end." Enoch must have received a special revelation at the time of Methuselah's birth regarding the fate of his child. The name could be composed of two words מַת (*mat*), meaning "man" or "male," and שֶׁלַח (*šelaḥ*), meaning "missile" or "weapon." In this case, his name would be translated as "man of the weapon" or "man of the javelin (dart)." Alternatively, the name could be a composition of the words מוּת (*mût*), meaning "die" or "kill," and שָׁלַח (*šālaḥ*), meaning "sent," "sent away," or "let go." In this case, *Methuselah* would mean "when he is dead, it shall come (be sent)."[21] According to a tale from those times, every village had a guard who, with a spear in hand, protected the village. If this guard died, the village became vulnerable to attacks from outside forces and thus could be destroyed. The name *Methuselah* suggests that perhaps he was a protector of his village and that it was believed that his death meant the end of their world.

Enoch received the revelation about the destruction of the world at the time of Methuselah's birth; God revealed that the flood would come after the death of his son. Thus, either at God's explicit direction or as an act of his own faith, Enoch named the child *Methuselah*, mean-

20. Morris, *The Genesis Record*, 155.

21. James Montgomery Boice, *Genesis: An Expositional Commentary*, vol. 1 (Grand Rapids: Zondervan, 1982), 292.

ing "when he is dead, it shall come." The flood would be held back while Methuselah lived, but when he died, it would come.[22]

What kind of parent would want to give a name that is related to the end time? Nonetheless, Enoch spread the message regarding the coming judgment and named his son according to the word in order to prepare faith for the end.

Finally, the long-prophesied flood came upon the earth 1,656 years after Adam, on the seventeenth day of the second month of the year that Noah turned six hundred years old. This was the year of Methuselah's death at the age of 969 (Gen 5:27; 7:11).

(1) Through Methuselah, Enoch came to a sure awareness of the end.

Enoch experienced a turning point in his life with the birth of Methuselah and began to walk with God. The Bible emphasizes that Enoch began his walk with God after the birth of Methuselah (Gen 5:21–22). The meaning of Enoch's son's name, "when he is dead, the end of the world shall come," probably was a constant reminder of the coming judgment that prompted Enoch to prepare his faith for the end each time he called his son by name.

Enoch did not withdraw from the world to live in seclusion. He lived among his fellow men. He fathered children, raised them, and educated them. He also labored to support his family. Undoubtedly, it was difficult to walk with God during dark times governed by the sinful cultures of the secular world. Enoch's awareness of the impending judgment and his consciousness of the end made the walk possible (Luke 21:32–36).

Jude 14–15 supports the notion of Enoch's eschatological faith. He lived prophesying about God's impending judgment against the ungodly deeds and the ungodly speech of his time.

(2) Methuselah enjoyed the greatest longevity in all human history.

Excluding Enoch, who was taken up to heaven, the life span of the descendants of Adam in Genesis 5 ranged from 777 years to 969 years (an average of 912 years). This is an unimaginably long life span by today's standard. Life spans that lasted almost a thousand years demonstrate

---

22. Ibid.

that mankind was originally created for eternity. This gives rise to the hope that mankind will live eternally in a spiritual body in the future (1 John 2:25; Rev 22:5). At the same time, it is a demonstration of God's mercy toward mankind. God planned judgment when He saw that sins of all sorts had invaded every corner of the earth, but He delayed judgment for the 969 years of Methuselah's life. Even after Noah's ark had been built, God granted one last chance for repentance by giving notice of the impending judgment seven days prior to the flood. In essence, Methuselah's longevity represents God's patience and His great mercy and compassion for mankind (1 Tim 2:4; 2 Pet 3:9).

(3) Methuselah enjoyed the special privilege of witnessing God's amazing providence of salvation.

Methuselah was a sure witness to the entire redemptive work until the flood. How much of redemptive history did Methuselah live to see?

① He heard Adam's account of the Garden of Eden for 243 years.

② He witnessed his father Enoch's walk with God for three hundred years and saw him being taken up to heaven alive.

③ He saw the birth of Noah, the archetype of the Savior, during times of overflowing sin and wickedness. He lived contemporaneously with Noah for six hundred years.

④ Methuselah lived from the beginning to the end of the construction of Noah's ark and probably offered the greatest amount of help with the ark. In addition, he was presumably the greatest source of strength, courage, and hope for Noah. It is most likely that Methuselah understood the ominous meaning of his name—God's judgment would come upon his death. Consequently, he lived a godly life with keen sensitivity regarding the end time until the very last day of his life and presumably expended all his efforts in testifying that God's judgment was near. As prophesied, he died at the age of 969 in the year of the flood.

⑤ He witnessed the birth of Shem, Noah's eldest son, who would continue the godly lineage after the great flood. He lived contemporaneously with Shem for ninety-eight years (Gen 5:32; 7:6; 11:10).

9. Ninth Generation: Lamech

לֶמֶךְ (*lemek*): strong youth[23]

Lamech was the son born to Methuselah at the age of 187 (Gen 5:25; 1 Chr 1:3-4). He was born 874 years after Adam. He became the father of Noah at the age of 182. He lived 595 more years and had other children. He died at the age of 777 (1,651 years after Adam), five years before the flood (Gen 5:28–31). He lived 113 years contemporaneously with Enoch, 595 years with Noah, and 56 years with Adam. The tenth generation Noah, however, did not meet Adam because he was born 126 years after Adam's death.

His name is recorded in the genealogy of Jesus in Luke 3:36 as Λάμεχ (*Lamech*).

Methuselah was born to Enoch at the age of sixty-five, and his grandson, Lamech, was born to him at the age of 252. Lamech probably was 113 years old when Enoch was taken up to heaven. Thus, both Methuselah and Lamech witnessed Enoch's godly life and walk with God. Surely, this son and grandson had been raised under the godly influence of Enoch.[24]

Two sets of people with the same names appear in Genesis 4 and Genesis 5. They are Enoch (Gen 4:17) and Lamech (Gen 4:18) from the line of Cain, and a different Enoch (Gen 5:21) and Lamech (Gen 5:28) from the line of Seth. These two sets of figures are distinguished from one another in the genealogy through the use of additional biographical notations. The Lamech from Cain's line was a man of grief and despair, while the Lamech from Seth's line was a man of hope. Certainly, they took two diverging paths in life.

In addition, the meaning of the name *Lamech* from the line of Cain is understood as "conqueror" or "strong one in confronting God." These meanings are derived from the Arabic origin of his name, which means "oppressor" or "strong one." He deserted God and boasted of his own strength. He wanted to conquer the world with evil and challenged

23. Spence and Exell, *Genesis*, 96; Suh, *Book of Genesis*, 242.

24. Hee Bo Kim, *Patriarchal Fathers in the Old Testament* (Seoul: Presbyterian Theological Seminary Press, 1979), 31.

God's will. Although they have the same name, the meaning "conqueror" or "strong one" is adequate for Lamech the son of Methushael from the line of Cain, but not for Lamech the son of Methuselah from the line of Seth.

The meaning "powerful one" is more appropriate for the Lamech from the line of Seth. Furthermore, "a man of prayer"[25] is another derivation given to the name of Lamech because only through prayer can one attain the power of faith to cast out demons and defeat the forces of evil (Mark 9:29).

The Lamech in Genesis 5 is distinguished by an additional description that underscores the importance of his son. In other words, attention is given more to his son than to Lamech himself.

(1) Lamech had a son and named him *Noah* ("comforter" or "giver of peace").

The name *Noah* was Lamech's confession of faith and his desire toward the will of God.

> **Genesis 5:28–29** And Lamech lived one hundred and eighty-two years, and became the father of a son. [29]Now he called his name Noah, saying, "This one shall give us rest from our work and from the toil of our hands arising from the ground which the Lord has cursed."

This passage contains Lamech's anguished cry regarding the fragility of mankind that he so acutely recognized through his own deep suffering on this earth. This Lamech was a godly man. He acknowledged man's inability to overcome suffering. He recognized that suffering and sadness in life were the result of the fall of man and God's subsequent curse. Thus, he did not rebel against God or give up under the duress of suffering and affliction; rather, they motivated his faith. He trusted solely in God and hoped that the curse would be lifted through his son (Gen 5:29).

Only those who sincerely repent, acknowledging that the evil of the times is the result of their sins, can possess true faith to conquer this world.[26]

---

25. Spence and Exell, *Genesis*, 96.
26. Boice, *Genesis*, 255–56.

(2) Lamech earnestly anticipated the coming of the Messiah.

Lamech longed for the end of man's sorrowful fallen state and for the restoration of Eden. He hoped that someone would lift the death sentence pronounced upon man (Gen 3:24; 4:16) and open the path for recovery to the original state. He understood all too keenly the pain associated with life and the frailty of mankind and hoped that true peace and consolation from God would come with the birth of his son. Accordingly, Genesis 5:29 expresses Lamech's sincere longing for the Messiah and the joyful news for all mankind. His hope was similar to Paul's confession in 2 Corinthians 1:5: "For just as the sufferings of Christ are ours in abundance, so also our comfort is abundant through Christ."

Lamech's son, Noah, promised a new beginning for mankind; he was a gift from the "God of all comfort" (2 Cor 1:3-7). He was the archetype of Jesus Christ whom God had sent. Jesus Christ is the one who gives true comfort and rest to this earth (Isa 9:6; John 14:27). Lamech's burning hope for the Messiah was evident in his confession of faith.

(3) Lamech lived the shortest life (777 years) among the ten generations since Adam.

Lamech lived the shortest life among the ten patriarchs from Adam to Noah. Considering that "seven" is the number of completion, however, it is plausible to think that he completed all his tasks in life during the 777 years. He probably helped his son Noah to build the ark, as he longed to see the day when the revelation he received would be fulfilled. Presumably, God took Lamech abruptly five years before the flood, before evil came (Isa 57:1), because he had offered the best of his entire life for the fulfillment of His will.

(4) Like other patriarchs, Lamech had many other children until he was 777 years old.

> **Genesis 5:30** Then Lamech lived five hundred and ninety-five years after he became the father of Noah, and he had other sons and daughters.

Lamech's children were Noah's biological siblings. They were all loved, raised, and trained by the same godly father. However, none of his many siblings were to be found at the time of the flood; only the eight members of Noah's immediate family were saved. All the other children born to Lamech had rejected their father's teachings and refused to listen to the Word of God. They followed after the wickedness of the times. Because they were Noah's siblings, they probably received additional appeals to enter the ark, but they rejected them all. They enjoyed life in the world, yielded to their own desires, and did not cooperate with the building of the ark. Although they were so close to the actual builder of the ark, all of Noah's siblings were washed away by the waters of judgment. In other words, they had the channel of salvation very close to them, but they could not be saved because they did not believe.[27]

In Matthew 24:37 it is written, "For the coming of the Son of Man will be just like the days of Noah." We must not become so foolish as to disregard the Word of God and miss the ark of salvation as Noah's siblings had done.

---

27. Morris, *The Genesis Record*, 161.

10. Tenth Generation: Noah

נֹחַ (*nōaḥ*): rest, comfort

Noah was the son born to Lamech at the age of 182 (Gen 5:28; 1 Chr 1:4). He was born 1,056 years after Adam. He became the father of Shem at the age of 502 and later of Ham and of Japheth. He lived 350 years after the flood, but he did not have any other children. He died at the age of 950 (2,006 years after Adam [Gen 5:32; 9:28–29; 11:10]).

His name is recorded in the genealogy of Jesus in Luke 3:36 as Νῶε (*Nōe*).

The name *Noah* is derived from the Hebrew word נוּחַ (*nûaḥ*), which means "to settle down," "appease," or "rest" (Deut 5:14; 2 Kgs 2:15; Lam 5:5). The derived meanings from this word are "Sabbath," "rest," and "comfort."

The godly descendants who lived in the world abounding with iniquity earnestly longed for God's comfort through the birth of this son (Gen 6:5). Genesis 5:29 states, "Now he called his name Noah, saying, 'This one shall give us rest from our work and from the toil of our hands arising from the ground which the LORD has cursed.'" The word "rest" is in the Piel stem of the Hebrew verb that emphasizes the meaning "surely bring us consolation." This demonstrates their desire to be consoled by God.

Lamech did not name his son *Noah*, with the messianic meaning "comfort" and "consolation," out of personal desire or through human discernment. The name is a reflection of a newly revealed providence of redemption from God.[28] The end to the long period of suffering had come; it was now time for God's comfort and rest. In his commentary on Genesis, Yune Sun Park notes on Genesis 5:29 that Lamech had named his son "rest" because he mistook this child to be the Messiah. In other words, he suggests that Lamech thought that this child was the Savior, who was to come and deliver all mankind from the curse of

28. Suh, *Book of Genesis*, 245; Boice, *Genesis*, 256.

sin. Park deduces that people of the early times must have placed their hope in the coming of the Messiah according to the promise of God (Gen 3:15).[29]

The Bible states that Noah's time was so wicked that God was sorry that He had made man (Gen 6:5–7). Accordingly, the verse "But Noah found favor in the eyes of the LORD" (Gen 6:8) emphasizes that Noah was God's bright lamp during this dark and wicked time and reveals the total depravity of a world in which not one godly person lived except for Noah and his family. This is why 2 Peter 2:5 states, "And [God] did not spare the ancient world, but preserved Noah, a preacher of righteousness, with seven others, when He brought a flood upon the world of the ungodly."

Noah's time was so ungodly that there was not one person who received Noah's message of warning as the truth or in any way attempted to understand it, until all were destroyed by the flood (Matt 24:38-39). Likewise, God will also seek out the godly during the ungodly times of the end. Like Noah, we must also find favor in God's eyes so that we may stand before the Son of Man (Ps 12:1; Mic 7:2; Luke 21:36).

(1) Lamech had a son at the age of 182 (Gen 5:28).

> **Genesis 5:28** And Lamech lived one hundred and eighty-two years, and became the father of a son.

This verse deviates from the usual structure of this genealogy. For the previous patriarchs, it was written "gave birth to," followed by the son's name. For Lamech, however, it was written "gave birth to a son," without mentioning the son's name. Genesis 5:29 also makes mention of this son.

> **Genesis 5:29** Now he called his name Noah, saying, "This one shall give us rest from our work and from the toil of our hands arising from the ground which the LORD has cursed."

The word *son* is used distinctively in Genesis 5:28. The author makes the extra effort to suggest that this was not just another son among many, but rather a *unique son* much like the "only begotten Son"

29. Park, *Commentary on Genesis*, 124.

(John 1:14, 18; 3:16, 18; 1 John 4:9). Just as Eve gave birth to a son and rejoiced, saying, "I have gotten a manchild with the help of the LORD" (Gen 4:1), so Noah's birth gave rise to a special expectation, a special joy, and a special meaning because this son was the archetype of Jesus Christ, who was to come as the Only Son (John 3:16).

The name *Noah* foreshadows Jesus Christ, who would come to save this world and give the true Sabbath rest. In obedience to God's Word, Noah prepared the ark and saved his family from God's judgment that destroyed the fallen world. As a result, they obtained Sabbath rest. Jesus is the comforter who came in the flesh to the fallen world to declare the true Sabbath (John 14:27). When, in his second coming, Christ arrives to judge the world by fire, He will once again save His chosen people and lead them to heaven, the kingdom of the true Sabbath.

(2) Noah lived at the junction of two ages.

There is no mention of Noah's age or the remaining years of his life in Genesis 5. This implies God's holy will to establish the work of redemption in a new light through Noah (Gen 5:32). Primeval history was to end with Noah, and a new world was to commence after the flood, leading to the emergence of Abraham (Gen 12:1–3). Noah lived contemporaneously with Abraham for fifty-eight years.

Calculation:

Year of Noah's death (2,006 years after Adam)
– Year of Abraham's birth (1,948)
= 58 years

Noah met with all but three of the ten generations of patriarchs before the flood: Adam, Seth, and Enoch. Among the ten generations after Adam, he lived the third-longest life with a life span of 950 years (Gen 9:28–29). He lived to see all ten generations after the flood down to Abraham. Altogether, Noah lived contemporaneously with seventeen generations of patriarchs including his own.

The following are facts related to Noah's birth:

① Noah was born 126 years after Adam's death.

Calculation:
Year of Noah's birth (1,056 years after Adam)
– Year of Adam's death (930)
= 126 years

② Noah was born 69 years after Enoch's ascension.

Calculation:
Year of Noah's birth (1,056 years after Adam)
– Year of Enoch's ascension (987)
= 69 years

③ Noah was born 14 years after Seth's death.

Calculation:
Year of Noah's birth (1,056 years after Adam)
– Year of Seth's death (1,042)
= 14 years

(3) During the 136-year period between the death of Jared (sixth generation) and the birth of Shem, all the patriarchs in the line of Seth had died except for Methuselah, Lamech, and Noah.

Calculation:
Year of Shem's birth (1,558 years after Adam)
– Year of Jared's death (1,422)
= 136 years

Noah was 502 years old when he became the father of Shem. At the time, all the patriarchs in the line of Seth had already died, and only three patriarchs were alive during the 136 years. After the birth of Shem, Ham and Japheth were also born to Noah (Gen 5:32; 6:10). It was after all three sons were married that God appeared to Noah and gave him precise instructions for the construction of the ark in preparation for the flood (Gen 6:14–18).

(4) The prediluvian world in which Noah lived was completely corrupt.
Genesis 6:2 states, "The sons of God saw that the daughters of men were beautiful; and they took wives for themselves, whomever they chose." This refers to how the godly descendants of Seth (Gen 5) inter-

married with the corrupt descendants of Cain (Gen 4), deserted God, and became men of the flesh (Gen 6:3). Consequently, God declared, "My Spirit shall not strive with man forever" (Gen 6:3).

Since then, the wickedness of the world accelerated and the earth abounded with all types of sin, leaving no place left uncorrupted (Gen 6:5). Here, "the wickedness of man was great on the earth" implies that sin had seeped into every corner of the human heart so that wickedness sprung forth and overflowed. All the intents of their thoughts and plans were always against faith, evil from the beginning to the end; they totally rejected God's rule and involvement (Gen 6:5).

Genesis 6:11 describes the extent of the corruption: "Now the earth was corrupt in the sight of God, and the earth was filled with violence." The English word *corrupt* comes from the Latin word *corruptus*, past participle of *corrumpere*, from *com* + *rumpere* ("to break"), and it means "to change from good to bad in terms of morals, manners, or actions," or "to degrade with unsound principles or moral values." Violence is the exertion of physical force so as to injure or abuse (as in warfare, or effecting illegal entry into a house).[30] Thus, to say that the earth was corrupt and filled with violence means that abuse, injury, murder, robbery, rape, and other violent illegal activities were rampant. This is why God said, "The end of all flesh has come before Me" (Gen 6:13), declaring that this age was about to encounter the impending judgment by flood.

The world just before the flood was so desperately corrupt that God was sorry that He had made man, and He grieved (Gen 6:6). This surely is a shocking statement. The flood was God's fearful punishment against the dissipated world that did not place God in its heart. Noah, however, found favor in the eyes of God despite the corruption of his times (Gen 6:8). Genesis 6:9 explains, "Noah was a righteous man, blameless in his time; Noah walked with God."

This age in which we are living is also rapidly following the path of extreme corruption and violence. Jesus said that the time of the Son of Man is like the days of Noah (Matt 24:37; Luke 17:26). Noah built the ark as God had commanded (Gen 6:22; 7:5), and as a result God said, "You alone I have seen to be righteous before Me in this time" (Gen 7:1).

---

30. Boice, *Genesis*, 256.

We need to receive God's grace as Noah did. In 1 Peter 1:13 we are urged, "Therefore, gird your minds for action, keep sober in spirit, fix your hope completely on the grace to be brought to you at the revelation of Jesus Christ." We need to receive this grace in order to prepare the ark of faith (Heb 11:7) and stand in the order of the saved ones when He comes to judge by fire in the end (2 Pet 3:7, 12).

(5) There are three notable traits about the birth of Noah's sons.

① Until Noah, the patriarchs' average age at procreation was 118 (Gen 5). Noah was unique. He became the father of his sons after the age of five hundred (Gen 5:32). The Bible gives the exact year of Shem's birth. He was born ninety-eight years before the flood, when Noah was 502 years old.

> **Genesis 11:10** These are the records of the generations of Shem. Shem was one hundred years old, and became the father of Arpachshad two years after the flood.

Noah lived until he was 950 years old. Comparing the period of time he lived after becoming a father to his three sons with the period of time that the previous patriarchs lived after becoming fathers to their sons, we can conclude that Noah lived long enough to see the birth of six generations (Jared, the sixth generation from Adam, was born 460 years after Adam).

② Unlike the other patriarchs who gave birth to children until they died, there is no scriptural record of Noah having additional children after he had his three sons. It is only recorded that he lived another 350 years (after he was six hundred years old), for a total of 950 years, and died (Gen 5:32; 6:10; 9:28–29). This pattern repeats once again with Terah, the nineteenth generation from Adam (Gen 11:26). He had Abraham, Nahor, and Haran at the age of seventy, and there are no records of him having additional children.

③ Noah's three sons were married before the flood but did not have any children until they entered the ark and the flood began.

> **Genesis 6:18** But I will establish My covenant with you; and you shall enter the ark—you and your sons and your wife, and your sons' wives with you.

Only eight people entered the ark, and Noah's three daughters-in-law gave birth to sons after the flood (Gen 7:7, 13; 8:18; 1 Pet 3:20; 2 Pet 2:5).

> **Genesis 10:1** Now these are the records of the generations of Shem, Ham, and Japheth, the sons of Noah; and sons were born to them after the flood.

When Moses recorded the genealogies of the godly line of Seth, he probably recorded in detail the ages of the patriarchs at procreation of the firstborn because it was significant matter. This is a precise reflection of the circumstances of their times as well as the lives of the patriarchs in the genealogy of faith.

Noah had children at an old age (after he was five hundred years old [Gen 5:32]) and did not have additional children after the three sons that God gave to him. His sons began to have children only after the flood. These facts reveal that they had wholeheartedly believed in the message of judgment received by Noah and fully participated in the preparation work. This is also evident in the verse "And Noah did according to all that the LORD had commanded him" (Gen 6:22; 7:5). God was bringing the corrupt age to a close; its end was near.

> **Genesis 6:13** Then God said to Noah, "The end of all flesh has come before Me; for the earth is filled with violence because of them; and behold, I am about to destroy them with the earth."

(6) Noah built the ark with reverence for God.

After God warned Noah about the corruption of his time (Gen 6:1–8), He directed him to build the ark (Gen 6:14–16). Of course, God Himself supplied Noah with precise instructions and design. The Bible testifies that Noah built the ark according to the plan that God had given to him (Gen 6:22; 7:5).

Hebrews 11:7 reveals why Noah was able to complete all that God had commanded him: "In reverence [he] prepared an ark." The word *reverence* describes a heart that strives to abide by God's Word with fear until the very end. Noah did not envy the prosperity of the wicked. He believed it was man's rightful duty to revere God (Prov 23:17; Eccl 12:13), and the more he revered God, the more God poured His wisdom upon Noah so that he could complete the ark. This is because the fear of God is the beginning of wisdom (Job 28:28; Ps 111:10; Prov 1:7;

9:10; 15:33). In truth, the ark was the perfect manifestation of Noah's faith and reverence for God.

Noah's ability to spend such an extended period of time building the ark without a change of heart is proof of his reverence and firm belief in God's promise. While he was building the ark, people merely watched, ridiculing him and shaking their fingers at him in reproach. One can only imagine Noah's heartache and his emotional and physical fatigue during that long period of time.

Having seen how Noah so patiently built the ark through all those years, God said, "For you alone I have seen to be righteous before Me in this time" (Gen 7:1). God's praise must have felt like a long-awaited rain during a drought. Faith is not about words, but rather about deeds, such as Noah's act of building the ark. The greater the faith, the better the preparation. Jesus also commanded, "For this reason you be ready" (Matt 24:44). Those who are ready can enter the wedding feast (Matt 25:10). Let us stay alert and prepare the lamp and the oil to welcome the bridegroom (Matt 25:1–13). There is no other way for believers to stand before the Son of Man in the end except by being alert in prayer (Luke 21:36).

(7) After the flood, God made a covenant with Noah as the second ancestor of mankind after Adam.

God completely tore down the structure of the entire wicked world through the flood and prepared for a new beginning. The flood did not bring an end to the world. Although God knew that the evil heart of man remained even after the flood (Gen 8:21), in His absolute grace and mercy He enacted the eternal covenant of the rainbow, vowing that He would never again destroy the earth by flood (Gen 9:9–17).

Thus, history will be preserved by the grace of God until the end predetermined by God and until salvation is perfected through Jesus Christ. God blessed Noah and his sons to be fruitful, to multiply, and to fill the earth (Gen 9:1, 7) just as He had blessed Adam (Gen 1:28; 2:15). The *blessing of the beginning*, "be fruitful and multiply," was renewed in Noah's time and remained effective in the new world after the flood.

From the time of Noah, the world entered into the period of rest from God's wrath. Now, true rest will be given through Jesus Christ, the Lord of the Sabbath (Matt 12:8; John 14:27).

CHAPTER 11

The Genealogy from Shem to Abraham

The second genealogy, from Shem to Abraham, continues in Genesis 11, following the genealogy from Adam to Noah in Genesis 5. This genealogy illustrates how mankind had multiplied to fill the earth and focuses attention on the one figure chosen from among the multitude to lead the work of redemption. Genesis 10 introduces Noah, his three sons, and their seventy descendants. In Genesis 11, Shem is chosen among Noah's three sons, and from his line emerges Abraham, the starting point of redemptive history.

What is heartbreaking in the genealogy of Shem's descendants in Genesis 11 is the fact that mankind became sinful once again after the flood and erected the Tower of Babel and that the descendants of Shem participated in their sins when they should have guarded their godliness. As a result, the life span of mankind was abruptly shortened from the time of Peleg and thereafter as they continued to sin.

It was during these spiritually dark times that God chose Abraham and called him out of the land of Ur of the Chaldeans, where sin had prevailed (Gen 11:31–32). Ultimately, he made the firm decision in faith to leave his father in his old age and departed from Haran at the age of seventy-five to finally set foot on the land of Canaan (Gen 12:1–5).

11. Eleventh Generation: Shem

שֵׁם (*šēm*): name, reputation, fame[1]

Shem was born 1,558 years after Adam (before the flood, when Noah was 502 years old). He became the father of Arpachshad at the age of 100 (2 years after the flood) and lived 500 years more and had other children. He died at the age of 600 (2,158 years after Adam [Gen 11:10–11]). Shem lived 448 years contemporaneously with his father Noah (1 Chr 1:4). He lived 35 years more after Abraham's death, until Isaac was 110 years old and Jacob was 50 years old. Shem was 98 years old when the flood occurred and lived to the age of 600. He lived a long life and witnessed the world before and after the flood. He lived contemporaneously with fifteen generations of patriarchs, from Methuselah (eighth) to Jacob (twenty-second).

His name is recorded in the genealogy of Jesus in Luke 3:36 as Σήμ (*Sēm*).

Shem was Noah's firstborn, but the narrative of the genealogy in Genesis 10 lists Noah's sons in the order of Japheth, Ham, and Shem. This was done to focus attention on Shem and his descendants, who would become the center of the redemptive history. Just as Noah prophesied, "Blessed be the LORD, the God of Shem" (Gen 9:26), the descendants of Shem are the central figures in the history of redemption, for Jesus Christ would come through this lineage.

Shem was born to Noah before the flood at the age of 502 (Gen 11:10), 1,558 years after Adam. Noah was six hundred years old at the time of the flood, and Shem was ninety-eight years old.

> **Genesis 11:10** These are the records of the generations of Shem. Shem was one hundred years old, and became the father of Arpachshad two years after the flood.

The name *Shem* means "honor" and "renown." The name of his brother Ham means "black" and "hot," and the name of his brother

1. Gordon J. Wenham, *Genesis 1–15*, Word Biblical Commentary 1 (Waco, TX: Word, 1987), 129; Ernest Klein, *A Comprehensive Etymological Dictionary of the Hebrew Language for Readers of English* (New York: Macmillan, 1987), 664.

Japheth means "extend" and "enlargement."[2] Shem's name hints that Noah's desire was for his son to become renowned, but not for the sake of family honor. Rather, his expectation was for his son to live a life that exalted the name of God and upheld His honor throughout the earth.

(1) Shem lived to honor God's name.

The word *honor* is derived from the Latin word *honos* and means "high regard or great respect."[3] This word generally refers to the state of being highly esteemed by others and to the glory that comes along with it. People in this world erect monuments and set up halls of fame in order to commemorate persons who have made noteworthy contributions to the world.

A person's honor is in his or her name, character, and identity. Likewise, the fullness of God's awesome glory, authority, and honor is in His holy name. This is because God's name contains His creation (Ps 33:6; Heb 11:3), divine providence (Rom 11:36; 1 Cor 8:6), and salvation (Acts 2:21; 4:12; Rom 10:13). Above all, the Word that proceeds from His mouth will not return empty (Isa 55:11); when God speaks, His words bear fruit. Thus, God's name has the highest authority and honor.

> **Isaiah 55:8-13** "...And it will be a memorial [שֵׁם, šēm] to the LORD, for an everlasting sign which will not be cut off."
>
> **Psalm 135:13** "Thy name [שֵׁם, šēm], O LORD, is everlasting, Thy remembrance, O LORD, throughout all generations."
>
> **Isaiah 42:8** "I am the Lord, that is My name [שֵׁם, šēm]; I will not give My glory to another, nor My praise to graven images."
>
> **Hosea 12:5** "Even the LORD, the God of hosts; the LORD is His name [שֵׁם, šēm]."

Just as a person is liable for the defamation of another's name or character, God holds people liable for the defamation of His great name, for taking the name of God in vain (Exod 20:7). Taking the Lord's name in vain means to mock, ridicule, or neglect His name (Gal 6:7).

---

2. A. R. Fausset, *Fausset's Bible Dictionary* (Grand Rapids: Zondervan, 1949).

3. Victoria Neufeldt, ed., *Webster's New World College Dictionary*, 3rd ed. (New York: Macmillan, 1996), 648.

Acknowledgment from the world and praise from other human beings have temporal effects. Honor received through the name of God, however, is a spring of eternal joy and blessings (Mal 4:2). Solomon's fame was great, because it was "concerning the name of the LORD" (1 Kgs 10:1; 2 Chr 9:1). Therefore, those who guard the name of God with all their hearts, minds, and lives will also see their names lifted high and will live honorable lives.

Shem also lived a faithful life, not for his own honor but rather for the glory and honor of God's name. He lived a life that merited the glorious title "the God of Shem" (Gen 9:26).

(2) Shem received the testimony "Blessed be the LORD, the God of Shem" (Gen 9:26).

A particular child in a family may be considered the family's "lucky charm." The parents may say, "This child is our lucky charm because all the good things started happening to our family after this child was born!"

Likewise, the exclamation "Blessed be the LORD, the God of Shem" expresses Noah's vision in faith regarding God's continual blessings that would blossom through Shem. He sang praises in hope that God's name would be made renowned through the descendants of Shem and that they would continue to glorify God and call upon His name. What a great honor it is for Shem to have God Almighty, sovereign over the whole universe, declare that He would be glorified through his descendants! There could be no greater honor for any individual.

The descendants of Shem continued to call on God's name just as Noah had prophesied. God was identified as the God of Abraham (a descendant of Shem), the God of Isaac, and the God of Jacob; Abraham had fully passed down his legacy of faith to his children (Exod 3:6, 15; Matt 22:32; Mark 12:26; Luke 20:37; Acts 3:13; 7:32). He did precisely what God had called him to do (Gen 18:18–19).

It was prophesied that Shiloh (i.e., the Messiah) would come through Judah (Gen 49:10), the fourth of Jacob's twelve sons, whose name means "this time I will praise the LORD" (Gen 29:35). This praise began with the descendants of Shem and echoed through the later generations.

The coming Messiah has a name above all names (Phil 2:9) and is worthy to receive all the honor, glory, and praise (Rev 5:12). The name of the returning Lord is the "King of kings" and "Lord of lords," who will be renowned with glory and fame most high (1 Chr 16:27; 1 Tim 6:15; Rev 17:14; 19:16).

(3) Lamech died when Shem was ninety-three years old, and Methuselah died five years later, when Shem was ninety-eight years old in the year of the flood.

Shem lived thirty-five years longer than Abraham and was alive during Isaac and Jacob's time. This was an amazing blessing of longevity. During the six hundred years of his long life, he lived contemporaneously with Methuselah (eighth generation from Adam) down through Jacob (twenty-second generation from Adam)—a total of fifteen generations, including himself (Gen 5:25–32; 11:10–32; 25:7–26; 35:28; 41:46; 45:11; 47:9, 28).

① Born before the flood (8th–11th generations): Methuselah, Lamech, Noah, Shem.

② Born after the flood (12th–22nd generations): Arpachshad, Shelah, Eber, Peleg, Reu, Serug, Nahor, Terah, Abraham, Isaac, Jacob.

12. Twelfth Generation: Arpachshad

אַרְפַּכְשַׁד (ʾ*arpakšad*): boundary[4]

Arpachshad was born 1,658 years after Adam. He became the father of Shelah at the age of 35 and lived 403 more years and had other children. He died at the age of 438 (2,096 years after Adam [Gen 11:12–13; 1 Chr 1:24]). He lived 348 years contemporaneously with Noah. He lived until Abraham was 148 years old and Isaac was 48 years old.

His name is recorded in the genealogy of Jesus in Luke 3:36 as ᾿Αρφαξάδ **(*Arphaxad*).**

Shem had five sons after the flood: Elam, Asshur, Arpachshad, Lud, and Aram (Gen 10:1, 22). Arpachshad was the third son. The Bible enumerates the five sons and reveals that the will of God would continue to be fulfilled through the third son and not the first.

After Shem became the father of Elam and Asshur, he had a third son and named him *Arpachshad*, meaning "boundary" (Gen 10:22). In faith, Shem hoped that his blessings and spiritual boundaries would be passed down to the future generations through Arpachshad.

The genealogy in Genesis 10 does not provide an answer as to why God's will was carried on through Arpachshad. However, the Bible's description of the relationship between the chosen people of Israel and the nations of Elam and Asshur at a later point in time reveals why these two sons were set aside from God's chosen line.

Isaac Asimov states, "The first two sons of Shem are Elam and Asshur, the eponyms of the Elamites and the Assyrians, which at the time that Genesis was reduced to writing were the most powerful nations of the 'Semitic' world."[5]

---

4. Francis Brown, *The New Brown, Driver, Briggs, Gesenius Hebrew and English Lexicon: With an Appendix Containing the Biblical Aramaic* (Peabody, MA: Hendrickson, 1979), 75; *The Oxford Bible Interpreter* (Seoul: Bible Study Material Publisher, 2007), 1:594.

5. Isaac Asimov, *Asimov's Guide to the Bible*, 2 vols. in 1 (New York: Avenel Books, 1981), 53.

(1) The reason Shem's first and second sons were not included in the genealogy of redemptive history.

Shem's first son was Elam.

Elam (עֵילָם) is an Assyrian word meaning "high" or "highlands." Elam is the ancestor of the Elamites, who lived in the highlands located between the Persian Gulf and the Caspian Sea on the right bank of the Tigris River in the time of the ancient Near East. Due to geopolitical reasons, Elam had continuously engaged in battles with Sumer, Babylon, Assyria, Media, Persia, and other Mesopotamian nations in the surrounding area. During Abraham's time, Chedorlaomer, the king of Elam, led an invasion into Canaan, and Abraham was forced to attack him and his allies (Shinar, Ellasar, Elam, and Goiim) with his 318 men in order to rescue Lot, whom they had taken captive (Gen 14:1–17). The Elamites, who had originally lived to the east of Mesopotamia, had quickly expanded westward to the Jordan.

The Elamites were skilled archers (Jer 49:35). As a nation, they were belligerent and militant, and the people of the world feared them (Ezek 32:24). When Assyria attacked Judah, Elam sent soldiers to assist in the destruction of Jerusalem (Isa 22:6). God declared that He would directly send plagues, pour out His anger, and send the sword to consume Elam and destroy the king and the princes who had assaulted His chosen people (Jer 49:36–38; Ezek 32:24–25).

The Elamites were also one of the nations that had interfered with the reconstruction of the temple upon Israel's return from the Babylonian exile (Ezra 4:1-9). The region of Elam in those days is the current highlands of the Khuzestan province in the southwest part of Iran.

Shem's second son was Asshur (Assyria, Assyrians).

The name *Asshur* (אַשּׁוּר) means "a prosperous place" and is derived from the verb that means "to prosper" or "to rejoice." Assyria took advantage of every opportunity to expand and enlarge its territory; it erected the most powerful city-state of the ancient Near East. The power of the Assyrian Empire was at its peak from the ninth century BC until the seventh century BC. The capital city at the time was Assyria, but it was moved to Nineveh during the reign of King Sennacherib (705–681 BC).

After being conquered by Nimrod, the people of Assyria did not carry on the faith of Shem, but instead turned into a belligerent nation like the descendants of Ham and afflicted the chosen nation of Israel. In the words "From that land he went forth into Assyria" in Genesis 10:11, the pronoun "he" refers to Nimrod, Ham's grandson (Gen 10:6–8). Nimrod was the first mighty man on the earth, and it was he who invaded the land of Asshur (Gen 10:8). He was a "mighty hunter" before the Lord, a hero mighty enough to establish four great cities (Gen 10:9, 11–12). In accordance with the meaning of his name, "rebel," he turned away from faith in God, which had been passed down from Noah, and erected the Tower of Babel. He stood on Satan's side, against the work of God.

In relations to the chosen nation of Israel, King Shalmaneser of Assyria destroyed Samaria, the capital of the northern kingdom of Israel, in 722 BC during the reign of King Hoshea (2 Kgs 18:9–10). After the conquest of the land of Israel, the Assyrians began to occupy the land and lived among the Israelites, accelerating the corruption of the Israelites (2 Kgs 17:27–33). Moreover, King Sennacherib, who had already invaded the northern kingdom of Israel, brought his army of 185,000 men down to the southern kingdom of Judah and surrounded the city of Jerusalem during King Hezekiah's reign. God, however, struck them dead (2 Kgs 18:13–19:37).

Regarding the Assyrians, God said through Isaiah, "Woe to Assyria, the rod of My anger and the staff in whose hands is My indignation" (Isa 10:5). Isaiah prophesied that judgment would eventually come upon Assyria because they also did not acknowledge God and were proud (Isa 10:12–16; 14:24–25).

The people of Assyria were originally of the line of Shem but became "a racially mixed people, combining the cultures, languages, and religions with that of their joint Shemitic and Hamitic (Nimrod) stock."[6] As a result, they drew farther and farther away from faith, eventually becoming enemies with God. This is why the channel of redemptive history continued through Shem's third son, Arpachshad.

---

6. James Montgomery Boice, *Genesis: An Expositional Commentary*, vol. 1 (Grand Rapids: Zondervan, 1982), 335.

(2) Arpachshad was born to Shem at the age of one hundred, two years after the flood, 1,658 years after Adam (Gen 11:10).

Shem was one of the eight people who witnessed God's judgment, the consequence of sins, through the great flood. After the flood, God blessed not only Noah, but also his three sons, saying, "Be fruitful and multiply, and fill the earth."

> **Genesis 9:1** And God blessed Noah and his sons and said to them, "Be fruitful and multiply, and fill the earth."
>
> **Genesis 9:7** And as for you, be fruitful and multiply; populate the earth abundantly and multiply in it.

Shem lived through judgment and persevered through the days of suffering in the enclosed ark. In the process, he matured spiritually to possess a *God-first* faith. This is evident from his actions not long after the flood when his father, Noah, became drunk with wine and lay in his tent. When his younger brother, Ham, saw his father's nakedness, he went out and spread rumors.

> **Genesis 9:22** And Ham, the father of Canaan, saw the nakedness of his father, and told his two brothers outside.

The word "told" in this verse is נָגַד (*nāgad*) in Hebrew, meaning "to announce," "to denounce," or "to explain" (Gen 41:24). Ham exposed his father's conduct in exaggerated detail. Shem's actions, however, were prudent and careful. He entered the room humbly walking backwards and covered his father's nakedness, displaying the depth of his filial respect and duty (Gen 9:23).

After waking up, Noah pronounced severe judgment upon Ham's son, Canaan. Conversely, he blessed Shem, saying, "Blessed be the LORD, the God of Shem." He prophesied, "And let Canaan be his servant. May God enlarge Japheth, and let him dwell in the tents of Shem" (Gen 9:25–27). Consequently, Shem received the inheritance of faith from Noah.

(3) Shem hoped that the boundary of faith would be secured through Arpachshad.

Shem received God's grace and blessings in full and had a third son, whom he named *Arpachshad*. The meaning of the name, "boundary," hints at Shem's fervent hope that the spiritual boundary, the foundation for the work of redemption, might be established through his son.

Shem's expectation for Arpachshad to secure the boundary of faith and to set up a bridgehead for the gospel is reminiscent of the time when the dove was sent out from the ark the second time. It found a small resting place for the sole of its tiny foot and brought back a freshly picked olive leaf (Gen 8:8–11). From this, Noah realized that dry ground was finally appearing and breathed a sigh of relief and kept his hope.

God began His work of redemption by first marking out His boundaries. He chose the small country of Israel in the land of Palestine as a foothold for His work. The chosen Israel became His own boundary and territory (John 1:11). From among all the nations that rose after the flood (Gen 10:31–32) He chose one nation for His work and made its people His own precious people (Deut 7:6; 10:15; 26:18; 32:9). The prophet Amos gives an account of the birth of the chosen nation: "You only have I chosen among all the families of the earth" (Amos 3:2). God chose Israel not because it possessed any unique qualities or by merit, but rather by His absolute grace (Amos 9:7). Amos warned that they would not be able to escape God's fierce judgment if they forget the grace by which they were chosen (Amos 3:2).

At the fullness of time (Gal 4:4), God sent Jesus to the land of Israel, which He had chosen and prepared from long ago to receive the Messiah. This land was rightfully His own (John 1:11). This was the boundary that He chose and set apart as His own since the time of Abraham, but the Son of Man had no place to rest His head when He came (Matt 8:20; Luke 9:58).

In reality, Jesus' ministry did not expand far outside of the small boundary of Israel. He spent most of His time in His land. A good example is the account of his encounter with the Canaanite woman, a Gentile (Syrophoenician [Mark 7:26]) who had traveled a long distance to bring her sick daughter to Jesus. He responded coldly to her request, saying, "I was sent only to the lost sheep of the house of Israel" (Matt 15:24). When Jesus sent His disciples out to evangelize, He instructed them, "Do not go in the way of the Gentiles, and do not enter any city of the Samaritans; but rather go to the lost sheep of the house of Israel" (Matt 10:5–6).

The size of the land of Israel was inconsequential compared to the rest of the world. However, just as a bridgehead is strategically secured during a battle, God also secured His land to act as the central ground for His work. Geographically, the land of Judah, which God chose, was situated at the center of the world, connected to Europe, Africa, and Asia (Ezek 38:12). We should also strive to become God's "boundary," which He consecrates and establishes to advance His will (1 Pet 2:9).

13. Thirteenth Generation: Shelah

שֶׁלַח (*šelaḥ*): send away or sent, sprout (shoot), outstretching (undertaking)

Shelah was born 1,693 years after Adam. He became the father of Eber at the age of 30 and lived 403 years more and had other children. He died at the age of 433 (2,126 years after Adam [Gen 11:14–15; 1 Chr 1:24–25]). He lived 313 years contemporaneously with Noah. Shelah outlived Abraham by 3 years. He lived until Isaac was 78 years old and Jacob 18 was years old.

His name is recorded in the genealogy of Jesus in Luke 3:35 as Σαλά (*Sala*).

The name *Shelah* is derived from the Hebrew word שָׁלַח (*šālaḥ*) and means "to throw (out)," "to send," or "to spread out."

Arpachshad named his son *Shelah* with the hope that God would send godly descendants out to all parts of the world so that the power of faith may expand its reach. Accordingly, it was during Shelah's time that the descendants of Shem spread out to the different regions. God's boundaries (or central base) were secured during Arpachshad's time and enlarged during Shelah's time in order to spread the gospel to all parts of the world. This was the fulfillment of the "multiply" part of God's command to "be fruitful and multiply, and fill the earth" (Gen 9:1, 7), which He gave immediately after the flood. Similarly, the chosen people of Israel, which began with one man, Abraham, whom God first called out from Ur of the Chaldeans, had multiplied greatly by the time the Israelites left Egypt. Exodus 1:7 testifies, "The sons of Israel were fruitful and increased greatly, and multiplied, and became exceedingly mighty, so that the land was filled with them."

(1) Israel was God's first boundary, but this was expanded to encompass the Gentiles, furthering the boundaries of the gospel in accordance with Jesus' command as He ascended into heaven (Matt 28:18-20).

Another Hebrew origin for the name *Shelah* is שֶׁלַח (*šelaḥ*), from which comes the meaning "young branch," "shoot," or "new branch." A sprouting branch is a new shoot containing the hope that one day it will grow into a large tree. Jesus is the spiritual shoot who opened the path to salvation through His death and resurrection. Just as new shoots in the spring season quickly grow into fresh green leaves and clothe a big forest, Arpachshad hoped that the gospel would spread and expand just as swiftly.

With his crucifixion and resurrection as the turning point, the work of the gospel of Jesus Christ expanded out from the Jews in the land of Judea to the lands of the Gentiles (Matt 28:18-20; Acts 1:8; 13:46–47). The time had come to gather the sheep from outside the pen (i.e., the Gentiles) to one shepherd (John 10:16). Paul was also called for this ministry—to become a vessel to hold the Gentiles (Acts 9:15). The movement of the gospel, which began in Jerusalem, spread to nearby Samaria and farther out to all the ends of the earth (Acts 1:8).

(2) The progression of the work from Arpachshad to Shelah corresponds to the growing gospel movement during the early church era after Jesus' resurrection and ascension.

It is important for us to examine how the boundaries of the gospel were enlarged after the advent of the Holy Spirit upon the 120 people during Pentecost. The unbelieving land of Israel became a land of the gospel through the small group of 120 people who gathered in Mark's upper room. Additionally, the great expansion and growth of the Word of God began when these believers were sent out to witness the gospel (Acts 2:41, 47; 4:4; 5:14, 28; 6:7; 9:31; 11:21; 12:24; 19:20). The gospel yielded abundant fruit and increased all around the world (Col 1:5–6).

The growth and expansion of the gospel movement during the early church era is the foreshadowing of the Word movement in the end time. The task of spreading the gospel has been entrusted to us today (Matt 24:14). As people entrusted with the Word of God (Rom 3:2), we must diligently teach the Word to our children and to our neighbors and friends until the earth is filled with the knowledge of the Lord. Our hope and prayer is to see the day when everyone in this world, from the least to the greatest, comes to the knowledge of God (Heb 8:10–11; 10:16–18; Isa 11:9; Hab 2:14).

Jeremiah 31:31–34 "Behold, days are coming," declares the LORD, "when I will make a new covenant with the house of Israel and with the house of Judah, 32not like the covenant which I made with their fathers in the day I took them by the hand to bring them out of the land of Egypt, My covenant which they broke, although I was a husband to them," declares the LORD. 33"But this is the covenant which I will make with the house of Israel after those days," declares the LORD, "I will put My law within them, and on their heart I will write it; and I will be their God, and they shall be My people. 34And they shall not teach again, each man his neighbor and each man his brother, saying, 'Know the LORD,' for they shall all know Me, from the least of them to the greatest of them," declares the LORD, "for I will forgive their iniquity, and their sin I will remember no more."

14. Fourteenth Generation: Eber

עֵבֶר (*ʿēber*): the one who crossed over

Eber was born 1,723 years after Adam. He became the father of Peleg at the age of 34. He lived 430 more years and had other children. He died at the age of 464 (2,187 years after Adam [Gen 11:16–17; 1 Chr 1:25]). He lived 283 years contemporaneously with Noah. Eber outlived Abraham by 64 years. He lived until Isaac was 139 years old and Jacob was 79 years old.

His name is recorded in the genealogy of Jesus in Luke 3:35 as Ἔβερ (*Eber*).

The name *Eber* derives its meaning from the Hebrew word עָבַר (*ʿăbar*), which means "to pass over" or "to cross over." Thus, "Eber" means "one who crossed over" or "region across or beyond." The meaning of his name hints at how he would cross over the Euphrates River from the land of sin and embark on a walk of faith.

The word *Hebrew* is derived from the same root word as *Eber*. This is an attestation to the fact that Eber is the ancestor of the Hebrew nation and that the Hebrews followed in the steps of their ancestors Abraham and Eber and crossed the Euphrates to separate themselves from the sinful land (Gen 14:13).

The Bible makes a peculiar statement regarding Eber: "And also to Shem, the father of all the children of Eber" (Gen 10:21). John Calvin emphasizes the importance of Eber: "Moses, being about to speak of the sons of Shem, makes a brief introduction, which he had not done in reference to the others."[7]

The Bible highlights Eber's significance by praising him even before enumerating the descendants in Shem's genealogy. Arpachshad and Shelah were also Shem's descendants, but they were set aside, and only the children of Eber are described as descendants of Shem.

The first purpose of the verse is to praise the merits of Eber's faith and

7. John Calvin, *Commentaries on the First Book of Moses Called Genesis*, vol. 1, trans. John King (Grand Rapids: Baker, 1989), 320.

to call attention to Eber immediately after Shem. Furthermore, Genesis 10:21 can be interpreted as "and all the children of Eber are born of Shem," awarding value also to the faith of his descendants. God's title had changed from "the God of Shem" (Gen 9:26) to "the God of the children of Eber" (Gen 10:21), focusing more specifically on the children of Eber. In this manner, Eber is highlighted as an important link to Abraham, the father of faith, in the line of Shem (Gen 11:10–27).

(1) Although Eber enjoyed the greatest longevity among the direct descendants of Shem, there was a trend of decreasing human life span to about two hundred years after the generation of his son Peleg.
The abrupt decrease in human life span by half is directly related to sin (Prov 10:27).

> **Psalm 55:23** But Thou, O God, wilt bring them down to the pit of destruction; men of bloodshed and deceit will not live out half their days. But I will trust in Thee.

Eber enjoyed the blessing of longevity because he protected his faith and distanced himself from sin even as the perverse movement to build the Tower of Babel was well underway. Contrary to Eber, the life span of his descendants was cut in half, as a curse, because they did not follow their ancestors across the river. Rather, they intermingled with the descendants of Ham to participate in the building of the Tower of Babel (Gen 10:6–10; 11:1–9).

(2) Eber crossed the Euphrates River and established the kingdom of Ebla.[8]
Many people turned away from God during the movement to build the Tower of Babel. It was at this time that Eber crossed over the Euphrates River from Mesopotamia to Haran and erected the large city of Ebla to maintain orthodox faith in God. As a godly descendant, Eber crossed the river and waved the banner of spiritual reformation and religious purification.

According to the clay tablets discovered around this region, the kingdom of Ebla was a highly civilized city-state established in the region

---

8. "A Letter to the Readers: [Discoveries at Ebla]," *The Biblical Archaeologist* 40, no. 1 (March 1977): 2–4.

known today as Aleppo in Syria. It is believed that Eber was probably its founding king. It is likely that the city-state had previously existed as a small city but was established as a large city-state during Eber's time. Thus, Eber the godly descendant from the line of Shem became the first king, and the kingdom was named after him. According to the clay tablets, the kingdom of Ebla flourished in the arts and academic scholarship and reached its peak around 2300 BC when Eber ruled. In fact, records of the receipt of tributes from nations in the Euphrates region were excavated from this region, leading to the speculation that the kingdom of Ebla was the most powerful kingdom in the ancient Near East.

According to the calculation of the years in the Bible, Eber was born 1,723 years after Adam (c. 2391 BC). He became the father of Peleg 1,757 years after Adam and lived until 2,187 years after Adam (1927 BC). Thus, the years of the kingdom of Ebla coincide with the years of Eber's time.

This information was discovered when over fifteen thousand clay tablets were excavated from the southwestern region of Syria and subsequently deciphered. The deciphering process was made possible with the excavation of the world's greatest Sumerian-Eblaite dictionaries, containing some one thousand words. According to the tablets, the kingdom of Ebla's dominance expanded to the south, encompassing the entire area of Palestine, Lebanon, Syria, and Sinai. To its west it expanded to Cyrus, and to its east to Mesopotamia. There were impressive correspondences with places such as Megiddo, Gaza, Melchizedek, Sodom, and Gomorrah, which are mentioned in other texts reporting shipment of goods and receipt of payments. Based on this evidence, it seems reasonable to propose that the kingdom of Ebla had enjoyed great prosperity and prestige as well as a large territory.[9]

(3) The name of the river that Eber and Abraham crossed is "Euphrates."
Amazingly, *Euphrates* means "abundant" or "storage house of heaven." During harvest time, wheat is gathered into the barn, but the chaff is thrown into the unquenchable fire. Likewise, only people like Eber who set themselves apart from the place of sin by crossing the Euphrates

9. "A Letter to the Readers"; Sung Il Kim, *Exploring Origin of the Korean Nation: Discovering the Route of the Shemites* (Seoul: Research Institute for Creation History, 1997), 88–93.

River will become the spiritual wheat that enters heaven's storehouse. Those who remain in the sinful world to partake in building the Tower of Babel are like the chaff and cannot enter heaven.

> **Matthew 3:12** And His winnowing fork is in His hand, and He will thoroughly clear His threshing floor; and He will gather His wheat into the barn, but He will burn up the chaff with unquenchable fire.

God's judgment will also fall upon the Euphrates in the last days. Among the seven trumpet plagues, the sixth will fall upon the great river Euphrates (Rev 9:13–15).

> **Revelation 9:13–14** I heard a voice . . . saying to the sixth angel who had the trumpet, "Release the four angels who are bound at the great river Euphrates."

According to Revelation, the sixth bowl will be poured out upon the great river, the Euphrates.

> **Revelation 16:12** And the sixth angel poured out his bowl upon the great river, the Euphrates; and its water was dried up, that the way might be prepared for the kings from the east.

The book declaring Babylon's destruction was thrown into the Euphrates (Jer 51:61–64). In the last days, those who cross the Euphrates will be able to escape the last great tribulation.

(4) The "God of Eber" later became the "God of Abraham."

Like Eber, Abraham crossed the Euphrates to enter the land of Canaan when he left Ur of the Chaldeans. In doing so, Abraham completely departed from his ancestors Peleg, Reu, Serug, Nahor, and Terah, who had intermingled with the sinful world and plunged into darkness after the time of Eber (Gen 11:31–12:4; Josh 24:2–3; Acts 7:2–4).

Abraham's contemporaries identified Abraham as a "Hebrew" (Gen 14:13), meaning "one who crossed the river," acknowledging that he was a descendant of Eber. Both *Eber* (עֵבֶר) and *Hebrew* (עִבְרִי) are derived from the verb *ʿăbar* (עָבַר) and have the same meaning. Abraham, who was Eber's seventh generation, reconnected the branch of orthodox faith that had been severed after Eber. Therefore, the "God of Shem" became the "God of Eber," and now the "God of Abraham."

15. Fifteenth Generation: Peleg

פֶּלֶג (*peleg*): division, separate, split

Peleg was born 1,757 years after Adam. He became the father of Reu at the age of 30. He lived 209 years more and had other children. He died at the age of 239 (1,996 years after Adam [Gen 11:18–19; 1 Chr 1:25]). His life span was shortened to about half compared to Eber's time. Thus, Peleg was the first one to die among the 10 generations after the flood. He lived 239 years contemporaneously with Noah.

His name is recorded in the genealogy of Jesus in Luke 3:35 as Φάλεκ (*Phalek*).

The name *Peleg* originates from the Hebrew word פָּלַג (*pālag*), which means "to split" or "to divide." His name thus means "division," "separation," and "split." Genesis 10:25 confirms that the world was divided during his time in accordance with the meaning of his name. The godly man Eber probably named his son *Peleg* with the hope that he would live a holy life, separated and consecrated from the sinful world. Peleg's life, unfortunately, fell short of his father's expectations.

(1) It was during Peleg's time that languages were confused and mankind became scattered as a result of the construction of the Tower of Babel (Gen 11:1–9).

The phrase "for in his days the earth was divided" in Genesis 10:25 describes the result of the construction of the Tower of Babel and the confusion of languages by God. Because it was impossible to build such a complex structure without being able to communicate with one another, their plans were thwarted and they were scattered abroad (Gen 11:9). This is how the city in which the tower was being built earned its name.

> **Genesis 11:9** Therefore its name was called Babel, because there the LORD confused the language of the whole earth; and from there the LORD scattered them abroad over the face of the whole earth.

Men forgot about the fierceness of God's judgment even after experiencing the great flood, and they stirred up God's wrath once again with the construction of the Tower of Babel.

(2) The most peculiar characteristic of Peleg's time was that the human life span was shortened by about half compared to that of his father Eber's time. Peleg was the first one to die among the ten generations of patriarchs since Noah.

Eber lived 464 years, but Peleg lived only 239 years. Reu lived 239 years, and Serug lived 230 years. They did not live much over two hundred years and did not enjoy the longevity that their ancestors did; rather, they lived only about half the life span of their ancestors. After the flood, Peleg died suddenly, before all the other godly patriarchs in the line of Shem who were still alive and healthy. The shortening of life span during Peleg's time indicates that Peleg and his descendants did not fear God and sinned before Him (Ps 55:23; Prov 10:27).

> **Ecclesiastes 8:13** But it will not be well for the evil man and he will not lengthen his days like a shadow, because he does not fear God.

Judging from Genesis 10:25, "for in his days the earth was divided," the construction of the tower was the great sin of challenging God. Man was supposed to cherish the memory of the fearful flood and seek to draw closer to God. Instead, they gathered all human wisdom to build the tower in an attempt to escape God's judgment in case there was to be another (Gen 11:3–4). The underlying message of this challenge against God was that they believed His judgment by the flood to have been unjust. Even Peleg, the offspring of godly Eber, had fallen into the temptation of making concessions for worldly gain and power; ultimately, he also participated in the construction of the tower and committed a grave sin against God.

Sung Il Kim, in his writings about the ancient biblical times, notes that Nimrod had lifted his name high among his followers and wanted to construct the tower in order to keep them from rebelling against him. However, because it was impossible to do so without the sophisticated construction skills of the descendants of Shem, they must have taken part in this work.[10]

After the flood, the tides of sin and corruption swept away even the godly descendants of Shem. The situation was similar to Noah's time, when sin had so filled the world that the sons of God saw the beauty of the daughters of men and intermarried with them (Gen 6:2). The fall of the descendants of Seth truly brought sorrow and pain to God's heart, to the point that He was sorry that He created them. This became the deciding factor for the judgment of the flood (Gen 6:5–7). Peleg was supposed to carry on the faith in the line of Shem, but he stood in the path of sin. Sin grew great enough to merit another catastrophe similar in scale to the flood, but God's covenant of the rainbow promised that no such flood would occur again. Therefore, the sudden decrease in the average life span during Peleg's time can be interpreted as a form of God's judgment upon man. Even Noah (Adam's tenth generation) outlived Peleg (Adam's fifteenth generation) by ten years. Peleg's life was shortened because he took part in sinning against God.

(3) Peleg lived contemporaneously with Abraham (his sixth generation) for forty-eight years.

Ten generations of ancestors in the line of Shem from Noah to Terah were all alive during Abraham's lifetime. It is probable that Noah, Shem, Arpachshad, Shelah, and Eber had already migrated toward Haran during Abraham's time.[11] Hence, Abraham probably lived with Peleg, Reu, Serug, Nahor, and Terah until he left Ur of the Chaldeans.

At the age of forty-eight, Abraham witnessed the unprecedented early death of his ancestor Peleg at the age of 239. The next year, when Abraham was forty-nine years old, he again witnessed the early death of his grandfather Nahor at the age of 148. God had forsaken them because they had strayed too far away from faith. Their deaths must have left a lasting impression on Abraham. It was while Abraham was living among these ancestors that God called him out and consecrated him.

---

10. Kim, *Exploring Origin*, 120.
11. Yong Kuk Wone, *A Dictionary of Biblical Archaeology* (Seoul: Lifebook, 1984), 701–5.

16. Sixteenth Generation: Reu

רְעוּ (*rĕʿû*): friend, neighbor[12]

> **Reu was born 1,787 years after Adam. He became the father of Serug at the age of 32. He lived 207 more years and had other children. He died at the age of 239 (2,026 years after Adam [Gen 11:20–21; 1 Chr 1:25–26]). He lived 219 years contemporaneously with Noah.**
>
> **His name is recorded in the genealogy of Jesus in Luke 3:35 as Ῥαγαύ (*Rhagau*).**

The name *Reu* is derived from the noun רְעִי (*rĕʿî*), meaning "pasture" or "pasturage," and the verb רעה (*rāʿâ*), meaning "to pasture," "to tend," "to associate with," and "to be a friend of."

Unstable times followed after the death of Eber because there was no spiritual leader to provide guidance. Realizing this, Peleg named his son *Reu*, hoping that he would develop good relationships in this world and find success. Instead of teaching his son to become a friend of God, he foolishly desired for his son to develop good social relationships with people of the sinful world.

(1) Reu probably lived a nomadic life.

According to the origin of the name *Reu*, meaning "to pasture," "to tend," or "to graze," he must have lived a nomadic life. Raising live-stock and farming were the two greatest means of livelihood in the ancient agrarian societies.

Characteristic of nomadic life, people migrated from one place to another in search of water and grazing fields. They generally engaged in vast migrations in the spring or summer season and even moved around within pastures. A great migration probably occurred after the incident of the Tower of Babel, and it was probably at this time that they chose to live their lives as nomads. Reu's dedication to this kind of life is evident in his name. He probably migrated from place to place

12. Ludwig Koehler and Walter Baumgartner, *The Hebrew and Aramaic Lexicon of the Old Testament: Study Edition*, vol. 2, trans. and ed. M. E. J. Richardson (Boston: Brill, 2001), 1264; *Oxford Bible Interpreter*, 1:637.

in search for green pastures as he raised livestock and secured grounds for his life.

The lives of saints on this earth also involve continuous migration. The Bible describes such people as "strangers" (1 Pet 2:11) and "sojourners" (1 Chr 29:15). The word *sojourn* refers to a "temporary stay." Saints are on this earth temporarily; eventually they will move on to their eternal home in heaven (Heb 11:13–16).

(2) Reu was faithful in his friendships with other people.

Reu also has a derived meaning of "to associate with" or "to be a friend of." Before the incident of the Tower of Babel, everyone lived in one community and spoke one language.

> **Genesis 11:1** Now the whole earth used the same language and the same words.

However, God squelched their foolish rebellion by confusing their language and scattering them across the earth. Human beings exist within relationships; relationships are established mainly through communication; and language is considered the main means of communication. The confusion of languages was thus a detrimental impediment because it not only affected daily conversation, but also led to differences in ways of thinking eventually resulting in disorder.

By raising the level of differences, misunderstandings, and hostility toward one another, God nullified their plans to challenge Him. This probably led to the formation of new communities as people began to migrate from place to place looking for others who spoke similar languages. Within these new communities, new relationships probably developed between people who shared similar interests. Presumably, establishing new relationships and ties was the first priority in the newly founded communities. Thus, Reu's name is an accurate reflection of a time in which friends who shared common interests and spirit were in desperate need.

It is essential to remember, however, that friendships outside of God are Satan's snares; they bind the legs of saints to this earth. If Reu had focused on holding hands with God and reconciling his relationship with Him, he would not have gotten so caught up with earthly relationships. It would have been easier for him to leave the land of his dwelling behind, just as Abraham had done, in order to begin a new life as a true sojourner to restore his faith.

What became of mankind after being scattered across the earth? As people settled down and built communities, they began to once again erect invisible cities of sin. People who were accustomed to sinning drew closer to one another in a special bond; they joined forces and built up their strength for the purpose of opposing and sinning against God.

(3) A true believer must be worthy of being called a "friend of God."

Eber and other godly ancestors from the line of Shem probably crossed the river and established a holy community of faith (i.e., the kingdom of Ebla) during Reu's lifetime. Peleg and his descendants probably were confident that they could continue their lives of faith without crossing the river to the other side. However, they could not maintain the purity of faith in the humanistic society full of idolatry. Not too long after the Tower of Babel incident, around the time of Abraham, the tides of evil provoked the godly descendants of Shem to corruption and idolatry (Josh 24:2).

These were the circumstances under which God called Abraham. Just as God called Noah to build the ark at a time when sin had filled the earth, He also called Abraham in times of great apostasy in order to establish His kingdom.

In response to God's calling, Abraham forfeited all that was life to him and severed his family ties and friendships. He did not know where he was headed (Heb 11:8), but he obeyed God's calling (Gen 12:4) and began his new life as a sojourner. Neither Peleg nor Reu nor Serug nor Nahor had been able to do this, but Abraham was resolute. He gave up his friendship with this world and yearned for a close friendship with God (Jas 4:4). As a reward, he gained the title "friend of God" (Ps 25:14) and became the only person in the Bible to earn such a noble title (2 Chr 20:7; Isa 41:8; Jas 2:23). We need to ask ourselves whether we are friends with this world or with God.

17. Seventeenth Generation: Serug

שְׂרוּג (*śĕrûg*): vine-shoot,[13] firm strength,[14] bow[15]

Serug was born 1,819 years after Adam. He became the father of Nahor at the age of 30. He lived 200 more years and had other children. He died at the age of 230 (2,049 years after Adam [Gen 11:22–23; 1 Chr 1:26]). He lived 187 years contemporaneously with Noah.

His name is recorded in the genealogy of Jesus in Luke 3:35 as Σερούχ (*Serouch*).

The name *Serug* (שְׂרוּג) originates from the word שָׂרַג (*śārag*), which means "to mesh together," "to be intertwined," and "to intertwine themselves."[16] The purpose of meshing together and intertwining is to build strength. Tendrils growing on walls are strong and sturdy because they have so many well-intertwined branches growing out to the sides. An arrow fitted onto the bow of an archer also symbolizes strength. Thus, it can be inferred that Reu named his son *Serug* with the hope of strengthening his community in order to survive in the chaotic world after the confusion of languages.

This strength, however, was neither spiritual strength nor strength from above; it was human strength built by intertwining with the world and by taking part in it.

(1) Serug relied totally on his own power and strength.

This is evident from the derived meaning of his name: "arrow."

① In the Bible, arrows were used as offensive weapons in battle. The Bible speaks of bows and arrows in relations to wars and battles: "the bow of war" (Zech 9:10), "the bow of battle" (Zech 10:4), "bow of Elam, the finest of their might" (Jer 49:35), "he who sat on it had a

13. H. D. M. Spence and Joseph Exell, eds., *The Pulpit Commentary*, vol. 1, *Genesis*, *Exodus* (Peabody, MA: Hendrickson, 2004), 171.

14. Ibid.

15. Disciples Publishing House, *The Grand Bible Commentary: With Comprehensive and Synthetic Exegetical Study Methods*, vol. 1 (Seoul: Bible Study Material Publisher, 1991), 457.

16. Wenham, *Genesis 1–15*, 251–52.

bow . . . and he went out conquering, and to conquer" (Rev 6:2), and "[men] who shot with bow, and were skillful in battle" (1 Chr 5:18).

② It was common for those who had fallen away from the line of faith to become archers or to become belligerent. Shem's first son Elam was one of the finest archers (Jer 49:35). Ishmael, the son of Abraham's maidservant, was an archer (Gen 21:20), and Isaac's son Esau also hunted with bow and arrow (Gen 27:3). All of them were aggressive and militant and gave birth to belligerent nations that attacked and afflicted the chosen people of God later in history.

It appears that Serug possessed nothing that could help him settle in the land immediately after the Tower of Babel incident. Because threats from foreign nations were commonplace, it is likely that he built military power in preparation for wars and used bows and arrows as weapons. Instead of arming himself with faith in God, he acted as did the Gentile nations and sought to protect himself by building a unified military force armed with bows and arrows.

Isaiah prophesied that those who do not seek the Lord but instead rely on strong nations, taking comfort in large numbers of horsemen and chariots, will be cursed and destroyed (Isa 31:1–3). This is because they, too, are neither spirit nor God, but are mere flesh.

(2) A true believer must rely on God's strength.

A soldier may prepare for battle with swords and spears, but all these instruments of war mean nothing without God, because victory belongs to Him (Prov 21:30–31). The battle is the Lord's (1 Sam 17:47), and His salvation is not based on external factors (1 Sam 14:6). At times, the Lord Himself fights battles for His people (Exod 15:3, 14:13-14).

Well aware of this, the psalmist confessed, "For I will not trust in my bow" (Ps 44:6). There are so many things that seem impossible when done by our own human strength, although they are ostensibly achievable at the outset. Experience proves that things do not work out as easily as we think. Human strength eventually succumbs to greater powers. A believer must trust in the power and might that come from the Word of God and sincerely seek His grace (Acts 19:20; Heb 4:12). The joy of the Lord is the strength of His people (Neh 8:10). He fills those who believe and trust in His Word with amazing new strength so that they can overcome any crisis.

Psalm 119:133 Establish my footsteps in Thy word, and do not let any iniquity have dominion over me.

Isaiah 40:31 Yet those who wait for the LORD will gain new strength; they will mount up with wings like eagles, they will run and not get tired, they will walk and not become weary.

Zechariah 4:6 Then he answered and said to me, "This is the word of the LORD to Zerubbabel saying, 'Not by might nor by power, but by My Spirit,' says the LORD of hosts."

18. Eighteenth Generation: Nahor

נחוֹר (*nāḥôr*): to snort, to blow out[17]

Nahor was born 1,849 years after Adam. He became the father of Terah at the age of 29. He lived 119 more years and had other children. He died at the age of 148 (1,997 years after Adam [Gen 11:24–25; 1 Chr 1:26]). He lived the shortest life among all twenty generations of patriarchs. He lived 148 years contemporaneously with Noah.

His name is recorded in the genealogy of Jesus in Luke 3:34 as Ναχώρ **(*Nachor*).**

The name *Nahor* (נחוֹר) means "to be out of breath," "to pant," and "to snort." The root of this word is (נָחַר) (*naḥar*), which means "snorting." Judging from the fact that Peleg lived 239 years, Reu 239 years, Serug 230 years, and Terah 205 years, we can conclude that Nahor, who died at the age of 148, did not fully live out his years. He must have been cursed by God and must have experienced sudden death from an accident or disease. His sudden death was probably a shock to his family and the patriarchs in the line of Shem.

(1) Nahor's life appears to have been shortened due to sin.

Peleg was the first to die among the ten generations after the flood, but Nahor lived the shortest life. He died suddenly only a year after Peleg at the age of 148. In the Bible, sudden deaths are associated with sin (Job 22:15–16; Ps 55:23; Prov 10:27; Eccl 7:17; 8:13). The Bible presents two cases in which people suddenly perish.

First, the proud will perish.

> **Proverbs 29:1** A man who hardens his neck after much reproof will suddenly be broken beyond remedy.

17. Ibid., 252.

Second, liars will perish.

> **Proverbs 6:12–15** A worthless person, a wicked man, is the one who walks with a false mouth, [13]who winks with his eyes, who signals with his feet, who points with his fingers; [14]who with perversity in his heart devises evil continually, who spreads strife. [15]Therefore his calamity will come suddenly; instantly he will be broken, and there will be no healing.

Nahor was enjoying the prime of his life when he was struck with a plague and immediately perished. The meaning of his name indicates that he had dedicated his whole life to being preoccupied or obsessed with something. Whether it was in terms of wealth or honor, he probably dreamed of being great and stopped at nothing to achieve his goals. He poured out his wealth, his time, and his youth into the world. In today's terms, he had made it big in his prime years, whether it was with regard to his business or to fame. He found satisfaction in his own calculations and was deceived by his own wit. Ultimately, he was so engrossed in the secular life (wealth, honor, and fame) that he lost himself and thoroughly lost sight of the importance of his spirit and life.

(2) Nahor probably was a man of greed deeply immersed in secularism. In accordance with Proverbs 28:16, Nahor would have enjoyed longevity if he hated greed, but his life came to an abrupt end because he could not overcome his greed.

> **Proverbs 28:16** A leader who is a great oppressor lacks understanding, but he who hates unjust gain will prolong his days.

In Luke 12:15, Jesus said, "Be on your guard against every form of greed." In Ephesians 5:3, Paul said, "But do not let immorality or any impurity or greed even be named among you." Greed leads to all sorts of lies and even to forsaking God or to using God to achieve selfish desires. At times, it manipulates a heart devoted to faith for evil purposes, filling it with the greed of the flesh, which is idolatry (Col 3:5). Nahor was this kind of person.

Although Nahor expended all his energy to achieve his goals and busied himself traveling to all parts of the world, the result was futile because God suddenly took his soul back. Nahor boasted as if he possessed the whole world, but he was a fool who lost himself in the end (Matt 16:26; Luke 9:25). In Luke 12:20, Jesus deplored such fools:

"You fool! This very night your soul is required of you; and now who will own what you have prepared?"

God would have been greatly pleased if Nahor had expended all his energy to guard his faith, to consecrate himself holy in this world, and to battle against the sinful world. The principle of faith based on the fact that we came into this world naked (Job 1:21; Eccl 5:15; 1 Tim 6:7–9) dictates that we become accustomed to constantly leaving things behind for a new place. Nahor, however, found satisfaction only when honor, wealth, and riches adorned him; he felt comfort and great joy when he placed his trust in them and looked upon them. This was why he was so busy all his life, panting and gasping in order to satisfy his desires.

The meaning of Nahor's name reveals no trace of godliness. It only shows that he had lived his life totally separated and alienated from God. God said in Genesis 6:3 that the end of such a person is just flesh, without the spirit of God. Although Nahor confessed that he believed, his life was immersed in sensuality and hedonism, where God is not present.

The apostle Paul said that the wrath of God is revealed from heaven against all those who are ungodly, unrighteous, and more detestable than unbelievers (Rom 1:18). His indictment of heathens found in Romans 1:21–32 is as follows:

> Even though they knew God, they did not give thanks (1:21).
>
> Even though they knew God, they became futile in their speculations (1:21).
>
> Even though they knew God, they became fools without wisdom (1:22).
>
> Even though they knew God, they exchanged His glory for idols (1:23).
>
> Even though they knew God, they exchanged the truth for a lie (1:25).
>
> Even though they knew God, they were filled with degrading and indecent thoughts (1:26–27).
>
> Even though they knew God, they did not see fit to acknowledge God any longer (1:28).
>
> Even though they knew God, they planned only evil and were ungrateful (1:29–31).
>
> Even though they knew that such practices are worthy of death, they not only continued to do the same without feeling any shame, but also gave hearty approval to those who practice them (1:32).

It is warned that the wrath of God will be revealed from heaven against all ungodliness of men who suppress the truth in unrighteousness (Rom 1:18).

This is exactly what happened to Nahor. Regardless of how great one's possessions may be, one will pant heavily and meet the end of life the way Nahor did if God takes away the breath of life that He had breathed into Adam's nostrils (Gen 2:7).

The corruption of the descendants in the godly line of Shem accelerated with the passage of time: Reu placed more importance on human relationships than on his relationship with God; Serug trusted in his own strength; and Nahor's life was immersed in secularism and greed. It was not that they did not know God, but rather that they completely forsook their faith and tragically fell into worshiping detestable idols (Josh 24:2, 15). They were totally corrupted; they relapsed into the fleshly lifestyle.

It was the desires of the flesh that stood against the Holy Spirit and turned them away from the Word of truth (Gal 5:17). This is the act of sowing two types of seeds in a vineyard (Deut 22:9). This is the act of making the ox and the donkey plow together (Deut 22:10). This is the act of mixing wool and linen together (Deut 22:11). This is the detestable faith that attempts to bind believers with nonbelievers, Christ with Belial, and the temple of God with idols (2 Cor 6:14–16).

We must do away with greed, which is idolatry (Col 3:5), and boldly remove the carnal faith that has been mixed with the greed of the world. As God's people, if we pant, it should be from working zealously to fulfill His will.

19. Nineteenth Generation: Terah

תֶּרַח (*teraḥ*): to stay, to delay

Terah was born 1,878 years after Adam. He became the father of Abram at the age of 70. He lived 135 more years and had other children. He died at the age of 205 (2,083 years after Adam [Gen 11:26–32; 1 Chr 1:26–27]). He lived 128 years contemporaneously with Noah.

His name is recorded in the genealogy of Jesus in Luke 3:34 as Θάρα (*Thara*).

The name *Terah* (תֶּרַח) means "to stay" or "to delay." He left Ur of the Chaldeans with Abraham and moved to Haran en route to the land of Canaan, but he tarried in Haran (Gen 11:31–32). He died forty years before Abraham in the land of Haran. He was the nineteenth generation from Adam, and he lived 128 years contemporaneously with Noah, the tenth generation, although this does not mean that he lived with Noah in the same place for 128 years.

(1) Terah was an idol worshiper (Josh 24:2–5, 14–15).

Terah was a descendant of faith; he had inherited the faith of Noah, Shem, and Eber. In truth, although he boasted of the faith of his ancestors, he became so deeply immersed in idolatry that his own faith shook from its roots. Joshua 24:2 specifically states, "From ancient times your fathers lived beyond the River, namely, Terah, the father of Abraham and the father of Nahor, and they served other gods."

(2) Terah left Ur of the Chaldeans, the city of idols, but he settled in Haran.

> **Genesis 11:31** And Terah took Abram his son, and Lot the son of Haran, his grandson, and Sarai his daughter-in-law, his son Abram's wife; and they went out together from Ur of the Chaldeans in order to enter the land of Canaan; and they went as far as Haran, and settled there.

The chief event noted in Terah's genealogy in Genesis 11:27–32 is Abraham's departure from Ur of the Chaldeans for the great journey to the land of Canaan. This was the dramatic scene where God totally separated Abraham from the home of evil where the Tower of Babel had been built so that He might use him.

God appeared to Abraham in Ur of the Chaldeans as the God of glory and commanded him, "Depart from your country and your relatives, and come into the land that I will show you" (Acts 7:2–3). Apparently, when Terah heard about the encounter from Abraham, he got caught up in the grandeur and enthusiasm of the calling and took an even greater initiative to obey the calling by *taking* Abraham and leaving with him from Ur of the Chaldeans. Genesis 11:31 states, "Terah took Abram his son, and Lot the son of Haran, his grandson, and Sarai his daughter-in-law . . . and they went out together from Ur of the Chaldeans." The unfortunate part was that Terah did not enter the land of Canaan. He died in Haran at the age of 205 (Gen 11:32). Terah's life was true to the meaning of his name: "to delay." While Terah and Abraham were tarrying in the land of Haran, God appeared to Abraham once again and commanded, "Go forth from your country, and from your relatives and from your father's house, to the land which I will show you" (Gen 12:1). This time, Abraham fully obeyed and departed from Haran for the land of Canaan (Gen 12:5). From this point, Abraham became the focal point of God's new work of salvation.

(3) After Terah, Abraham came to the forefront of the history of redemption.

The genealogy of Shem in Genesis 11 lists who gave birth to whom, at what age, and how many years he lived and had children (Gen 11:10–26), but unlike the genealogy in Genesis 5, it does not list how many years each ancestor lived before he died. In Terah's case, however, this information is provided in order to emphasize his death.

> **Genesis 11:32** And the days of Terah were two hundred and five years; and Terah died in Haran.

Genesis 11 concludes with the death of Terah. The sound of the Tower of Babel being built up—the sound of betrayal and opposition against God—has been silenced. The odor from the carnal faith of the supposed descendants of faith (e.g., Peleg, Reu, Serug, and Nahor) has gone. All came to an end with Terah's death. Now, the focus was on one man: Abraham.

In a world where even the descendants of faith (i.e., of Shem) were tainted by idol worship, God found one man, Abraham, and urgently called him out. After the Tower of Babel incident, mankind fell into a mire of sin so great that God's work of salvation was almost cut off. With the death of Terah, however, darkness that had loomed over the line of Shem was lifted, and a new work of salvation began through Abraham.

The "God of Shem" (Gen 9:26) became the "God of Eber" (Gen 10:21), and now He was the "God of Abraham." Ham's sin after the flood had cast a pall of dark clouds over the line of faith, but the words of hope, "Blessed be the LORD, the God of Shem," were fulfilled when Abraham was singled out from the line of Shem. He opened wide the path of salvation for all mankind.

20. Twentieth Generation: Abraham

אַבְרָהָם (*ʾabrāhām*): father of the multitude, father of nations

Abraham was born 1,948 years after Adam. He became the father of Isaac, the covenantal son, at the age of 100. He died at the age of 175 (2,123 years after Adam [Gen 17:1–22; 21:5; 25:7; 1 Chr 1:27–28]). He lived 58 years contemporaneously with Noah. Within the ten generations after Noah, the patriarchs who died before Abraham were Arpachshad, Peleg, Reu, Serug, Nahor, and Terah. The patriarchs who died after Abraham were Shem (died 35 years after Abraham), Shelah (died 3 years after Abraham), and Eber (died 64 years after Abraham).

His name is recorded in the genealogy of Jesus in Luke 3:34 as ʼΑβραάμ **(*Abraam*).**

The name *Abram* (אַבְרָם) means "exalted father" or "honorable father," but the name "Abraham" (אַבְרָהָם), which God gave to him at the age of ninety-nine, means "father of the multitude" and "father of nations" (Gen 17:5). The name underscores the crucial role that Abraham would play in fulfilling God's divine administration of redemption.

Adam was the first father of mankind, Noah became the father of the new world after the flood, and Abraham was the father of the chosen people of Israel. He is also the father of faith of the spiritual nation in Jesus Christ.

The history of redemption that began with Seth and continued through Noah during the age of the flood now reached Abraham. Failure, betrayal, and corruption had seeped even into the line of Shem after the Tower of Babel incident, but God chose Abraham from the house of Terah. By the time Abraham was born, it had only been 292 years since the flood, and only one hundred years since the building of the Tower of Babel, but sin was once again overflowing.

(1) Abraham received God's calling in Ur of the Chaldeans (Gen 11:31; Acts 7:2–4).

Abraham was first called by the God of glory in Ur of the Chaldeans. *Ur* (אוּר) originally means "light" or "fire." Scholars suggest that this name reflects the reverence and worship of fire during those times, which is further evidence that Abraham had lived during a highly idolatrous age. In Joshua 24:2, Joshua said to the people, "From ancient times your fathers lived beyond the River, namely, Terah, the father of Abraham and the father of Nahor, and they served other gods." One day, the God of glory appeared to Abraham and commanded him to leave Ur of the Chaldeans (Acts 7:2–3). Hence, Abraham followed his father, Terah, out of Ur of the Chaldeans and settled in Haran (Gen 11:31).

(2) Abraham fully obeyed God's second calling in Haran and became a blessing (Gen 12:1–3, Heb 11:8).

Haran was one of the magnificent cities of Paddan-aram located in the northern region of Mesopotamia. It is presumed that a significant number of people from the line of Shem lived around this area (Gen 10:22; 24:4; 25:20; 28:5).

Abraham, after leaving Ur of the Chaldeans, settled in Haran. Haran was supposed to be a mere stop on the way to Canaan, but Abraham's filial piety for his father kept him from leaving. Terah was born among the sins of his fathers; he was raised eating and drinking in the midst of sin. He had become so accustomed to sinning that he could not sever ties with sin during the stopover in Haran, so he settled there. This was the fulfillment of the meaning of his name: "to delay" and "to stay."

Abraham had lived a long time in Haran with Terah when God called him yet a second time, at the age of seventy-five, to finally leave Haran for Canaan (Gen 12:5). God commanded Abraham, "Go forth from your country, and from your relatives and from your father's house, to the land which I will show you" (Gen 12:1).

Abraham obeyed this command and let go of his hold on Terah. It took great resolve to totally break his attachment from his father in order to follow God's command (Gen 12:4). Acknowledging Abraham's faith, the author of Hebrews testifies, "By faith Abraham, when he was called, obeyed by going out to a place which he was to receive for an inheritance; and he went out, not knowing where he was going" (Heb 11:8). Abraham was seventy-five years old when he departed from Haran. He lived one hundred more years and became the father of Isaac and the grandfather of Jacob before he died at the age of 175.

(3) Abraham lived with Isaac for seventy-five years, and with Jacob for about fifteen years.

Hebrews 11:9 states, "By faith [Abraham] lived as an alien in the land of promise, as in a foreign land, dwelling in tents with Isaac and Jacob, fellow heirs of the same promise." What was Abraham's primary duty as he dwelt in his tent? Abraham occupied himself with the work of passing down his faith to his descendants. According to Genesis 18:18–19, this was precisely the reason why God had called Abraham. To Abraham's credit, he had fully completed this task and yielded the fruit of faith through his son Isaac. This was evident in Isaac's obedience when God commanded Abraham to offer Isaac, his only son of the covenant whom he had begotten at the age of one hundred, as a burnt offering (Gen 22:1–2, 9).

During the fifteen years that he spent living with Jacob, Abraham presumably passed down his faith by recounting stories about God's calling in Ur of the Chaldeans, his delay in Haran, his departure from Haran, all of God's amazing works during the one hundred years after he left Haran, and the fulfillment of God's covenant regarding the land and the descendants. Abraham's faith revealed through his life, however, probably had a greater impact than his words.

Three generations—Abraham, Isaac, and Jacob—had become one in faith. God was now called the God of Abraham, the God of Isaac, and the God of Jacob, and His amazing work of redemption began to unfold through them (Exod 3:6, 15–16; Matt 22:32; Mark 12:26; Luke 20:37; Acts 3:13; 7:32).

(4) Abraham lived fifty-eight years contemporaneously with Noah.

Abraham became the father of Isaac at the age of one hundred, and he died at the age of 175. According to the biblical genealogies, all ten generations after Noah were alive at Abraham's birth. Abraham was born 290 years after Arpachshad, and all his ancestors were still alive then.[18] According to the chronology of the patriarchs, Noah was 892 years old and still alive when Abraham was born. Abraham lived fifty-eight years contemporaneously with Noah until Noah died at the age of 950. This is an amazing fact. Although there were 390 years between

18. Ibid., 251.

the generations of Shem and Abraham, God's covenant that began with Shem after the flood had been passed down until it reached Abraham. Noah's faith probably had a positive influence on Abraham.

God's work of salvation, which began with Adam, passed through Noah (Adam's tenth generation) and finally reached Abraham (Noah's tenth generation) to encounter a new beginning. Afterwards, it unfolded with a new people of God (descendants of Abraham) and the new land of God (land of Canaan).

לכל בר דעת דרך המסעות ארבעים שנה במדבר והרוחב והאורך של ארץ הקדושה מנהר מצ
עמלק
מדבר צין הוא קדש
ים המלח
עתר
מקדה
עיר כרמל
שבט
חצור
ענב
מדבר פארן
מדבר סיני
מדבר שור
בתול
אלהולד
מולדה
שרוחן
באר שבע
שמעון
שבט
ארץ פלשתים
רמסס
ארץ גשן
פתם
אלכסנדרי
לוח המסעות במדבר
אשר על פי ה׳ יסעו ועל פי ה׳ יחנו
א׳ רעמסס	טו׳ רתמה	כט׳ חרהגדגד
ב׳ סכת	טז׳ רמן פרץ	ל׳ יטבתה
ג׳ אתם	יז׳ לבנה	לא׳ עברנה
ד׳ פיהחירת	יח׳ רסה	לב׳ עציןגבר
ה׳ מרה	יט׳ קהלתה	לג׳ מדבר צין
ו׳ אילם	כ׳ הרספר	לד׳ הרההר
ז׳ ים סוף	כא׳ חרדה	לה׳ צלמנה
ח׳ מדבר סין	כב׳ מקהלת	לו׳ פונן
ט׳ דפקה	כג׳ תחת	לז׳ אבת
י׳ אלוש	כד׳ תרח	לח׳ דיבן גד
יא׳ רפידם	כה׳ מתקה	לט׳ עלמן דבלתים
יב׳ מדבר סיני	כו׳ חשמנה	מ׳ הרי עברים
יג׳ קברות התאוה	כז׳ מסרות	מא׳ ערבת מואב
יד׳ חצרת	כח׳ בני יעקן

PART FIVE

A New Work of Salvation

The Bible contains God's divine administration for the redemption of fallen mankind. The genealogies in the Book of Genesis clearly illustrate this divine administration through the two distinct spiritual lines: the line of Seth and the line of Cain. The incredible contrast between these two lines clearly shows that the saints who fulfill God's plan for redemption are to lead lives set apart from the world. The genealogies in Genesis 5 and Genesis 11 conclude the generations of the line of Seth with Abraham and at the same time open up a new era in the history of redemption through him. The flow of the lineage from Seth until Abraham can be summed up as the process of being *set apart* from the world through adherence to the Word of God. The Bible teaches us that those who consecrate themselves from this world will become central figures in the history of redemption and the fulfillment of God's divine administration.

Now, we will examine the differences between the line of Seth and the line of Cain, and the redemptive significance of the process in which Abraham is *taken out* from the world.

> **Genesis 18:17–19** And the LORD said, "Shall I hide from Abraham what I am about to do, [18]since Abraham will surely become a great and mighty nation, and in him all the nations of the earth will be blessed? [19]For I have chosen him, in order that he may command his children and his household after him to keep the way of the LORD by doing righteousness and justice; in order that the LORD may bring upon Abraham what He has spoken about him."

CHAPTER 12

The Differences between the Line of Cain and the Line of Seth

Adam and Eve had two sons, Cain and Abel, after they were expelled from the Garden of Eden. When Cain committed the evil act of killing Abel, God appointed another seed, Seth, to replace Abel (Gen 4:25). Adam's two sons were now Cain and Seth. Although they were from the same parents, these two sons became ancestors of two very distinct lines. Seth became the ancestor of the genealogy of the chosen people who obeyed God's Word and advanced the fulfillment of His plan for salvation. Cain became the ancestor of the genealogy of people who challenged God's will, persecuted His chosen people, and hindered the work of salvation. These two spiritual lines flow distinctly through the Old and New Testaments.

According to our studies thus far on the line of Seth and the line of Cain, the descendants of Seth had their roots in God and were active participants in His work of redemption. As a reward, they enjoyed longevity on this earth. Conversely, the descendants of Cain flourished and gloried in the secular world, but they were cut off from God. They stood on the side of the wicked and afflicted the chosen people, hindering the flow of redemptive history. What are the specific differences between the two lines?

1. The Genealogies of Cain and Seth Have Different Beginnings

The beginning of all things is important; a bad start increases the probability of a bad ending. The two genealogies had very different beginnings.

The genealogy of the line of Cain began with Cain's departure from the presence of God. Genesis 4:16 states, "Then Cain went out from the presence of the LORD, and settled in the land of Nod, east of Eden." He gave birth to his son Enoch after his departure from God and set the tone for the rest of his line: a genealogy with no ties to God. Regardless of the notable achievements in the world, those who leave God will perish (Ps 73:27). Jeremiah 17:5 states, "Thus says the LORD, 'Cursed is the man who trusts in mankind and makes flesh his strength, and whose heart turns away from the LORD.'"

In contrast, the genealogy of the line of Seth began with God. Genesis 5:1–3, which introduces the genealogy of the descendants of Adam, states that God had created Adam and to Adam was born a son at the age of 130 whom he named *Seth*. Thus, the genealogy of Seth traces back to Adam and ultimately to God.

The genealogy of Jesus in Luke 3 also traces its roots back to God, "the son of Seth, the son of Adam, the son of God," testifying that God's plan for salvation was being fulfilled through the line of Seth. Another affirmation of this fact is that the descendants of Seth who were alive during Noah's time were given the honorable title "the sons of God" (Gen 6:2).

There are also many verses in the Bible that clearly state that we are sons of God and that He is our Father.

> **References:** Exodus 4:22; Deuteronomy 1:31; 14:1; 32:5–6; 2 Samuel 7:14; 1 Chronicles 22:10; Isaiah 1:2; 9:6; 63:16; 64:8; Jeremiah 3:4, 19, 31:9; Hosea 11:1; Malachi 2:10; Psalm 2:7; 68:5; 89:26–27; Matthew 5:45; 6:4; 7:11; 10:20, 29, 32; 11:25; 23:9; Mark 11:25; Luke 2:49; 6:36; 10:21–22; 11:2; 12:30; John 1:12; 4:21; 8:41, 54; 20:17; Galatians 4:6; Ephesians 1:17; 1 Peter 1:17

Applying this truth to the lives of believers today, we can conclude that those who do not pray have departed from God, while those who pray to God have their beginnings with Him (Deut 4:7). Those who distance themselves from the Word of God have forsaken Him, while those who draw near to His Word have their beginnings with Him (Ps 1:1–3).

2. The Genealogies of Cain and Seth Demonstrate Different Lifestyles

Among the differences between the descendants of Cain and the descendants of Seth, we must focus on the differences in their ways of life. Generally, there are two ways in which human beings live their lives on this earth. One way is to live a self-centered life focused on one's own success and happiness. The other way is to live a God-centered life focused solely on glorifying Him.

The descendants in the line of Cain lived self-centered lives. These men introduced in Genesis 4 were founders of new cultures, civilizations, and professions. They were considered successful from the world's perspective. After Cain departed from God's presence, he built the first city and named it *Enoch* after his son (Gen 4:17). His way of life involved building a city to protect himself and to exalt his own name. This kind of way of life reached its climax with Lamech, the seventh generation. Lamech was an extremely self-centered man who murdered a young boy for inflicting a small wound on him.

Lamech's sons achieved fame by becoming originators of various civilizations. Genesis 4:20-22 tells us that Jabal became the father of those who dwell in tents and have livestock. His brother Jubal became the father of all those who play the lyre and pipe. Tubal-cain was a forger of sharp implements made of bronze and iron. However, their lives did not exalt God's name; their lives were completely self-centered and had absolutely nothing to do with God. The Tower of Babel was a clear manifestation of their lifestyle. Their main purpose for building cities and towers was to make a name for themselves (Gen 11:4).

In contrast, the descendants in the line of Seth lived God-centered lives. For these men who appear in Genesis 5, there is no mention of earthly achievements, new discoveries, or anything else that involved making a name for themselves. Their lives were focused on glorifying God. Enosh called upon the name of the Lord and worshiped Him. Mahalalel sang His praises. Enoch walked with God for three hundred years. As his name indicated, Methuselah lived his life with his eyes fixed firmly upon God's judgment that would bring the world to an end. Lamech hoped that God's rest would be established through his son Noah. Noah built the ark and lived a life of obedience to the Word of God. Their lives were all God-centered lives that manifested His glory.

Since the beginning of the history of mankind, all lives took either of these two paths—the path according to the line of Cain or the path according to the line of Seth. The path according to the line of Cain may have been enriched with wealth, honor, power, and fame through various earthly achievements. However, no matter how extravagant their lives may have been, the Bible warns that woe will be upon those who go the way of Cain. Those who follow the path of Cain are like trees doubly dead and uprooted, like wild waves of the sea casting up their own shame like foam, and like wandering stars for which the black darkness has been reserved forever (Jude 11–13). They are like oak trees whose leaves have dried up, like a garden with no water (Isa 1:30), and like broken cisterns that cannot hold water (Jer 2:13). No matter how much water they drink, they will become increasingly thirsty. Furthermore, they are like a bush in the desert that does not see when prosperity comes (Jer 17:5-6). Worries, concerns, sadness, and pain will not cease to engulf them. All this will happen to them because they have forsaken God, the fountain of living waters.

However, the descendants of the line of Seth will continue to yield fruit in their old age. They will be full of sap and very green because they glorified God's name (Ps 92:14). Why? Because the God of their faith is the fountain of living waters (Jer 2:13; 17:13). He watches over their lives from beginning to end, exalts their name above every name, and ensures that their names are never erased (Phil 2:9).

3. The Genealogies of Cain and Seth Have Different Records of Birth and Death

The genealogy of the line of Seth in Genesis 5 was recorded in a specific format: "He became the father of X, he lived Y years, and all his days were Z." This genealogy accurately records the time of birth, death, and life span. The genealogy of the line of Cain, however, has no record of birth, death, or life span. What does this mean?

First, it signifies that there are lives that God acknowledges and lives that He does not acknowledge. The genealogy of Cain does not record when each person was born, how long he lived, or when he died, because their lives were not esteemed by God. The people of this world may have acknowledged their success, but they were meaningless in God's eyes. There was not one moment of their lives that was worthy to be acknowledged by God or to be recorded in the Bible.

On the other hand, there are exact records of the births, lives, and deaths of the descendants of Seth because their years were esteemed by God. God carried out His plans through this line that He acknowledged. Psalm 1:6 states, "For the LORD knows the way of the righteous, but the way of the wicked will perish."

Second, it indicates that there was a difference with regard to the succession and continuation of faith. Faith in God and the spiritual inheritance were not passed down through the generations of the line of Cain. Their lives were extremely individualistic. They were all deeply engrossed in themselves and obstinate in their own ways. They built up *personal strongholds* until their lives faded into vanity.

The stream of faith, however, continued to flow without a break down through the generations of the line of Seth. The descendants of Seth diligently passed down to their children the Word of God and the works of faith, which they had also inherited from their fathers (Ps 78:3–8; Isa 38:19; Joel 1:3).

For this reason, the record of the line of Cain came to an abrupt end after only seven generations, while the record of the line of Seth continued from Adam to Abraham, the twentieth generation. Although there were slight digressions along the way, there were no interruptions in the lineage of the godly descendants or in the works of faith until the coming of the Messiah. It continued from Adam to the Messiah and to us today. This enduring genealogy shows that although individuals died, God's work of life committed to overcoming the curse of death continued without rest through the godly descendants.

Third, it distinguishes the lives of "beasts" from the lives of true "men." The lives of the men in the line of Cain were like those of beasts. For beasts, the repetition of the cycle of birth and death is meaningless. The children in the line of Cain never once gave thought to the redemptive significance of the times in which they lived. They did not live their lives by grace; they lived for themselves and for their own satisfaction. The Bible says that those who lack understanding are no different than beasts (Ps 49:12, 20; Eccl 3:18–19).

However, the children in the line of Seth were awarded the status of men, not of beasts. Genesis 5:2 says, "[He] named them Man." Genesis 5:3 also says that Adam gave birth to Seth. These verses underscore the fact that the line of Seth was passing down the form of the true "man" whom God had created in His own likeness.

4. The Genealogies of Cain and Seth Have Different Records of Longevity

There are no records of the year of birth or death for the descendants in the line of Cain. Hence, there is no way to know how long they lived on this earth. On the contrary, records show that the descendants in the line of Seth enjoyed longevity on this earth. The blessing of longevity was God's special privilege awarded to the descendants of Seth but not to the descendants of Cain. The phrase "So all the days that X lived were Y," which appears at the end of each patriarch's record, is an illustration of this blessing (Gen 5:5, 8, 11, 14, 17, 20, 27, 31). "So all the days that X lived were Y" did not mean only that they lived long lives, but that the blessing was marked by both spiritual and physical well-being. Longevity did not mean long life in a frail or diseased body; it was accompanied by good health and blessings. The word "live" (חיה) in this verse means "to live prosperously" and "to revive from sickness, discouragement, or death."

Living out all the years that God had determined for them is testimony of His grace and protection. The descendants in the line of Seth had children even when they were well advanced in years. This is another indication that they had enjoyed good health through God's blessings (Prov 4:20–23). What was the secret behind their longevity?

First, they feared God.

The Bible explains that the secret to longevity is the fear of God (Deut 4:40; 5:16; 6:2–3; 11:9, 22:7; Exod 20:12; 1 Kgs 3:14; Job 22:15–

16; Ps 21:4; 55:23; 91:16; Prov 3:1–2, 7–8, 16; 4:20–23; 9:11; 10:27; 16:31; Eccl 7:17; 8:12–13; Eph 6:1–3).

Proverbs 10:27 states, "The fear of the LORD prolongs life, but the years of the wicked will be shortened." "To fear God" means to wholeheartedly revere and serve Him, acknowledging that He is the One to be awed. The author of Ecclesiastes draws this conclusion when he writes, "The conclusion, when all has been heard, is: fear God and keep His commandments, because this applies to every person" (Eccl 12:13). The command to fear God appears in many places throughout the Bible (e.g. Lev 19:14, 32; Deut 5:29; 6:2; 10:12, 20; Prov 3:7; 23:17). The fear of the Lord is the beginning of all wisdom (Job 28:28; Ps 111:10; Prov 1:7; 9:10). Those who fear God keep away from evil and turn away from its path (Job 28:28; Prov 3:7; 8:13; 16:6, 17). The fear of God is the path to blessings without want (Ps 34:7–9; 128:1; Prov 14:26–27, 22:4; Isa 33:6). In 2 Corinthians 7:1, the end time is described as a world covered with filthy sins. The only way for us to preserve our spirit and body blameless and unblemished is to have the fear of God. The fear of God perfects holiness and allows us to see God (Heb 12:14).

Second, they distanced themselves from sin.

If we want to enjoy longevity, we must immediately do away with sins that are close around us in our lives. Sin shortens our lives and prevents the blessings of heaven from reaching us (Jer 5:23–25). The descendants in the line of Seth enjoyed longevity because they repented and distanced themselves from sin. In the Bible, Methuselah enjoyed the greatest longevity (969 years; eighth generation from Adam), then Jared (962 years; sixth generation from Adam), and then Noah (950 years; tenth generation from Adam). Their longevity calls for a reflection upon the truth that mankind was originally created to live eternally (1 John 2:25).

Man was originally created for eternal life, but death came by way of sin (Rom 5:12; 6:23). Man, however, did not immediately die, but lived a long life because God delayed the punishment of sin to a certain extent. Their life spans, however, grew shorter and shorter as they continued to sin despite God's love. It was abruptly shortened once after the flood. Later, when man attempted to exalt his own name and challenge God by constructing the Tower of Babel, God responded by shortening life span by half. In the beginning, the descendants of Adam enjoyed astonishing life spans close to one thousand years, but after the flood the number of years diminished to between four hundred and six hundred, and then to about two hundred years after the Tower of Babel incident. After Abraham, no one lived past two hundred years. Moses said that his eyes did not grow dim until he was 120 years old, but in Psalm 90 he sang, "As for the days of our life, they contain seventy years, or if due to strength, eighty years" (Ps 90:10).

Shortened life spans are a sure indication that sin had seeped deeply into the lives of mankind (Ps 55:23). Furthermore, sin had a staggering impact not only on man's life span, but also on the environment—the natural resources that man breathes, eats, and drinks. According to God's principle of creation, the earth rotates around its own axis while simultaneously revolving around the sun, maintaining twenty-four-hour days and four beautiful seasons of the year (Gen 1:14). The countless stars also keep their place and maintain order in the universe. Their strict yet wondrous order is a display of God's great love and His marvelous works (Ps 139:14).

The universe was originally created to benefit mankind. As the wickedness of man was great on the earth and the earth was filled with violence (Gen 6:5-7, 11-12), God was sorry that He had made man on the earth. He judged the world with the flood. The harmonious workings of nature, climate, and temperature, which once had been perfectly suitable for life, were altered after the flood (Gen 8:22). Changes in the climate meant that nature no longer provided only good things to mankind. Unlike the prediluvian days, the abnormal changes in the climate and seasons (severe cold or extremely intense heat) sped up the aging process and caused diseases leading to significantly shortened life spans. Genesis 8:21–22 explains that such changes took place because "the intent of man's heart is evil from his youth." From this point on, nature did not just bestow benefits; it also brought harm to mankind (Jer 5:23–25). This clearly was the result of sin. Regarding this, God said to Adam, "Because you have listened to the voice of your wife, and have eaten from the tree about which I commanded you, saying, 'You shall not eat from it'; cursed is the ground because of you; in toil you shall eat of it all the days of your life" (Gen 3:17).

Third, they honored their parents.

The Bible states that those who honor their parents will enjoy longevity (Deut 5:16; Eph 6:1–3). The fifth commandment also states, "Honor your father and your mother, that your days may be prolonged in the land which the LORD your God gives you" (Exod 20:12). Accordingly, the descendants in the line of Seth who had enjoyed longevity must have also honored their parents. Why is it so important to honor parents? It is a way of confessing that we remember the origin of our existence. Furthermore, honoring parents is equivalent to honoring God the Creator. Among the Ten Commandments, the fifth through the tenth commandments outline relationships between people. Among these, the fifth is the only commandment that includes the phrase "the LORD your God." This is because honoring our parents leads to honoring God. By honoring our parents, we acknowledge that the one who gave us life, the one who is the origin of our existence, is God.

We have learned, thus far, that those who obey the Word of God and keep from sinning will receive the blessing of longevity (Prov 3:1–2). When we distance ourselves from sin, realizing how miserable and fearful its consequences are, and when we fear God and live diligently, good opportunities will come along, good things will happen, spiritual works of life will occur, and our lives will prosper and advance. As we have confirmed through the descendants of Seth, the eternal Word of God must continue to be passed down not only to the current generation, but also to all future generations until the second coming of the Lord.

Why did God show His love and mercy by granting the blessing of longevity despite the inevitability of death for all mankind after Adam? There was a deeper reason for this than the multiplication of species.

First, it was for the fulfillment of God's blessing to be fruitful and multiply and to fill the earth (Gen 1:28; 9:1, 7). In accordance to this blessing, there was no break in the generations of the line of Seth, so they grew in number and formed the nation of Israel through the descendants of Abraham. Ultimately, a countless number of spiritual descendants of Abraham are born through Jesus Christ, who came as a descendant of Abraham (Gal 3:7–9, 29).

Second, it was for the preservation of the holy seed so that God's plan for redemption could be passed down through the generations of godly descendants. The godly patriarchs spent the long years of their lives properly instructing their descendants on the Word of God (Gen 18:18–19) and enjoying a more intimate and holy fellowship with God. Through their longevity, God achieved His plan for the succession of His Word and the fulfillment of His covenant.

In Genesis 5 the phrase "became the father of" (or "begot") appears twenty-eight times in the Hebrew Hiphil stem,[1] indicating that God had played an active role in influencing their births in order to further His plan. The continuity of the godly line of Seth is proof that God's absolute sovereign work had sustained it.

The day will come when the issue of sin is finally resolved and when creation is restored to its original state so that there may be eternal life without death (Rev 21:1–4). Isaiah prophesied that the day will come when nature will not harm mankind (Isa 11:6–9; 65:17–25; cf. Ps 121:6). This day will come when the earth is filled with the knowledge of the glory of the Lord (Hab 2:14). This will be the day when all creation will be made new through the second coming of Jesus Christ (Rev 21:5). This is the day that all creation has been anxiously longing for (Rom 8:19–23). A new world will be created in which there will no longer be tears, death, lamenting, or weeping.

God chose and called Abraham from the line of Seth to prepare for the coming of this glorious day. In truth, until Abraham appeared at the forefront of the history of redemption, God's work focused mainly on calling His chosen people out from the sinful world in order to set them apart.

---

1. Causative verbal form. For example, "He is great" is derived in the Hiphil stem as "He caused to be great" (J. Weingreen, *A Practical Grammar for Classical Hebrew*, 2nd ed. [Oxford: Clarendon Press, 1959], 112).

CHAPTER 13

The Work of Separation

> **Genesis 12:1** Now the LORD said to Abram, "Go forth from your country, and from your relatives and from your father's house, to the land which I will show you."

In reality, the history of Israel began with God's command for separation. God commanded Abraham, "Go forth from your country." During the long period of time preceding Abraham, God channeled His focus on separating and segregating His people.

Separation from what? It was separation from a pervasively wicked world. The chief purpose of the genealogy of the line of Seth (Gen 5:1–32) and of Shem (Gen 11:10–32) was to demonstrate how God had set apart and protected His chosen lineage from Adam to Abraham.

The ultimate purpose for separation was to carry forward the work of salvation, which began with Adam and continued through Abraham, the first direct ancestor of the chosen nation of Israel, until the coming of the Savior. God wanted to prevent the lineage of godly faith from being cut off before the final hour of the history of redemption (Hos 11:4; Mal 2:15). This was precisely why He diligently segregated His people from the powers of darkness through His love and protection and, at times, with a stick or whip.

The work of separation, however, is always accompanied by pain. It cannot be carried out or even understood without painful tears. Abraham, the father of faith, was the fruit of God's tears and sweat, the steadfast offspring dedicated to the work of salvation.

1. The Work of Separation among the Patriarchs after Noah

The names of the patriarchs in the line of Seth, especially from Arpachshad to Abraham, progressively reveal the process of separation essential for the establishment of faith. God opened up a new era after the flood and wanted the godly patriarchs to completely overcome the battle against idolatry and set out on a pilgrim's journey to preserve the tradition of faith. It was only after this that the "God of Shem" could also become the God of his descendants (Gen 9:26). Unfortunately, the descendants of Shem who came after Peleg did not live according to the positive meanings of their names. Instead of setting themselves apart from the world, they intermingled with the world.

From this point, we will examine God's methods of separation suggested in the meaning of their names and how they apply to us today.

(1) Arpachshad

Arpachshad was Shem's son, and his name means "boundary." He and his people separated themselves from the land of their origin and set up new boundaries. Israel was originally a small nation, but God chose the Israelites as His holy people and marked Israel as His own territory (Exod 19:6; Deut 7:6–7). When Jesus left the glory of His throne in heaven and came to this earth, He came to His own land and to His territory (John 1:11). We are also God's sacred territory and His heirs. As such, how must we live?

First, we must obey God's Word.

Just as a citizen of a country is expected to abide by the laws of that country, so also we must abide by the law of His Word if we are truly His territory. God spoke to His people in Exodus 19:5, "Now then, if you will indeed obey My voice and keep My covenant, then you shall be My own possession among all the peoples, for all the earth is Mine."

Second, we must become a holy territory.

Exodus 19:6 calls those who have become God's territory a "holy people," and 1 Peter 2:9 calls them a "holy nation." God is holy, and thus we too must be holy (Lev 11:45). We must sanctify ourselves so that the hands of sin and darkness may not touch us (1 John 5:18), until the coming of our Lord (1 Thess 5:23).

When we set ourselves apart from the world, we are no longer under Satan's rule. We are under God's boundless care and endless counsel. For this reason we are called "Thy people, Thine inheritance" (Deut

9:26, 29), "His people" (Deut 32:43), "a treasured possession" (Deut 26:18), and "a consecrated people to the LORD" (Deut 26:19). God promised that He would set His nation high above all nations (Deut 4:6–8; 26:19; 28:1). Thus, we who are under His sovereign rule are the most blessed on this earth (Deut 33:29).

(2) Shelah

Shelah was Arpachshad's son, and his name means "throw out" or "send away." This refers to separation caused by being thrown toward a determined location or by being sent out with a specific purpose. If it is for the will of God, we must make the resolute decision to leave our current dwelling place and head toward the newly designated place no matter how lowly, how unfamiliar, or inconvenient the place may be. Whether "Achor's Valley" (Isa 65:10; Hos 2:15) or desolate waste, if that is where God's will lies, then we must take the gospel and run to the place to which we have been sent.

As Jesus was ascending into heaven after His resurrection, He commissioned His disciples not to leave Jerusalem, but to stay there (Acts 1:4); Jerusalem was His marked territory. After they received the Holy Spirit, however, He commanded them to leave Jerusalem, saying, "But you shall receive power when the Holy Spirit has come upon you; and you shall be My witnesses both in Jerusalem, and in all Judea and Samaria, and even to the remotest part of the earth" (Acts 1:8). God wanted the members of the early church to be *thrown* toward all of Judea, to Samaria, and to the ends of the earth with the gospel in hand. For this purpose, God gave rise to the great persecution that scattered the believers throughout Judea, Samaria, and the ends of the earth after the advent of the Holy Spirit at Pentecost (Acts 8:1). This was God's *holy throw*.

The act of being thrown or sent away from one's current dwelling place to a different one marks the beginning of a lonely journey. In reality, it is hard to accept and obey the command to leave for a specific place. If, however, we are *thrown* for the sake of gospel, we will receive the blessing of the enlargement of our borders and the expansion of our boundaries, much like the blessing of Jabez (1 Chr 4:10).

Today, we need to be *thrown out* with the gospel in hand toward places of unbelief where the gospel has not yet been preached. We must conquer lands governed by Satan in order to expand God's boundaries. God delights in the feet of those who preach the gospel (Isa 52:7; Rom 10:15; Eph 6:15). Instead of taking comfort in "our boundaries," we must take the gospel of life and salvation and bravely throw it to the world (Matt 4:18–22; 28:18–20). Through this work, God's boundaries will expand to the farthest ends of the earth.

(3) Eber

Eber means "to cross the river and continue advancing toward a certain place." The meaning of the name conjures up the image of a person sent out with a mission, overcoming all the fierce obstacles, jumping over hurdles, and marching forward without looking back.

The journey of faith is a long-distance race with many obstacles along the way. No matter what kind of obstacles may stand before us, we must continue forward until we reach our destination. The obstacle that we face can be ourselves, our family or relatives, our friends, the threat of death, or the riches of this world. We must be separated out from these obstacles of life. We must neither avoid nor complain about the obstacles; rather, we must hold on to the Word of God for the power to overcome them and continue on. In order to do this, we must continuously overcome ourselves, battling against our own thoughts and bearing the pain of cutting off human relationships if necessary (Luke 9:61–62).

There were innumerable rivers and barriers standing in Paul's way (2 Cor 11:23–30) when he broke out of the boundaries of the Law and was thrown out as a vessel for the Gentiles (Acts 9:15). However, Paul leapt over these obstacles by relying only upon God. He confessed in 1 Corinthians 15:10, "I labored even more than all of them, yet not I, but the grace of God with me."

King David encountered many obstacles in each of the battles that he fought, but he was victorious because he trusted in God. Regarding his feats, King David declared in Psalm 18:29, "For by Thee I can run upon a troop; and by my God I can leap over a wall." Today, we hope to become *spiritual Ebers* by crossing over rivers of sin and setting ourselves apart so that the boundaries of the gospel may greatly expand.

(4) Peleg

Peleg means "separate" or "divide." Foremost, this is a reference to the division of nations resulting from the Tower of Babel incident (Gen 11:9), but it is also a reflection of God's desire for separation. At a time when faith had been commingled and defiled, God called for the separation of faith and disbelief, of good and evil, of light and darkness, and of the spirit and the flesh (2 Cor 6:14–16). Although Peleg was a descendant of the godly line of Shem, he participated in the construction of the Tower of Babel. Those who built the tower possessed arrogant desires to exalt their own names rather than God's and the desire to protect themselves by building their own city. Satan coaxed the people to build towers of arrogance and complacency in order to prevent the will of God from advancing. Peleg had commingled with such people.

God's work of separation began when men united to build their own city and tower. God intervened by confusing their language (Gen 11:7). Through His intervention and separation, God prevented the people from committing even greater sins and prepared for the birth of Abraham through the lineage of Peleg many years thereafter.

The patriarchs from Peleg until just before Abraham (i.e., Peleg, Reu, Serug, Nahor, and Terah) could not completely separate themselves from sin. They were not able to fulfill God's hope of separation bound in the meaning of their names. Consequently, their names mainly serve the function of a guide to understanding how God separated and set Abraham apart for His redemptive purpose.

The pain of separation is mandatory for those who seek to enter the kingdom of heaven, the spiritual Canaan. We must separate ourselves and come out from the city of Babel, the city that epitomizes all disbelief (Rev 18:2–4). This means separation from a double-sided faith that seeks the counsel of the wicked. It is separation from the path of sinners who compromise with evil; it is separation from the seat of scoffers (Ps 1:1).

At the end of the painful struggle for separation, we will find God standing and waiting for us. God will take care of us and wipe away all of our tears. He will untangle all of our problems in one sweep (Luke 18:8). Hallelujah!

(5) Reu

Reu means "friend" or "special relationship." This suggests that we need to be called a "friend of God" in order to separate ourselves from this world (Gen 18:17; John 15:14–15). God is the Creator, but He is a personal God who wants to build an intimate relationship with His chosen people (Job 29:4; Ps 25:14; Amos 3:7). Abraham was reckoned a "friend of God" after he left his father's house and became consecrated through faith (2 Chr 20:7; Isa 41:8; Jas 2:23). There are no secrets between friends; Abraham knew in advance about the judgment that would fall upon Sodom and Gomorrah (Gen 18:17). John 15:14–15 teaches us how we can also be called a "friend of God."

> **John 15:14–15** You are My friends, if you do what I command you. [15]No longer do I call you slaves, for the slave does not know what his master is doing; but I have called you friends, for all things that I have heard from My Father I have made known to you.

What must we do to become a friend of God? We need to totally obey and do exactly as Jesus commands. John 15:14 states, "You are My friends, if you do what I command you." Faith without works is dead (Jas 2:26). A true friend is one who can be by our side at any time or hour. Let us draw closer to God our eternal friend (Ps 73:28; Jas 4:8). God draws near to us when we pray (Deut 4:7). If the president of our country were to become our friend, our status in society would change overnight. How much more so if we become friends of God?

(6) Serug

Serug means "intertwined tendril" or "firm strength." This is a great way to separate ourselves from the world and to restore our relationship with God. It depicts how a believer's soul, like the tendrils, should be intertwined and bound in God's will and His Word so as to prevent a falling into the world (John 15:7). It also refers to the firm strength with which God holds believers. Believers cannot consecrate themselves from the world by their own will or strength; they can be made holy only through the Word of God and prayer (1 Tim 4:5). Separation is possible only when God's sovereign love is poured out through grace.

In 2 Corinthians 5:14 the apostle Paul tells us, "For the love of Christ controls us." The word "control" in this verse is also translated as "attract." The New International Version translates this verse as "For Christ's love compels us." *To control* is συνέχω (*synechō*) in Greek, meaning "to hold fast," and is used with reference to the act of herding cattle from all sides. The love of Jesus Christ has a strong hold of our hand and will guide us forward just as a shepherd guides his sheep.

The love of Christ also had a strong hold on the apostle Paul. Christ's love constrained him so that he did not live for himself; it enabled him to walk the path of a difficult calling with relative ease. Paul remained focused on God until He was fully satisfied. God's love was so great that Paul could not help but go out and evangelize; he could not help but offer his whole body in faithfulness. God's love was so great that Paul forfeited all his possessions, all his honor, and all his knowledge. For Paul, everything was rubbish before the love of Christ (Phil 3:8). Christ's love was so great that Paul did not hesitate to give up his life in Rome; he offered up his life with joy.

Yes, true separation is possible only when we are crazy for the love of Christ. Once we truly experience His love, we will have no regrets with regard to the immeasurable pain, the suffering, and the personal loss that come with separation. When we are led by the love of Christ, we will be able to walk the path of separation with joy, even if it may be the path of martyrdom.

(7) Nahor

Nahor means "to be short of breath" or "to pant." On a positive note, the name depicts a person who, with every ounce of strength, confronts and battles the evil of this world until victorious. It describes a heart that seeks to protect and keep the Word of God from Satan. It describes the immense effort to resist being tainted by the sins of the world and to separate from the old habits and ways of life. The apostle Paul called this battle "the good fight" (2 Tim 4:7). This conflict is not with an external enemy; it is an internal struggle against the evil within (Rom 7:16–25). It is the act of "buffet[ing] my body and mak[ing] it my slave" (1 Cor 9:27). Paul advises us to "compete" aggressively for the final victory (1 Cor 9:25).

Even as we perform the Lord's work, there are many times when our zeal gets the best of us and we work to satisfy ourselves and our own greed (Matt 16:22–23). At times, our zeal is motivated by the awareness of other people's gaze; sometimes it comes from competitiveness. Human zeal gone astray displeases God. It may please other human beings for a moment, but God looks into our hearts, and He does not acknowledge this kind of zeal (1 Sam 16:7). It is all in vain. When this kind of zeal becomes the motivation for work, it will only lead to exhaustion without yielding fruit. As Paul stated, our zeal has to be a godly zeal and godly jealousy (2 Cor 11:2). When we receive the zeal of God's Spirit, God will do the work. He will provide us with all the strength, ability, wisdom, and wealth that we need (Phil 2:13).

Jesus always worked with godly zeal (John 5:17). This was especially evident in the Garden of Gethsemane when He prayed earnestly to resolve the issue of sin for each and every one of us. He shed so many tears for us; He vindicated us countless number of times. He fought intensely against Satan to the point of bloodshed on our behalf (Luke 22:44; Heb 5:7).

Paul also worked with this godly zeal and made seven exclamations in 2 Corinthians 7:11, six of which begin with the word "what." This word "what" is ἀλλά (*alla*) in Greek and means "more on the other hand" or "more besides." We must exhaust our efforts to be more faithful to the work entrusted to us, to pray more, to serve more, to evangelize more, to labor more, and to always persevere in God's service (1 Cor 15:58; 1 Thess 4:1; 2 Tim 4:2). Laboring harder is the way to live up to the grace that we have received and to separate ourselves from the path of sinners (1 Cor 15:10).

(8) Terah

Terah means "stay" or "delay." Terah lived a wretched life, worshiping idols in Ur of the Chaldeans, the seedbed of sin (Josh 24:2). However, he was enthralled by the fear of the God of glory, who appeared to his son Abraham (Acts 7:2–3). Momentarily, he repented and abandoned his old way of life to leave Ur of Chaldeans with Abraham and to separate himself from the city of idols (Gen 11:31).

Unable to totally cut ties with his old sinful ways, however, Terah settled in Haran and eventually died there (Gen 11:32). Nonetheless, just moving out of the Ur of Chaldeans and crossing the river to Haran was a great feat for Terah, who had lived a life totally immersed in idol worship.

Terah's life teaches us that we need to live a pilgrim's life if we want to become the source of blessings, to possess spiritual and material wealth, and to bear many descendants of faith as Abraham did. If Terah had moved from Haran to Canaan with Abraham, he would have become the father of faith along with Abraham. Furthermore, he would have become a great name, respected by his descendants just as Abraham was. As the meaning of his name "to delay" or "to stay" indicates, Terah had delayed and stayed behind. Satan often uses the abundance of wealth to keep us from entering the spiritual Canaan and to delay the fulfillment of God's will.

Haran was an important center of commerce due to its location midway between Canaan and Mesopotamia. It became a city of abundance because considerable commerce activity took place there. Like Terah, people's hearts are often held down by the treasures and riches of this world (Matt 6:21; Luke 12:34). If we dedicate our lives to following the path of wealth, bowing before money, and using money as a gauge of success, then our hearts have already forsaken God. We cannot serve both God and money (Matt 6:24). God tells us not to fix our hopes on the uncertainty of riches (1 Tim 6:17). The love of money is the root of all sorts of evil (1 Tim 6:10). Judas loved money and fell into temptation as a result (John 12:4–6). It led him to betray Jesus and hand Him over for money—a fatal mistake that could never be wiped away. In the end, he hung himself and died a tragic death.

The verb *separate* means "to disconnect," "to sever," to set apart," or "to make a distinction between." Doing this is not as easy as it sounds. We must first feel great indignation for the sins that we have committed and then pound our hearts in earnest repentance (Ps 32:3; 34:18; Prov 28:13). We cannot draw near to God as long as we are still connected to the world by sin. Sin will only work to separate us from God and accuse us before Him. The sins that we commit will follow us like a shadow throughout our lives; they will look for us and testify against us (Num 32:23; Isa 59:12). Revelation 17:16 explains that sin will make us desolate and naked and will burn us up with fire. So persistent and vicious is sin that Jesus, though He was without sin, fell on His knees and rubbed His forehead against the ground in fervent prayer until our sins were separated from us (Luke 22:44). Like Jesus, we must feel great scorn for sin, and we must repent thoroughly of our sins so that sin cannot adhere to us in any way. We must become totally separated from sin.

It is only then that we can fully obey the command "Leave!" If there is anything that keeps us from walking the path of a pilgrim, we must sever ourselves from it through faith. True faith is answering God's command with "Yes" and "Amen," followed by action even though His plan may not be immediately comprehensible (2 Cor 1:20). We must not become complacent in the fact that God has chosen us. We cannot advance one step without self-sacrifice, without faithfulness, and without our eyes focused on the final goal each and every day.

As biblical history shows, God will see the end of what He has determined—His plan for the salvation of mankind. If we do not take comfort in this world, if we do not hesitate or step backwards, then we can advance forward with each step and at last enter God's kingdom as holy saints set apart from this world.

2. The Work of Separation in Abraham's Life

There were four crucial levels of separation in Abraham's life. These four levels represent different levels of Christian faith.

The First Separation: separation from his homeland and relatives, separation from Terah (Gen 12:1, Acts 7:2–4).

Ur of the Chaldeans was the place where Abraham's ancestors lived and worshiped idols (Josh 24:2, 15). His departure from this land represents the first step in faith for Christians: separation from the world.

Ur of the Chaldeans was a fertile land located southeast of Baghdad and was the center of the ancient civilization as well as the center of idolatry. Idol worship had achieved its peak during Abraham's time, and Terah was more absorbed in worshiping idols than in worshiping the true God. This was when God commanded Abraham, "Depart from your country and your relatives" (Gen 12:1, Acts 7:2-4). He obeyed and departed from Ur of the Chaldeans with his father, Terah, and arrived in Haran. Terah, however, was tempted by the ease of life in Haran and settled there, though it should have been a mere rest stop on the way to Canaan.

At last, when Abraham was seventy-five years old, God called him a second time, but this time He commanded Abraham to leave not only his country and his relatives, but also his father's house (Gen 12:1). This was an intensified command spurred on by Abraham's failure to fully obey God's command when he was first called out of Ur. Genesis 12:4–5 clarifies that it was only after Abraham had fully obeyed God's command to separate from his father's house that he was able to enter Canaan.

> **Genesis 12:4–5** So Abram went forth as the LORD had spoken to him; and Lot went with him. Now Abram was seventy-five years old when he departed from Haran. [5]And Abram took Sarai his wife and Lot his nephew, and all their possessions which they had accumulated, and the persons which they had acquired in Haran, and they set out for the land of Canaan; thus they came to the land of Canaan.

Because Abraham lived in a patriarchal society, it was difficult for him to reject his father's wishes and leave him behind. He was seventy-five years old and Terah was 145 years old and alive when Abraham left Haran (Gen 11:26; 12:4). It must have been heartbreaking for the first-born in charge of the household to leave his father in his old age. Acts 7:4, "And from there, after his father died, God removed him into this country in which you are now living," shows how determined Abraham was to follow the Word of God. The word for "death" in Acts 7:4 is ἀποθνῄσκω (*apothnēskō*) in Greek, used to represent symbolic death or death in a spiritual sense (1 Cor 15:31). It is apparent that this word was used to signify Abraham's total separation from his filial affections for his father. Terah was as good as dead to him (Luke 14:26). Terah died sixty years later in Haran at the age of 205 (Gen 11:32). Abraham overcame the pain of such separation and followed the word with faith (Gen 12:4).

The Second Separation: separation from Lot (Gen 13).

Genesis 13:10–11 reveals that Lot had possessed secular greed. He chose the valley of the Jordan when he parted ways with Abraham because it was well watered everywhere all the way to the land of Zoar, like the garden of the Lord. God separated Abraham from such a person. This represents separation from lingering secular tendencies and continued instability even after initial separation from the world.

Genesis 13:10–12 And Lot lifted up his eyes and saw all the valley of the Jordan, that it was well watered everywhere—this was before the LORD destroyed Sodom and Gomorrah—like the garden of the LORD, like the land of Egypt as you go to Zoar. [11]So Lot chose for himself all the valley of the Jordan; and Lot journeyed eastward. Thus they separated from each other. [12]Abram settled in the land of Canaan, while Lot settled in the cities of the valley, and moved his tents as far as Sodom.

Lot had accompanied Abraham throughout his journey out of Ur into Canaan. Lot had been with him through the toughest times, from their arrival at Canaan, the foreign land of the Gentiles, until settlement. Hence, the separation must have been heartbreaking.

Only those who can overcome the pain of separation can become true disciples of Jesus. In Luke 14:26, Jesus says, "If anyone comes to Me, and does not hate his own father and mother and wife and children and brothers and sisters, yes, and even his own life, he cannot be My disciple." He continues in Luke 14:33, "So therefore, no one of you can be My disciple who does not give up all his own possessions." Today, we can also become true disciples when we cut our ties with the secular and materialistic things of this world.

The Third Separation: separation from Ishmael (Gen 21).

After Isaac, the covenantal son, was born, God commanded Abraham to drive out Ishmael, the first son, born to him through his maidservant by means of human effort and scheming (Gen 21:10–14). This represents the level of faith in which we surrender our own plans and powers to submit before the great will of God. It is the process in which we deny ourselves.

Galatians 4:30 But what does the Scripture say? "Cast out the bondwoman and her son, for the son of the bondwoman shall not be an heir with the son of the free woman."

In Genesis 17:18 Abraham confessed, "Oh that Ishmael might live before Thee!" Genesis 21:11 tells us, "And the matter distressed Abraham greatly because of his son," hinting at how much he had adored Ishmael during the thirteen years before Isaac was born. His affection for his son did not cause his commitment to obeying God's command to waver. He sent out his thirteen-year-old son along with his mother,

Hagar. Separation from Ishmael must have caused Abraham the greatest pain in his life, the pain of having his flesh torn away.

We must also drive out the "Ishmaels" in our lives today. We must deny ourselves of the things that we love—things that we cannot let go even though we know that they have nothing to do with the will of God—if those things will hold us back in our journey of faith. In doing so, we earn the right to possess the true inheritance of God.

The Fourth Separation: separation from Isaac (Gen 22).

After Abraham drove Ishmael out, God commanded Abraham to offer up Isaac, his only son whom he loved, as a burnt offering (Gen 22:1–12). In faith he obeyed. Of course, God ultimately saved Isaac from Abraham's hands, but this near-sacrifice required offering someone whom Abraham had loved and cherished the most. He had truly intended to offer up to God that which held the greatest value to him (Gen 22:16–17). For Abraham, this separation was equivalent to death; it shook the very foundation of his existence. Abraham was required to sever his bond not only with the son born to him according to the flesh, but also with Isaac, the covenantal son, who had been his sole object of affection at the time.

Abraham overcame this incomprehensible test through his total trust in God. This was a display of mature faith—the ability to return to God what belongs to Him. In essence, he had confessed that even the blessings that had originally come from God ultimately belong to Him. The twenty-four elders make a similar confession in Revelation 4:10–11; they glorify God by casting down before His throne the crowns that they had received from Him (Rev 4:4), confessing in song that all created things belong to God.

> **Revelation 4:10–11** The twenty-four elders will fall down before Him who sits on the throne, and will worship Him who lives forever and ever, and will cast their crowns before the throne, saying, [11]"Worthy art Thou, our Lord and our God, to receive glory and honor and power; for Thou didst create all things, and because of Thy will they existed, and were created."

The Christian journey of faith is similar to these steps of separation. Faith matures through separation (Isa 52:11). We cannot advance forward to the new place to which we have been called unless we depart from our sinful past, old habits, and old ways. If we cannot completely abandon them as God commands, then those very things will return to us in the future as thorns and snares (Josh 23:13; Judg 2:3).

When God first commanded Abraham to leave Ur of the Chaldeans, and again when God commanded him to leave Haran, where he had moved with his father, he submitted and departed on a pilgrim's journey not knowing his final destination (Gen 12:1; Heb 11:8). From a societal viewpoint, this path meant forfeiting his rights, losing his resting place, and living a sojourner's life. It was a journey impossible to take had he not endured the separations with tremendous determination and courage.

Abraham, by faith and fear of God, had overcome the pain of separation from his father, Terah; his nephew Lot; his son Ishmael; and his son of the covenant, Isaac. As a result, he achieved the apex of faith at last.

> **Genesis 22:12** And [the angel of the LORD] said, "Do not stretch out your hand against the lad, and do nothing to him; for now I know that you fear God, since you have not withheld your son, your only son, from Me."

God continues to fulfill the work of redemption through those who obey the call for separation. People of faith today must follow in Abraham's footsteps of faith in order to become true spiritual Hebrews and cross over the spiritual Euphrates River. In the eyes of some, this path may appear imprudent, like the journey of a wretched wanderer without a final destination, but this path is a holy and honorable path taken in obedience to the Word of God.

(1) What must we do to achieve holy separation?

First, we must come out from the world, the Babylon, and refrain from participating in its sins (Rev 18:4). Next, we must live lives consecrated from this world. In 2 Corinthians 6:14–7:1 we learn about the principles of holy consecration. Although we Christians physically live in this world, our lives must be thoroughly set apart from the world; we must not compromise with the world, but instead we must maintain holiness befitting the children of God (Lev 11:44–45; 1 Pet 1:15–16). In addition, we must reject various worldly philosophies and liberal theology. Compromising with these teachings will ultimately cause us to break away from the pure teaching of the gospel.

(2) What kind of blessing awaits those who walk the holy path of separation?

God gave a great blessing to Abraham, who walked the holy path of separation (Gen 22:17). This great blessing, according to the Living Bible translation, is an "incredible blessing"—an immense blessing unimaginable to the human mind. This blessing crosses over the boundaries of human understanding. This "great blessing" was fulfilled when Jesus came as the descendant of Abraham (Matt 1:1). God Almighty, the Lord over all the universe and creation, came upon this earth as a descendant of Abraham. What greater blessing could there be? Even today, those who follow the Word and overcome the pains of separation as Abraham had done will receive the same "great blessing" that Abraham had received (Gal 3:6–9). Hallelujah!

> **Genesis 22:15–18** Then the angel of the LORD called to Abraham a second time from heaven, [16]and said, "By Myself I have sworn, declares the LORD, because you have done this thing, and have not withheld your son, your only son, [17]indeed I will greatly bless you, and I will greatly multiply your seed as the stars of the heavens, and as the sand which is on the seashore; and your seed shall possess the gate of their enemies. [18]And in your seed all the nations of the earth shall be blessed, because you have obeyed My voice."

CHAPTER 14

Abraham from the Perspective of Salvation

The Bible was written by God and thus contains no meaningless narrative. The primary purpose of the genealogies recorded until this point was to reveal the root of Abraham; the intent was to make Abraham known. At the same time, it was a record of God's diligence in preparing for and electing Abraham, the passageway of the Messiah, who was to come for the salvation of mankind.

Most of the genealogies recorded in the Bible list the most important figure at the end so that a new era begins with that person. The genealogy in Genesis 11 was recorded with Abraham in mind and hints at the role that he would play in the future. This is similar to the genealogy in Matthew 1:1–17, which was recorded with the works of Jesus Christ in mind (Gen 17:19; 22:12–18; Gal 3:16).

Abraham, Adam's twentieth generation, was an important figure because he had opened the first gateway for the coming of the Messiah. This is why Jesus' genealogy begins with Abraham. Matthew 1:1 introduces Jesus as the "son of David, the son of Abraham," not as the son of Adam. Without hesitation, the Jews called Abraham their father (John 8:39). When Lazarus died, he went to heaven and was in Abraham's bosom, while the rich man went to hell. Even from hell the rich man dared to cry out, "Father Abraham" (Luke 16:24, 30). All nations of faith throughout the world began with Abraham. His importance carries on through the New Testament, as the Bible tells us that those who are of faith are blessed with Abraham (Gal 3:6-9).

1. The Work of Sin Proliferated until the Birth of Abraham

God's work that began with creation ran parallel with the major sinful events in the world until Abraham's time. Starting with the eating of the fruit (Gen 3), Cain's murder (Gen 4), Lamech's song (Gen 4), the marriage of the sons of God and the daughters of men (Gen 6), the judgment of the flood (Gen 7-9), and the construction of the Tower of Babel (Gen 11), sin amplified and man grew farther and farther away from God. Sin, which began with one individual, grew to the group level and expanded further to the national level.

After the flood, sin resurfaced for the first time through Ham, but its powers grew to infect all mankind, eventually leading to the construction of the Tower of Babel. Sin truly holds enormous power. Before the flood, it lured the sons of God to its own side, and just before the Tower of Babel incident, it built a powerful community that attempted to encroach upon heaven, where God resides, by building a city and a tower. The members of this humanistic community had cut themselves off from the line of salvation that God had given to mankind and relied on their own wit. The Tower of Babel incident took place only a little over one hundred years after the judgment of the flood. In so little time, sin had infected and covered the world like a poisonous mushroom.

Calculation:

The sum of the patriarchs' ages at the birth of their first son from the time Arpachshad was born to Shem (two years after the flood) until Peleg was born to Eber (Gen 11:10, 12, 14, 16).
2 (years after the flood) + 35 + 30 + 34 = 101

Noah and Shem had been saved from the dreadful flood and were alive when the Tower of Babel was being built. Noah had witnessed how the world was judged because of its overflowing sins. His righteous heart was torn once again as he watched men's evil intentions working to build up the tower. Noah probably spent the 350 years of his life after the flood the same way he had previously lived: expending all his energy in preaching to the succeeding generations about God's redemptive will that graciously preserved this earth.

2. God Preserved Faith throughout the History of Sin and Wickedness

God preserved the framework of faith, the last remaining holy stump, so that the history of redemption may not be cut short even in the midst of the ever-thickening work of sin after the fall of Adam until Genesis 11 (Isa 6:13; 2 Pet 2:5).

God clothed Adam and Eve with garments of skin before He banished them from Eden (Gen 3:21). For Cain, God appointed a sign of protection for a murderer after He cursed him to become a wanderer on the earth (Gen 4:15). He preserved Noah's family and proclaimed the message of blessings and prosperity once again through the covenant of the rainbow (Gen 8:17; 9:1, 7).

God did not fail to demonstrate the bright future of redemptive history even in the midst of continuous judgments, reaffirming His intention to save mankind. The light of God's grace and love shone even more beautifully through His judgments and punishments. His grace abounded even more where sin increased (Rom 5:20).

3. The Beginning of a New Work of Salvation through Abraham

The history of redemption that began to unfold in Genesis 12 after judgment upon the Tower of Babel encountered a revolutionary turning point. Until this point, God had been working universally with all of mankind. Now, He was working with one elect person: Abraham, the son of an idol maker from Ur of the Chaldeans. Consequently, it appears that the prospect of redemptive work has narrowed significantly in Genesis 12. However, the election of Abraham was a critical event in the history of redemption because it opened the first gateway for the coming of the seed of the woman promised in Genesis 3:15.

From this point, God's divine administration for the redemption of all nations on the face of this earth was fulfilled through Abraham, the chief focus of the genealogy of Shem and the genealogy of Terah. As God promised when He called him, Abraham began as one man, but he ultimately became the starting point for the salvation of all nations.

Ezekiel 33:23–24 Then the word of the LORD came to me saying, [24]"Son of man, they who live in these waste places in the land of Israel are saying, 'Abraham was only one, yet he possessed the land; so to us who are many the land has been given as a possession.'"

Genesis 12:3 [The LORD said to Abram,] "And I will bless those who bless you, and the one who curses you I will curse. And in you all the families of the earth shall be blessed."

Hebrews 11:12 Therefore, also, there was born of one man, and him as good as dead at that, as many descendants as the stars of heaven in number, and innumerable as the sand which is by the seashore.

When Abraham was ninety-nine years old, while he was still Abram, God renewed His covenant and gave him and his wife, Sarai, new names. Abram received the name *Abraham*, meaning "father of a multitude of nations" (Gen 17:4–5; Rom 4:17), and Sarai received the name *Sarah*, which means "mother of nations" (Gen 17:15–16). After the coming of Jesus Christ, Abraham's fatherhood expanded to include all those who believe (Rom 4:11–12, 16, 23–24; Gal 3:7, 29).

The God whom the Israelites had encountered through their own history is not just the God of the Jews. As evident in Genesis 1 to Genesis 11, He is the God of the universe. He created the universe; His providence is over all mankind; He sustains the world. In addition, after God's covenant with Abraham, the history of Abraham's descendants was not theirs alone. Their history was an extension of the history of redemption, which contains God's plans to fulfill His covenant with Abraham and eventually achieve salvation for all mankind.

The work recorded in Genesis 1 through Genesis 11 was only a prelude, a mere introduction, to Abraham's calling. The actual redemptive work began with Abraham in Genesis 12. The genealogy of Shem recorded in Genesis 11 was the dawning of the history of redemption that revealed "the appearance of Abraham for the salvation of the whole world."

Now, God had cut the ribbon for His plan to save all mankind through Abraham (Gen 18:18; 22:18). This was the glimpse of hope, a streak of daylight shining upon times of despair after the Tower of Babel incident, and Abraham stood at the center of that light. The advancement of God's redemptive work that began with the election of Abraham was completed through the coming of the Messiah from among the descendants of Abraham. God's covenant with Abraham, "And in your seed all the nations of the earth shall be blessed" (Gen 22:18), did not pertain only to Abraham; it was a covenant to be fulfilled when the Messiah comes as a descendant of Abraham.

The genealogy in Genesis 11 is testimony to the trustworthiness and faithfulness of God, who remembered and fulfilled His promise of salvation through the seed of the woman despite man's disbelief and disobedience (Rom 3:3; 2 Cor 1:18; 1 Thess 5:24; 2 Tim 2:13; Heb 10:23). The genealogy of the godly descendants will endure until the second coming of our Lord. We must strive to properly understand God's divine administration of redemption, which He seeks to fulfill in the end time, so that we may become godly descendants whom He is looking for.

Now, there is only one whose coming we must anticipate: Jesus Christ, who died on the cross and was resurrected for us. On the day He returns in all His glory, the work of redemption, which began with the calling of Abraham, will see its final completion. At that time, the devil, who stood against God and interfered with His work of salvation, will be thrown into the lake of fire and brimstone (Rev 20:10). I pray today that we gather all our strength to race toward the kingdom of heaven, with our hopes focused on that day of final victory.

ת לכל בר דעת דרך המסעות ארבעים שנה במדבר והרוחב והאורך של ארץ הקדושה מנהר מצ
עמלק
מדבר צין הוא קדש
ים המלח
צבוים
עמרה
הר ההר
עתר
מקדה
עיר כרמל
הצור
שבט
ענב
קדשברנע
מדבר סיני
מדבר פארן
מדבר שור
בתול
מולדה
אלהולד
שרוחן
באר שבע
שמעון
שבט
רמות
בית מרכבות
גת
אשקלון
ארץ פלשתים
ארבב גשן
פתם
שדה
צען
אלכסנדרי
לוח המסעות במדבר
אשר על פי ה׳ יסעו ועל פי ה׳ יחנו
א״ רעמסס
ב״ סכת
ג״ אתם
ד״ פיהחירת
ה״ מרה
ו״ אילם
ז״ ים סוף
ח״ מדבר סין
ט״ דפקה
יוד״ אלוש
יא״ רפידם
יב״ מדבר סיני
יג״ קברות התאוה
יד״ חצרת
טו״ רתמה
טז״ רמן פרץ
יז״ לבנה
יח״ רסה
יט״ קהלתה
כ״ הר ספר
כא״ חרדה
כב״ מקהלת
כג״ תחת
כד״ תרח
כה״ מתקה
כו״ חשמנה
כז״ מסרות
כח״ בני יעקן
כט״ חר הגדגד
ל״ יטבתה
לא״ עברנה
לב״ עציון גבר
לג״ מדבר צין
לד״ הר ההר
לה״ צלמנה
לו״ פונן
לז״ אבת
לח״ דיבן גד
לט״ עלמן דבלתים
מ״ הרי עברים
מא״ ערבת מואב

Conclusion

The history of God's work of redemption is not separate from the history of this world. The two are intertwined. The history of redemption has been developing and unfolding since before the beginning of time in accordance with God's pleasing will and by His absolute sovereignty. The significance of secular history lies in the fact that it is a means to fulfill God's purpose in the history of redemption. The history of this world transformed continuously from age to age as cultures developed. Yet, God's work of redemption continued to flow through this ever-changing history and will not cease until Jesus Christ's return. In light of this, we must discover the revelation of redemption that flows ceaselessly through the genealogies in Genesis. Then, we will be able to dig up the treasures of God's amazing providence of salvation hidden within.

Furthermore, God's divine administration of redemption is also hidden in the various corners of the Bible (Luke 24:25–27, 44; John 5:39, 45–47), and surely it will be fulfilled according to the Word of God (Isa 55:10–11; Matt 5:18; 24:35; Luke 21:33). The Word is the beginning, the plan, the blueprint, and the strong force that propels the fulfillment of God's history of redemption (Rev 1:17; 22:13). God created the entire universe through this Word (Ps 33:6, 9; John 1:3, 10), and the Word upholds it and guides it (Rom 11:36; Heb 1:3). It is also the Word that judges the fallen world in the end (2 Pet 3:7). As the end approaches, God's Word will fill all the earth (Isa 11:9; Hab 2:14), and this wonderful vision is prophesied in many places in the Bible.

Ezekiel 47 compares the evangelical movement of salvation manifested through Jesus Christ to the water flowing out of the temple. The temple was a reservoir, and the water in it was not still—it was flowing. This is symbolic of the ever-flowing living waters. This water increased, and as it increased, it trickled out little by little from the temple. In no time, it turned into a great body of water. It reached the great sea and gave life to the dying; it caused all kinds of trees to grow fresh and bear fruit. Everywhere this water reached, even the waters of the sea became fresh, and there were very many fish. Wherever this water went, everything prospered and lived (Ezek 47:8–9). Fishermen would come and go, for there were many fish according to their kinds, like the fish of the Great Sea (Ezek 47:10). By the river on its bank, on one side and on the other, grew all kinds of trees bearing fruit for food every month; they grew leaves for healing (Ezek 47:12). This was all "because their water flows from the sanctuary" (Ezek 47:12).

This is the prophecy that the living waters of God's Word will flow out from the church, the body of Jesus Christ, and give life to all the world and the nations in it (John 4:13–14; 6:63; Rev 22:1–2).

Even now, the spiritual water of life flowing from Golgotha, where Jesus Christ's cross stood, springs up endlessly and continues to flow to every corner of the entire universe to give life. Today, every church throughout the world that proclaims the gospel of the blood shed on the cross (the gospel of life) is a spiritual Golgotha. From there, the living waters continue to break through the grounds of sin to spring up and continuously flow out and increase. Life-giving works are occurring through the living waters in the churches that have the living Word of the cross (1 Cor 1:18), the Word of the precious blood shed on Golgotha for the atonement of all mankind. The soul of one who drinks from the living waters is like a "watered garden" because God directs the path of the water stream from deep underground toward the garden (Isa 58:11; Jer 31:12). The living waters do not cease to flow to the watered garden. The green pastures are endless. There is no suffering there (Jer 31:12). It is always full of vitality. Our souls are satisfied and our bones strengthened (Isa 58:11), so that our physical health is ensured. Only peace and joy overflow bountifully (Isa 66:12).

The prophet Zechariah received a revelation of the living waters flowing out of Jerusalem toward the eastern sea and the western sea (Zech 14:8; cf. Isa 2:2–4; Mic 4:1–2). The prophet Joel also saw that a spring would go out from the house of the Lord to water the valley of Shittim (Joel 3:18). The valley of Shittim was a barren and arid land where life could not survive, but this barren land will become abundant with grapes, greenery, and flocks of sheep giving milk through the overflowing waters (Joel 3:18). At one time, the priests mourned because there was nothing in the temple to give as an offering to the Lord (Joel 1:9, 13). But now, the dry land will become a fountain of the living waters that gives life.

A true church needs to become the altar from which the Word of the living waters springs forth so that souls may never thirst again. Jesus Christ is the source of the water of life (Rev 21:6). The Israelites drank the living waters from a rock in the wilderness (Ps 78:16; 105:41). Water poured out when Moses struck the rock. The New Living Translation translates it as "and water gushed out" (Num 20:11). When the water came out of the rock, it gushed out as from a waterfall and formed a river for the millions of people to drink in the wilderness (Ps 105:41). This rock foreshadows Jesus Christ. In 1 Corinthians 10:4 we read, "And all drank the same spiritual drink, for they were drinking from a spiritual rock which followed them; and the rock was Christ." Yes, only Jesus Christ is the source of the living waters.

> **John 7:37–38** Now on the last day, the great day of the feast, Jesus stood and cried out, saying, "If anyone is thirsty, let him come to Me and drink. [38]He who believes in Me, as the Scripture said, 'From his innermost being will flow rivers of living water.'"

Here, the work of the living waters signifies the work of God's Word and of the Holy Spirit. Both the Word and the Holy Spirit come from Jesus. The dry bones came together, received breath, came to life, stood on their feet, and became an exceedingly great army when Ezekiel prophesied as he was commanded (Ezek 37:7, 10). Likewise, the breath of life (i.e., the Holy Spirit) works through the Word, and where the living Word is proclaimed, the Holy Spirit works powerfully and works of life occur (Acts 10:44). Therefore, the church where Jesus is alive and His Word actively works is the church of the living waters. That is the kind of church that we strive to be because such is a church where the Holy Spirit powerfully, fervently, and abundantly dwells.

Amos 8:11–13 states,

> "Behold, days are coming," declares the Lord GOD, "When I will send a famine on the land, not a famine for bread or a thirst for water, but rather for hearing the words of the LORD. And people will stagger from sea to sea, and from the north even to the east; they will go to and fro to seek the word of the LORD, but they will not find it. In that day the beautiful virgins and the young men will faint from thirst."

Likewise, the world is falling deeper into a "famine of the Word," and it is becoming harder and harder to find the Word of the living waters. We need to arouse a fundamental movement within the church so that the Word of the living waters may overflow.

Only Jesus Christ is the true Shepherd, who leads us beside quiet waters and to the spring of the living waters (Ps 23:1; John 10:11, 14). He makes us lie down in green pastures, allowing us to eat in abundance without want. Revelation 7:17 states, "For the Lamb in the center of the throne will be their shepherd, and will guide them to springs of the water of life; and God will wipe every tear from their eyes." When we follow our true Shepherd, we will be able to live a life that overflows with blessings eternally.

Now we greatly anticipate the one who died for us on the cross and was resurrected, the one who leads us to the spring of the living waters, our true Shepherd, Jesus Christ. On the day our Lord gloriously returns, the history of redemption, which began and progressed through the genealogies of Genesis and was manifested through the calling of Abraham, will finally come to its complete fulfillment and fruition. On that day, the devil, who has been challenging God and interfering with His work of salvation until the very end, will be thrown into the lake of fire and brimstone (Rev 20:10).

Let us run our race toward the kingdom of God with our hope firmly focused on that final day of victory. Moses' sincere cry to "remember the days of old, consider the years of all generations" (Deut 32:7) in preparation for entry into Canaan is now resounding in our ears as we also prepare for our entry into the kingdom of God. This is God's firm command and the voice of His call for us to remember and understand the history of God's work of redemption through the years of all generations in the Bible.

The moment we come to an understanding of God's divine administration of redemption hidden in the Bible, He will acknowledge us as godly people of faith and as the burning lamp in a world covered with the dark clouds of sin and wickedness. God uses the spirit of the godly as His lamp, even in the present day (Prov 20:27). I pray with all my heart that the line of the godly offspring may continue until the prophecy of our Lord's return is fulfilled on this earth. Amen.

לכל בר דעת דרך המסעות ארבעים שנה במדבר והרוחב והאורך של ארץ הקודש
עמלק
מדבר צין הוא קדש
ים המלח
הר ההר
עתר
מקדה
עיר כרמל
שבט
הצור
ענב
בתול
מולדה
אלהולד
שרוחן
באר שבע
שמעון
שבט
גת
אשקלון
קדש ברנע
מדבר סין
מדבר פארן
מדבר שור
ארץ פלשתים
ארץ גשן
פתם
אלכסנדרי
לוח המסעות במדבר
אשר על פי ה׳ יסעו ועל פי ה׳ יחנו
א״ רעמסס טו״ רתמה יט״ הרהגדגד
ב״ סכת טז״ רמן פרץ ל״ יטבתה
ג״ אתם יז״ לבנה לא״ עברנה
ד״ פיהחירת יח״ רסה לב״ עציון גבר
ה״ מרה יט״ קהלתה לג״ מדבר צין
ו״ אילם כ״ הרספר לד״ הרההר
ז״ ים סוף כא״ חרדה לה״ צלמנה
ח״ מדבר סין כב״ מקהלת לו״ פונן
ט״ רפקה כג״ תחת לז״ אבת
יו״ אלוש כד״ תרח לח״ דיבן גד
יא״ רפידם כה״ מתקה לט״ עלמן דבלתים
יב״ מדבר סיני כו״ חשמנה מ״ הרי עברים
יג״ קברות התאוה כז״ מסרות מא״ ערבת מואב
יד״ חצרת כח״ בני יעקן

Commentaries

Dr. Kyung Bae Min, Th.D.
Distinguished Professor of Baekseok University
Honorary Professor of Yonsei University

I am grateful for this opportunity to share my thoughts regarding the work of our most honorable and respected pastor, Rev. Abraham Park.

Rev. Park is not the author of many books, yet in this remarkable book I saw his profound ability to write. This book explains the reason for his great ministry and the large church that he pastors, the Pyung Kang Che-il Presbyterian Church. I could not help but think it would be a shame if he does not put more of his great work in writing.

From the beginning pages of this book's profound message, my reaction was tearful prayers and thanksgiving. As I continued to read each page, I was assured, time and time again, that this book, its style and writing, manifests a careful study of the Scriptures and was penned by someone who possesses a profound, in-depth understanding of the Bible. I thought that the author surely has spent years in ceaseless meditation and prayer, for each page is filled with endless inspiration of love and truth. Rev. Park is a minister who has spent many years on his knees in prayer, reading the Holy Scriptures hundreds of times, studying the Hebrew language, and researching a wide range of theological texts. He completed all these works with the enlightenment of the Holy Spirit. His writing, page after page, is typified by his complete reliance on the Holy Scriptures. His writing is candid, absent of contrite and useless citations of other works or illustrations. It illuminates the fact that the gospel and message of salvation given to the church cannot be explained by anything other than the canon of the Holy Scriptures. It is rare to find writing like his, containing such a magnanimous message of truth and purity in every carefully selected word. This work is a masterpiece of clarity and truth rarely found in our time. This is why I boldly assure the reader that this book will remain a timeless work that warrants a place on the bookshelves of every church and university.

Rev. Park's knowledge and understanding of the Bible are incomparably profound. All the verses of the Bible seem to be chronologically indexed in his mind—like a vein in the Holy Scripture's inexhaustible gold mine that he has fully mapped. Rev. Park has the uncanny ability and insight to select the most appropriate text that will link and connect the most profound and complex passages that explain God's truth.

Another facet of this book that caught my attention is that it is well organized, written in a form that it is easy to follow and is filled with the fruit of his studies from as early as 1968. He has also shared this message and this method of study since 1983 through his preaching and ministry both at home and abroad. This book is the result of fifty wonderful years during which his ministry developed and has been supported by over forty years of prayer and extensive meditation. In this light, this book is a solemn notice to our academic world.

My description of this book's core value begins here. I had once given the excuse that I would have to think about writing a review of this book because I thought it impertinent for a "historical theologian" to write a review on a book that deals extensively with "biblical theology," and especially because it deals with Genesis and Old Testament theology. Nonetheless, to my own amazement, as I read the book, I saw that it is truly a work that ought to be deemed the "Magna Carta" of historical theology. The historical interpretations in this book spotlight the beauty of depth and insight found in the pages of the biblical commentary. I do not say this merely because I am a historical theologian, but because I found that the very premise and method of study for historical theology, its actual history, acute discernment of historical writing, and its descriptions are clearly evident in this book. This is a new revelation into the study of biblical history. Surely, this book sets a new precedent for all future studies of such history. I found this explicitly typified in the first three chapters.

What is even more astounding to me is that Deuteronomy 32:7-8 is the verse that I have always considered as the premise of all of my studies of history. This is the very Scripture verse that Rev. Park has used for the heading of part 1: "Remember the days of old; consider the years of all generations. Ask your father, and he will inform you, your elders, and they will tell you."

Rev. Park considers this verse as the landmark for this book, and it is a grand premise for his writings of history and theology as well. I have never read any of Rev. Park's writings prior to this occasion, and I am sure that most probably he has never read any of mine. Even if he has, I doubt that he would so easily find where I had made mention of this verse, since it was only a minute part of my work. Therefore, my heart was struck with admiration and wonder when I saw this verse used as the pillar of his work.

With this in mind, you may now understand why I could not put this book down, but read it through again and again. As I reflect back on my initial thoughts about this book, I realize that I would have been greatly disappointed if I had not been asked to write a review of such a great work. Even more disappointing would have been if readers also missed the chance to hear this important message from a person such as I, who has many great things to say about it. Although it may not have been the original intention of the author, this book introduces an innovative method and system of study that qualify it as a model for any study of biblical history in modern times. It is truly a Christian representation of historical philosophy.

The full title of this book is *The Genesis Genealogies: God's Administration in the History of Redemption*. The author affirms that the Book of Genesis is not only an introduction to the entire Bible, but also a blueprint of the history of the redemption of mankind and the world. In this illuminating view of the Genesis account, Rev. Park sees a picturesque and compact version of the Bible—a "micro-Bible." It is like a biblical parallel to the principle of modern biogenetic theory claiming that the development of a microscopic stem cell taken from flesh or bone can become the seed for recreating an entire body. He also purports that a thorough understanding of Genesis will uncover the mysteries of the redemptive history of mankind found elsewhere throughout the Holy Scriptures. Hence, this book can also be properly called "God's Work of Salvation as Viewed through the Genesis Genealogies." It truly is a work that deals with more than just the origin of creation, or Genesis, for it logically organizes the insight of God's work of redemptive history from the Scriptures.

Rev. Park states that faith comes from the past. He argues that the "days of old" refers to a history of God's love and compassion, including the entire process of His redemptive work. These words of wisdom pierce the soul and the core of the Scriptures. To Christians who would view the relationship between faith and history as the central theme of the Word as found in the Scriptures, the entire Bible can be defined as God's "history book." However, many may never have considered this vital point. It may have been avoided in theological discussions due to its relativity and presumed earthliness. The fallacy of pietistic theology, if there is any, is the belief that salvation comes from isolation or alienation from the world. Nonetheless, it is clearly revealed and explained in this book that salvation and God's providence are fulfilled in our day-to-day lives. In other words, this book does not treat faith as mere religious ritual, but makes it widely applicable to everyday life. This is the fulfillment of the long-cherished desire of Kwang Soo Lee, who in 1917 desperately hoped that the Korean church would adopt such thought and reflection. Thus, I say that this book is truly an achievement and work worthy of praise.

Rev. Park discovers the great foundation of historical salvation and redemption from the genealogies of the patriarchs. From his studies, he is able to distinguish God's redemptive plan in the hundreds of years in which each patriarch lived. Furthermore, the manner in which he precisely interprets the names of the patriarchs from the source language is most fascinating; he reveals how the names and their meanings are directly related to the historical circumstances of each patriarch's era. I could not help but marvel at his skill in subtly applying this new and fresh method of analogy. This perspective allows his readers to view the stories of the patriarchs as an archetype, not just in light of the stories of their lives, but in their connection to the current generation in our history. The intimacy between the message of the Bible and our reality cannot be explained any more vividly than this. Turning the Bible into a book that is "my story" is the outstanding achievement of this book.

The author unravels the mystery of God's work of redemptive history by connecting each of the many patriarchs' lives, one by one. This brings one to the conclusion that salvation is not accomplished either by accident or interruption. Rather, this kind of historical interpretation confirms that biblical history is a continually developing story in which salvation is fulfilled through a gradual progress, not by sudden change. Rev. Park construes this gradual progress in the revelation that

Ezekiel saw by the river Chebar, in which living water trickles from the temple of God, gradually becoming a stream of water, then a river, then a much greater river, and finally a sea. This interpretation allows us to view eschatology as a completion of redemptive history fulfilled in the glorious return of our Lord rather than a fearful judgment that comes abruptly at "the end time." Blessed with this understanding, one can look forward with thanksgiving and praise to the eschatological grace and blessings that are to come. This message reaffirms a gospel that marks Christianity as the religion of thanksgiving, joy, and bright hope. Simultaneously, it is an indirect exclamation of history on earth that exemplifies God's history of life and blessings.

Through devout faith and theology, the author has truly accomplished the great work of overlapping redemptive history with the history of the secular world. This surmounts the early Augustinian dichotomy of redemptive history and secular history that separated Christianity and the secular world. It is a monumental achievement of orthodox theology that avoids schismatic and mystical seclusion. It is amazing that this fact has been excluded from the customary studies of Genesis. If history progresses in a linear path and comes to its completion in the second coming of the Lord, then that in itself can become a general system for sacramental and incarnational theology, which are the mainstream theologies today. This belief is accurately highlighted and exalted in this book as the very foundation of the Christian faith, just like the meaning of Rev. Park's title "Hui Sun": the English meaning for *Hui* is "light" or "to shine," and *Sun* is "to spread," "to provide," or "to declare." It is essential for the Korean church to enhance, embrace, and adopt this kind of theology.

This book not only is a guide that takes us into the marvelous depths of the Holy Scripture, but also it will be a time-honored work of achievement and deserves attention from the Korean church for its great accomplishment in the theological and biblical study of the genealogies of Genesis.

Dr. Nam Sik Kim, Th.D.
Chief Editor of Kidok (Christian) Times
Visiting Professor of Chongshin University
Director of the Counseling Missions Research Center of Korea
President of the Presbyterian Church Korea History Association

A book is a summarization of the author's beliefs. It expresses the author's set of beliefs, knowledge, and ideologies, thus becoming the criterion upon which the author receives praise or criticism. An assessment of a person should be based upon primary sources such as his book, thesis, or other writings, not upon secondary sources, for those only serve to assist. I am not an acquaintance of the author. Not only have I not met him, but also I have not seen him from a distance or heard any recordings of his sermons. The only knowledge I had about him was from what I gathered from hearsay.

Coincidentally, I had the opportunity to read this book. Unlike other times, I assumed a critical attitude in reading this book, making underlines as I read. I read carefully and critically with curiosity. I thought, "What could he be saying in this book that is causing so many rumors about him?"

I would like to summarize the characteristics of this book in a few points. First, the book interprets the Bible from the perspective of God's work of redemption. The history of mankind is unfolding according to God's providence and plan for the redemption of mankind. Emphasizing this point, the author narrates the entire book from the perspective of God's work of redemption, in line with the title of the book. This is a clear expression of the author's creed and an indication of the philosophical foundation that he believes and follows.

Second, the author promotes proper understanding of the Book of Genesis. Genesis is the introduction to the Bible, and is the gateway to the study of the Bible. The author chose to explore the core of Genesis, the genealogies (*toledoth*). The genealogies in Genesis are more than simple chronological records of births and deaths, for they work to reveal God's providence for salvation. The author endorses proper understanding of Genesis through his in-depth study of the significance and the flow of the genealogies in view of the history of redemption.

Third, the author allows the Bible to interpret itself. The author indicates in the introduction that he does not intend this book to be "a theological or scholarly piece of work." He is a minister and evangelist. His purpose is not to introduce a theological doctrine, but to introduce subject matters found in the Bible and search for the interpretation within the Bible, which is the most fundamental method of interpretation. There are many books that blur the main point with enumeration of different theories. However, this book brings out the extraordinary from the ordinary by simply following the theme of redemption history and interpreting it through the Bible.

Fourth, the book contains helpful reference inserts. This book introduces other people's views on the subject matter and offers readers the grounds on which to make a proper judgment for themselves. At times, authors tend to assert that their view is the best and foremost, but this book introduces differing views along with the author's standpoint and thus broadens the readers' scope of understanding.

Fifth, the book is written in simple, everyday language. The author explains that the book is a compilation of his sermons. Perhaps this is why the book is written in colloquial style and contains the liveliness of a sermon, as if it were being preached from the pulpit. The language we use to communicate needs to be a language used in daily life, and this book does an excellent job at utilizing the advantages of such method of communication.

The book is soundly structured and well edited. The length of the book has the merit of being adequate for the readers to read without feeling burdened. However, I would like to suggest two places for improvement. First, as I noted, the book is written in colloquial form, but it uses some footnotes. Footnoting is not mandatory in this kind of book, and it could act as a distraction that breaks the book's equilibrium. It may have been better if the book had focused solely on the presentation of the message without using footnotes. Second, I wish that the book were longer. I believe that the book could have provided greater strength to the readers had it been written in greater detail.

I was left with many question marks after reading this book, and I wish to share a few. First, why is the author of this book the object of so much criticism? I too had a preconception about the author acquired from biased information. Nevertheless, I became confused and even bothered with the question of why he became subject to such criticism. For instance, most scholars generally claim that it took Noah 120 years to build the ark, but the book clearly demonstrates, on the basis of the Bible, that it did not take 120 years. I find it regrettable that the truth about an author who attempts to interpret the Bible by using the Bible has been so misunderstood by many people all this time.

Second, why are the critics silent now? This book was first released on October 27, 2007. If there is a problem with this book, the critics should have brought it up and indicated the specific problems with the author's beliefs by now. Why are they so quiet?

Third, is it not time for proper and just assessment to be made? Criticism should be based on the person's primary sources, not upon the basis of someone else's criticism. Although there are impartial critics out there, we cannot deny that there are also many ill-willed critics and those who make criticizing others their profession.

After reading this book, I was struck with disappointment as I realized that the Korean religious community does not make sufficient effort to confront the actual source or subject matter in order to gain proper understanding and make proper assessment of the truth. Furthermore, I find it regrettable that preconceptions, personal relationships, and politics play larger roles as the pivot point of judgment when the Bible, the Word of God, should be the criterion of all judgments.

Now, it is time for us to take the path of reconciliation. God has bestowed upon us the duty to live in harmony (2 Cor 5:18-19; Col 1:20; 1 Thess 5:13). We must reveal what must be revealed and apologize where apologies are necessary, so that we may walk hand in hand toward reconciliation. It is my desire that this book may become the priming factor that draws up the work of reconciliation.

Dr. Young Bae Cha, Th.D.
Former President of the Chongsin University

The Bible is the Word of the living God. If the Bible did not exist, all mankind would remain in darkness without any hope. The Book of Genesis is not only the introduction to the Bible, but also the basis of the principle of salvation recorded throughout the Bible. Without knowing Genesis, we cannot come to understand the core of the Bible. Genesis is composed of ten genealogies (*toledoth*). Thus, by studying these genealogies in Genesis, we can fathom God's will for salvation, which permeates the whole Bible.

This book examines the critically important Genesis genealogies from the perspective of salvation. What a welcoming shock it was to read this book for the first time! I could not contain my surprise, because although Rev. Abraham Park is over eighty years old, the depth of his book exceeds all imagination.

There have been many books, both domestic and international, dealing with the genealogies in Genesis. In many ways, this book stands on par with the other books. However, I regard *The Genesis Genealogies* as unrivaled in the subject of its study. Rev. Park's book chronologically organizes the lives of all the people who appear in the genealogies, from Adam to Abraham. This would have been a difficult task even for the expert theologians in this field of study. Therefore, it is an even greater feat for an aged pastor to organize such a complex genealogy and create an accurate timeline. Furthermore, because the book is Bible-centered and written from the perspective of salvation, Jesus Christ is unmistakably revealed in every corner of the book. Given that the author was able to organize such an extensive and sophisticated subject, it is evident that he has dedicated much time to conduct comprehensive research.

A book reveals an author's ideology. This book clearly manifests the fact that the author's faith is based on the Bible and the gospel. From my reading of *The Genesis Genealogies*, I believe that Rev. Abraham Park is a man of the gospel, and that his faith is sound because it seeks to reveal "only Jesus." This book will help wipe away all the misunderstandings about its author.

It is fortunate for the churches in Korea that a book containing such precious information is receiving the spotlight during increasingly dark times. It is a great blessing from God. I highly recommend this book with the sincere hope that it will become widely read by pastors and laypersons alike, and that it will play a critical role in the movement of the Korean churches' return to the Word of God. I pray for the overflowing blessing from the triune God for all those who read this book.

Dr. Young Yup Cho, Ph.D.
Professor of the Keyak Graduate School of Theology

I offer my sincere congratulations to Rev. Abraham Park for introducing his precious work *The Genesis Genealogies: God's Administration in the History of Redemption* to the church of Korea on this fiftieth year of his ministry.

I got a glimpse of the author's character, faith, and scholastic attitude as I read his introduction, where he says that although this book "may be inadequate as fruit presented before God" and "is certainly not a theological or scholarly piece of work," he asks readers to "read this book with a Christlike heart of understanding, forgive any awkward sentences, and give generous tolerance on any unintended mistakes." He continues, "When Peter asked, 'Lord, how often shall my brother sin against me and I forgive him?' Jesus answered, 'I do not say to you, up to seven times, but up to seventy times seven' (Matt 18:21). I ask that you overlook my shortcomings with the love and mercy of Christ. If anything has been accomplished through this inadequate servant, I confess that it was not the work of this eighty-year-old sinner, but completely the work of the Lord."

I started to read this book with skepticism, wanting to find out and understand who Rev. Park really is because I had come across writings of many people that accuse and criticize him in the United States and in Korea. By scrutinizing this book from the first page to the last, I was able to see that he has critically and accurately studied the Genesis genealogies from the perspective of the history of redemption. Moreover, he has compiled the book in conjunction with the Scripture verses. I believe that this is just one of the examples that show how Rev. Park has a proficient and thorough understanding of the Bible.

I joyfully recommend this book and pray that whoever reads it, whether professor, minister, theological student, or layperson, will be inspired and give thanks for the grace of God's work of redemption and return unto Him all the glory.

Rev. Tae Deuk Lim
Senior Pastor of Dae Myung Church in Daegu
Former Moderator of the Hap-dong General Assembly of the Presbyterian Church of Korea

I wholeheartedly congratulate Rev. Abraham Park, senior pastor of Pyung Kang Che-il Church, for completing and publishing *The Genesis Genealogies* in the year of "Jubilee," denoting fifty years of his ministry. Knowing that leaving behind a book of written words is a far more challenging and difficult task than mere utterances, I believe that this work is the fruit of a pastor who has read the Holy Scriptures hundreds of times.

The Genesis Genealogies chronologically sequences the various figures that appear in Genesis, examines the succession of faith and the succession of disbelief, profoundly probes into the environments and backgrounds of each and every period on the foundation of the Holy Scriptures, and imparts a clear understanding of the difference between Cain's genealogy in the succession of disbelief and Seth's genealogy in the succession of faith. In addition, from the lens of God's redemptive history, the book unravels the legendary course behind the separation of Abraham, the central figure of the Genesis genealogies, from the world, insightfully explaining it based on the Scriptures. Rev. Park's ability to present such profundity in a book that is interesting and easy for anyone to read and understand is truly the culmination of much toil.

The Genesis Genealogies considers the perplexing aspects of the genealogies posed by researchers of the Scriptures. Rev. Park carefully analyzes the confusion surrounding the view that since Noah's flood, man's life span was shortened to 120 years, which many have incorrectly understood as the time period that Noah took to build the ark; it explains this misperception without any bias by analyzing the Scriptures in a way that any layperson can easily understand. This book, partly because of its profound research of the Holy Scriptures, will powerfully convict those who are in doubt.

All these years, due to unjust misconceptions, Rev. Abraham Park has been negatively judged by the Korean Christian community and certain groups of people; this has resulted in a veiling of the truth about him and has thus prevented his faith and character from being known as they should be known. Those who actually meet him and directly witness his ministry often fall in love with the soundness and purity of his faith and with the power of the Word that he preaches as he preaches only of Jesus Christ. He is a man of humility who always speaks of how thankful he is that "such an unworthy man" like himself can serve by preaching the glorious gospel of Jesus Christ beyond his eighty years of age.

Personally, I had always hoped for Rev. Abraham Park's true character to be revealed as it should be; now, through this book, *The Genesis Genealogies*, it will be, albeit partially, known to the world.

I encourage all who desire to live a life of faith centered on the Scriptures, as well those who wish to inherit from the line of godly succession, to read this book many times. Having recognized the fact that the descendants of unbelief will gradually drift away from the realm of God's blessing, and with the sincere hope that those who read this book will continue the genealogy of the godly descendants, I recommend this book with the utmost joy.

Dr. Andrew J. Tesia, Ph.D.
President of the Research Institute of Reformed Theology

Everyone who has received salvation, including laypeople, pastors with a special calling, and theologians, must continue to study the inspired revelation, the Word of God, throughout their lives and apply what they have learned. Just as food is essential for the sustenance of life, this effort is essential for our spiritual survival. Among the various approaches available for correct understanding and application of the Word, total trust and faith in the Word as well as persistent effort and research are imperative. This is an absolute calling that all Christians must respond to in gratitude for the Lord's grace and love. Therefore, all Christians (including pastors and theologians), as debtors to God's grace, must always walk with the Word as the deer pants for the water brooks (Ps 42:1). It is not an easy task to discover a coherent theme and gain penetrating insight on the revealed Word. This is because of the long duration of time, historical circumstances, and the varied experiences and educational backgrounds of the authors during the recording of the inspired Word. It is impossible to comprehend God's profound will with our limited capacity, even through persistent readings and studies of the Word. At the second coming of the Lord, in the last days, when the perfect comes, the partial will be done away (1 Cor 13:10). I sincerely long for the day of the Lord's coming. Maranatha!

Recently, Rev. Abraham Park attempted something that no one has attempted before, through two books: *The Genesis Genealogies* and *The Forgotten Encounter* (soon to be published in English translation). They are sure to astonish the world.

I first met Rev. Park about ten years ago at a world missions conference that I attended through the invitation of my friend Rev. Andrew Phipps. I was greatly blessed as I listened to Rev. Park, through the powerful work of the Holy Spirit, preach vividly about Jesus Christ's suffering and crucifixion. I later heard some negative criticism against Rev. Park, and so I became reserved and watched him from a distance to discern what kind of person he is. Over the past ten years, I have heard his sermons about four times. I was greatly inspired and truly received grace each time I heard his messages. My soul, which had dried up from conventional faith, felt revived, like a fish thrown back into the water. The more I observed Rev. Park, the more I lamented that such a godly and faithful man and true pastor has to go through the frustration of being misunderstood. Then one day, Rev. Phipps gave me two manuscripts that Rev. Park authored. I read them right away. I could not put them down until I finished reading them. They are simply marvelous. After reading them, I was deeply ashamed that I had not completely accepted Rev. Park as a true servant of God. Hence, with an apologetic heart, I write this commentary.

Rev. Park uses the covenantal links to dynamically unfold the enormous biblical discourse, which no one can come close to endeavoring, from the perspective of God's redemptive plan. He logically and perfectly depicts this theme as the central theme of Christian theology as well as the theme of his own faith and theological belief. This surely is the result of his lifelong devotion to prayer and his study of the Word with gratitude for the Lord's grace. He has read the Bible hundreds of times since his calling, and his books are compilations of the Word of God and the spiritual mysteries of the Bible that he was awoken to through the process. Through the two books, we pastors and theologians will have to examine ourselves to see if we have lived our lives fulfilling the tasks we were given. At times, we must lend our ears to his discussions and confront the challenges.

First, by clearly organizing the Bible from the salvation and covenant perspective, Rev. Park has attempted something that has not been attempted during the two thousand years of the church's history. There are countless biblical commentaries and interpretations available. Furthermore, many pastors are studying and preaching the Bible based on various existing theological frameworks, typically those based on Calvinism and orthodox theology founded upon conservative faith. Nevertheless, one cannot help but be amazed at Rev. Park's work, which approaches the Bible, the original text of Christianity, as a great discourse and unfolds it coherently from the covenantal perspective. His two books truly reveal the essence of his immense theological beliefs and the perfect and logical development of his competence. More than anything, it is shocking to see a man of little scholarship (as he confesses to be) explain the profound Word in such a clear and easy way. It is amazing to see how both *The Genesis Genealogies* and *The Forgotten Encounter* are so perfectly arranged and harmonized. The mathematical calculations of the chronological years in history since the time of Adam cause readers to marvel at his immense effort and achievement, although further discussions may be needed as new archaeological discoveries are made. His achievement is truly a stern admonition to pastors and theologians who profess to be what they call "conservative" but have spent and are spending their time in denominational power struggles rather than working to fulfill their God-given tasks! A tearful, contrite heart is required.

Second, Rev. Park is now in his early eighties, but in both *The Genesis Genealogies* and *The Forgotten Encounter* he pours out the spiritual mysteries of the Bible that he was awoken to in a clear, detailed, and powerful literary style. Readers will be overtaken by a magical spell of continuous tension and anticipation that leaves them breathless and motionless. Above all, his literary style has powerful spiritual charisma that attracts the readers' attention. I believe that this is because Rev. Park himself has lived his whole life captured by the Word. Hence, his sermons call to mind the great "Prince of Preachers" who shook up not only England but also all the rest of the world in the mid-nineteenth century, Charles Haddon Spurgeon. Spurgeon was faced with the challenges of a time that was rapidly inclining toward the liberal left, and solitarily he poured out the Word of God into the minds of people through his sermons from the pulpit and his written works. The thousands who congregated at the London Central Baptist Church were captivated by his sermons as they listened breathlessly, with the exception of occasional bursts of acclamation and shouts of joy. The Word of grace that he had received he proclaimed with great strength and zeal, like a spiritual lion's roar. Unfortunately, he spent long, heartbreaking years facing much dissension, misunderstandings, disputes, and refutations. Nevertheless, with conviction in the Word of God, he pushed on with his pastoral ministry, standing firmly upon the orthodox belief of Calvinism.

Language represents one's beliefs. In that respect, Rev. Park may actually be the wizard of language that the Lord has sent to us during these turbid times where the Word of God has become scarce, and good and evil hard to distinguish. Despite his advanced age, his skill and ability to freely narrate the Word of God in his own words stand unrivaled. He is undeniably a faithful servant of God, completely captured by the Word and inspired by salvation.

Third, the foundation of Rev. Park's faith and theology was established through unspeakable suffering and affliction. Through times of trial and isolation he looked only upon God and trusted only in Him. He concentrated solely on faithfully raising his sheep—the congregation entrusted to him. He was captivated by a strong sense of calling and was unable to escape God's hands even for one moment. He spent many years in solitude as a result of unfounded accusations and jealousy. Nevertheless, he fully dedicated himself to the Lord and is a guardian of Calvinism, which holds biblical inspiration in one hand and God's sovereign authority in the other. As is well known, St. Augustine spent his youth in dissipation and pagan philosophy. He was even dedicated to Manichaeism at one time. However, after he met the Lord, he put an end to his old way of life and completely dedicated himself to the Lord. He gave thanks for the grace and love of the Lord of creation and found peace through repentance. Who among us today can criticize him, ostracize him, and condemn him as a libertine or a heretic? The grace and blessings that the church has received through him over the past fifteen hundred years of church history are immeasurable. How his *Confessions* have consoled many Christians, especially those who were struggling! He is considered one of the few preeminent figures of church history. There is no such thing as a perfect person in this world. I find Rev. Park's two books to be as moving as St. Augustine's *Confessions*, and readers will discover a yearning for God burning like an active volcano.

Fourth, the core of Christian theology is the progression from prophecy to fulfillment toward completion through the interpretation of the Bible using the Bible. At the center of this development is the variety of types that appear in the Old Testament, Christ's suffering and crucifixion, and completion through the second coming in the end. Through his great suffering and trials Rev. Park has developed a strong yearning for the return of the Lord and His glory. This is illustrated in his description of the patriarchs from Abraham to Isaac, Jacob, and Joseph, and to Moses and Joshua after the exodus. It will be depicted in greater detail in books to follow. Therefore, his understanding of the biblical history of redemption, which is the covenantal belief, is based completely on the Bible. This is possible because he was educated and trained in a conservative theological seminary and denomination. That is why, even in his advanced age, he has embarked on this great project that no one has dared to attempt. Truthfully, who among us, whether pastor or theologian, can coherently unravel this great discourse?

Rev. Park's well-versed knowledge of God's Word, the Bible, throws a great challenge to theologians whose knowledge is limited to one area of theology, for the Bible needs to be understood thoroughly and in its entirety. Theologians generally are very proficient in the areas of their study and research, but Rev. Park shows his spiritual power and knowledge in all areas of theology, which enables him to freely and appropriately use different parts of the Bible.

This is a lifelong project that Rev. Park has solely endeavored as part of his unyielding vow with God in response to the grace and love that he has received. His head and heart are filled with the Bible and the fervent zeal to think and live with the Word. In this sojourner's world we have discovered an old servant struggling to pour himself out as a drink offering on the Lord's altar, just like the apostle Paul.

Fifth, the well-organized logic and real challenges and applications of Rev. Park's work are distinguished yet natural. The details and motivating power come from his many years of experience and lifelong pastoral ministry.

His applications are concise and entirely based on the Bible. Although he uses very concise and plain language, his sentences contain a concentrated form of theological depth that no other pastor or theologian can mimic. He addresses highly debated issues that even theologians cannot easily address, such as the relationship between Abraham and Jacob, the relationship between Judah and Joseph, and the various themes that develop through Moses' life. His discoveries that the duration of the construction of Noah's ark was less than the well-accepted 120 years and of the forty-two camp sites during the Israelites' wilderness journey are the first of their kind since the time of Noah and Moses. This is a marvelous and celebrated achievement unimaginable even for a scholar who has dedicated his entire life to the study of the Bible and theology.

Unfolding the great discourse using a concise sermon format and storytelling style stands out in the world of theology, which places importance on logic and proof based on scholarship. Rev. Park unravels this discourse smoothly and with the sincerity of a grandfather narrating a story to his grandchild. His thorough insight of the Bible gives him the agility to maneuver through it and the ability to visually illustrate the Old and New Testaments as with a computer. His analysis of heretofore unresolved theological issues can easily be considered a masterpiece.

Finally, what is most urgently needed in all the churches today? Proper understanding of the Bible and its application in life are necessary to overcome the long period of stagnation. This is the goal that the church needs to pursue in the rapidly changing twenty-first century in order to recover the lost glory of old. For this purpose, we must first learn to live out the Word of God, develop our theological awareness, and revitalize the redemptive movement. Frankly, an understanding of the inspired Word of revelation, the Bible, and effective application in life are the universal hope of all pastors. Learning to effectively deliver the Word from the pulpit is a lifelong assignment for pastors. To be able to do this, they must first gain thorough knowledge of the Bible. This knowledge refers not merely to literal interpretation, but also to the ability to see the entire flow and to accurately reveal the meaning of each part. Another crucial task is to shed light on how the revelations of the Bible are fulfilled in history. Paradoxically, we are living in an age where the Word of God is overflowing and scarce at the same time. Thus, we must fathom the depth of God's will through the redemptive and covenantal approach. Thus, I joyfully recommend Rev. Park's *The Genesis Genealogies* and *The Forgotten Encounter* to all the churches of the world, for they not only satisfy the spiritual aspirations of thirsting Christians, but also they are an absolute necessity for those who desire a more mature life of faith. I pray that you read these books once and receive a double portion of blessings.

Bibliography

Allen, Clifton J., ed. *The Broadman Bible Commentary*. Vol. 1. Rev. ed. Nashville: Broadman, 1969.

Alter, Robert. *The Five Books of Moses: A Translation with Commentary*. New York: W. W. Norton, 2004.

Asimov, Isaac. *Asimov's Guide to the Bible*. 2 vols. in 1. New York: Avenel Books, 1981.

Boice, James Montgomery. *Genesis: An Expositional Commentary*. Vol. 1. Grand Rapids: Zondervan, 1982.

Brown, Francis. *The New Brown, Driver, Briggs, Gesenius Hebrew and English Lexicon: With an Appendix Containing the Biblical Aramaic*. Peabody, MA: Hendrickson, 1979.

Calvin, John. *Commentaries on the First Book of Moses Called Genesis*. Vol. 1. Translated by John King. Grand Rapids: Baker, 1989.

———. *Commentaries on the Gospel According to John [1–11]*. Translated by William Pringle Grand Rapids: Baker, 1989.

Cassuto, U. *A Commentary on the Book of Genesis: Part 1, From Adam to Noah*. Translated by Israel Abrahams. Jerusalem: Magnes, 1961.

Cho, David Yonggi. *Commentary on the Genesis I*. Seoul: Seoul Logos, 1996.

Delitzsch, Franz. *New Commentary on Genesis*. Vol. 2. Minneapolis: Klock & Klock Christian Publishers, 1978.

The Grand Bible Commentary: With Comprehensive and Synthetic Exegetical Study Methods. Edited by Disciples Publishing House. 16 vols. Seoul: Bible Study Material Publisher, 1991.

The Oxford Bible Interpreter. Edited by Disciples Publishing House. 130 vols. Seoul: Bible Study Material Publisher, 1989.

Driver, S. R. *The Book of Genesis*. London: Methuen, 1904.

Fausset, A. R. *Fausset's Bible Dictionary*. Grand Rapids: Zondervan, 1949.

Freeman, Travis R. "A New Look at the Genesis 5 and 11 Fluidity Problem." *Andrews University Seminary Studies* 42, no. 2 (2004): 259–86.

Hamilton, Victor P. *The Book of Genesis: Chapters 1–17*. Grand Rapids: Eerdmans, 1990.

Henry, Matthew. *Matthew Henry's Commentary*. 6 vols. Peabody, MA: Hendrickson, 1991.

Holladay, William L. *A Concise Hebrew and Aramaic Lexicon of the Old Testament: Based upon the Lexical Work of Ludwig Koehler and Walter Baumgartner*. Grand Rapids: Eerdmans, 1988.

Kang, C. H., and Ethel R. Nelson. *Discovery of Genesis: How the Truths of Genesis Were Found Hidden in the Chinese Language*. St. Louis: Concordia, 1998.

Kim, Eui Won. *Heaven, Earth, and the Toledoth of the Patriarchs*. Seoul: Presbyterian General Assembly Education Department, 2004.

Kim, Hee Bo. *Patriarchal Fathers in the Old Testament*. Seoul: Presbyterian Theological Seminary Press, 1979.

Kim, Suh Taek. *The Great Flood and the Covenant of the Rainbow*. Seoul: Hong Sung Sa, 1997.

Kim, Sung Il. *Exploring Origin of the Korean Nation: Discovering the Route of the Shemites*. Seoul: Research Institute for Creation History, 1997.

Klein, Ernest. *A Comprehensive Etymological Dictionary of the Hebrew Language for Readers of English*. New York: Macmillan, 1987.

Koehler, Ludwig, and Walter Baumgartner. *The Hebrew and Aramaic Lexicon of the Old Testament: Study Edition*. Vol. 2. Translated and edited by M. E. J. Richardson. Boston: Brill, 2001.

Külling, Samuel R. *Are the Genealogies in Genesis 5 and 11 Historical and Complete, That Is, without Gaps?* Riehen: Immanuel-Verlag, 1996.

Lange, John Peter. *A Commentary on the Holy Scriptures: Genesis*. Translated and edited by Philip Schaff. Grand Rapids: Zondervan, 1893.

Lee, Byung Kyu. *The Commentary on Genesis*. Seoul: Yum Kwang, 1986.

Lee, Sang Kun. *The Lee's Commentary on the Gospel of Matthew*. Seoul: Presbyterian General Assembly Education Deptartment, 1966.

"A Letter to the Readers: [Discoveries at Ebla]." *The Biblical Archaeologist* 40, no. 1 (March 1977): 2–4.

Leupold, H. G. *Exposition of Genesis*. Vol. 1. Grand Rapids: Baker, 1942.

McGee, J. Vernon. *Genesis: Chapters 1–15*. Nashville: Thomas Nelson, 1991.

Morris, Henry M. *The Genesis Record: A Scientific and Devotional Commentary on the Book of Beginnings*. Grand Rapids: Baker, 1976.

Neufeldt, Victoria, ed. *Webster's New World College Dictionary*. 3rd ed. New York: Macmillan, 1996.

Park, Yune Sun. *A Commentary on Genesis*. Vol. 1. Seoul: Yung Eum Sa, 1991.

———. *A Commentary on John*. Seoul: Yung Eum Sa, 1966.

Radmacher, Earl D., gen. ed. *The Nelson Study Bible: NKJV*. Edited by Ronald B. Allen. Nashville: Thomas Nelson, 1997.

Sailhamer, John H. *The Expositor's Bible Commentary with the New International Version*. Ed. Frank E. Gaebelein. Vol. 2. Grand Rapids: Zondervan, 1990.

Sarna, Nahum M. *Genesis: The Traditional Hebrew Text with New JPS Translation*. JPS Torah Commentary. Philadelphia: Jewish Publication Society, 1989.

Speiser, E. A. *Genesis*. Anchor Bible 1. Garden City: Doubleday, 1979.

Spence, H. D. M., and Joseph Exell, eds. *The Pulpit Commentary*. Vol. 1, *Genesis, Exodus*. Peabody, MA: Hendrickson, 2004.

Suh, Chul Won. *The Book of Genesis*. Seoul: Grisim, 2001.

Suk, Won Tae. *A Commentary on Genesis*. Seoul: Gyung Hyang, 2002.

———. *Complete Sermon Collection*. Vol. 2. Seoul: Gyung Hyang, 1985.

Walton, John H. *Genesis*. NIV Application Commentary. Grand Rapids: Zondervan, 2001.

Walton, John H., Victor H. Matthews, and Mark W. Chavalas. *The IVP Bible Background Commentary: Old Testament*. Downers Grove, IL: InterVarsity Press, 2000.

Weingreen, J. *A Practical Grammar for Classical Hebrew*. 2nd ed. Oxford: Clarendon Press, 1959.

Wenham, Gordon J. *Genesis 1–15*. Word Biblical Commentary 1. Waco, TX: Word, 1987.

Wone, Yong Kuk. *A Commentary of Genesis*. Seoul: Se Shin Culture, 1990.

———. *A Dictionary of Biblical Archaeology*. Seoul: Lifebook, 1984.

Reference 2

The Twenty Generations of the Patriarchs

1st **Adam** אָדָם 'Αδάμ	① Adam became the father of Seth at the age of 130. ② He lived 800 years and had other children. He died at the age of 930 (Gen 5:3–5). ③ Adam lived until 56 years after the birth of Lamech, his ninth generation.
2nd **Seth** שֵׁת Σήθ	① Seth was born 130 years after Adam. ② He became the father of Enosh at the age of 105. He lived 807 more years and had other children. He died at the age of 912 (1,042 years after Adam [Gen 5:6–8]). ③ He lived 800 years contemporaneously with Adam.
3rd **Enosh** אֱנוֹשׁ 'Ενώς	① Enosh was born 235 years after Adam. ② He became the father of Kenan at the age of 90. He lived 815 more years and had other children. He died at the age of 905 (1,140 years after Adam [Gen 5:9–11]). ③ He lived 695 years contemporaneously with Adam.
4th **Kenan** קֵינָן Καϊνάμ	① Kenan was born 325 years after Adam. ② He became the father of Mahalalel at the age of 70. He lived 840 more years and had other children. He died at the age of 910 (1,235 years after Adam [Gen 5:12–14]). ③ He lived 605 years contemporaneously with Adam.
5th **Mahalalel** מַהֲלַלְאֵל Μαλελεήλ	① Mahalalel was born 395 years after Adam. ② He became the father of Jared at the age of 65. He lived 830 more years and had other children. He died at the age of 895 (1,290 years after Adam [Gen 5:15–17]). ③ He lived 535 years contemporaneously with Adam.
6th **Jared** יֶרֶד 'Ιάρετ	① Jared was born 460 years after Adam. ② He became the father of Enoch at the age of 162. He lived 800 more years and had other children. He died at the age of 962 (1,422 years after Adam [Gen 5:18–20]). ③ He lived 470 years contemporaneously with Adam.
7th **Enoch** חֲנוֹךְ 'Ενώχ	① Enoch was born 622 years after Adam. ② He became the father of Methuselah at the age of 65. He walked with God for 300 years, had other children, and was transfigured and taken up to heaven without seeing death at the age of 365 (987 years after Adam [Gen 5:21–24; Heb 11:5–6; Jude 14–15]). ③ He lived 308 years contemporaneously with Adam.

8th **Methuselah** מְתוּשֶׁלַח Μαθουσαλά	① Methuselah was born 687 years after Adam. ② He became the father of Lamech at the age of 187. He lived 782 more years and had other children. He died at the age of 969 (1,656 years after Adam [Gen 5:25–27]). ③ He lived 243 years contemporaneously with Adam.
9th **Lamech** לֶמֶךְ Λάμεχ	① Lamech was born 874 years after Adam. ② He became the father of Noah at the age of 182. He lived 595 more years and had other children. He died at the age of 777 (1,651 years after Adam [Gen 5:28–31]). ③ He lived 56 years contemporaneously with Adam.
10th **Noah** נֹחַ Νῶε	① Noah was born 1056 years after Adam. ② He became the father of Shem at the age of 502, and the flood began when he was 600 years old. He lived 350 years after the flood and died at the age of 950 (2,006 years after Adam [Gen 5:32; 9:28–29]). Noah did not have more children after the flood. ③ Noah was born 126 years after Adam's death, so the two men did not meet. ④ The flood occurred 726 years after Adam's death. ⑤ Revelation regarding the flood and instructions for the ark were given after Noah's three sons were married (after Noah was 500 years old [Gen 5:32; 6:10–18]). ⑥ Revelation regarding the date of the flood: 1,656 years after Adam (when Noah was 600 years old), 10th day of the 2nd month. ⑦ Date of the flood = 1,656 years after Adam (when Noah was 600 years old). 17th day of the 2nd month (Gen 7:4, 6–12).
11th **Shem** שֵׁם Σήμ	① Shem was born 1,558 years after Adam (before the flood, when Noah was 502 years old). ② He became the father of Arpachshad at the age of 100 (2 years after the flood). He lived 500 more years and had other children. He died at the age of 600 (2,158 years after Adam [Gen 11:10--11]). ③ Shem lived 448 years contemporaneously with Noah, his father. ④ Shem lived 35 years more after Abraham's death, until Isaac was 110 years old and Jacob was 50 years old. ⑤ Shem experienced the flood at the age of 98 and lived a long life, until he was 600 years of age. He had witnessed the world before the flood, after the flood, and even the judgment of Babel. ⑥ He lived contemporaneously with 15 generations of patriarchs, from Methuselah (the 8th) to Jacob (the 22nd).
12th **Arpachshad** אַרְפַּכְשַׁד 'Αρφαξάδ	① Arpachshad was born 1,658 years after Adam. ② He became the father of Shelah at the age of 35. He lived 403 more years and had other children. He died at the age of 438 (2,096 years after Adam [Gen 11:12–13]). ③ He lived 348 years contemporaneously with Noah. ④ He lived until Abraham was 148 years old and Isaac was 48 years old.

13th **Shelah** שֶׁלַח Σαλά	① Shelah was born 1693 years after Adam. ② He became the father of Eber at the age of 30. He lived 403 more years and had other children. He died at the age of 433 (2,126 years after Adam [Gen 11:14–15]). ③ He lived 313 years contemporaneously with Noah. ④ Shelah outlived Abraham by 3 years, until Isaac was 78 years old and Jacob was 18 years old.
14th **Eber** עֵבֶר Ἔβερ	① Eber was born 1,723 years after Adam. ② He became the father of Peleg at the age of 34. He lived 430 more years and had other children. He died at the age of 464 (2,187 years after Adam [Gen 11:16–17]). ③ He lived 283 years contemporaneously with Noah. ④ Eber outlived Abraham by 64 years, until Isaac was 139 years old and Jacob was 79 years old.
15th **Peleg** פֶּלֶג Φάλεκ	① Peleg was born 1757 years after Adam. ② He became the father of Reu at the age of 30. He lived 209 more years and had other children. He died at the age of 239 (1,996 years after Adam [Gen 11:18–19]). ③ Man's life span was shortened to about half after Eber. Thus, Peleg was the first one to die among the 10 generations after the flood. ④ He lived 239 years contemporaneously with Noah.
16th **Reu** רְעוּ Ῥαγαύ	① Reu was born 1,787 years after Adam. ② He became the father of Serug at the age of 32. He lived 207 more years and had other children. He died at the age of 239 (2,026 years after Adam [Gen 11:20–21]). ③ He lived 219 years contemporaneously with Noah.
17th **Serug** שְׂרוּג Σερούχ	① Serug was born 1,819 years after Adam. ② He became the father of Nahor at the age of 30. He lived 200 more years and had other children. He died at the age of 230 (2,049 years after Adam [Gen 11:22–23]). ③ He lived 187 years contemporaneously with Noah.
18th **Nahor** נָחוֹר Ναχώρ	① Nahor was born 1,849 years after Adam. ② He became the father of Terah at the age of 29. He lived 119 more years and had other children. He died at the age of 148 (1,997 years after Adam [Gen 11:24–25]). He lived the shortest life among all 20 generations of patriarchs. ③ He lived 148 years contemporaneously with Noah.

19th **Terah** תֶּרַח Θάρα	① Terah was born 1,878 years after Adam. ② He became the father of Abram at the age of 70. He lived 135 more years and had other children. He died at the age of 205 (2,083 years after Adam [Gen 11:26–32]). ③ He lived 128 years contemporaneously with Noah. ④ Although Shem (11th), Shelah (13th), and Eber (14th) outlived Abraham (20th), his father, Terah (19th), died 40 years before Abraham.
20th **Abraham** אַבְרָהָם 'Αβραάμ	① Abraham was born 1,948 years after Adam. ② He became the father of Isaac, the covenantal son, at the age of 100. He died at the age of 175 (2,123 years after Adam [Gen 17:1–22; 21:5; 25:7]). ③ He lived 58 years contemporaneously with Noah. ④ Within the 10 generations after Noah: – Patriarchs who died before Abraham: Arpachshad, Peleg, Reu, Serug, Nahor, Terah. – Patriarchs who died after Abraham's death: Shem (outlived him by 35 years), Shelah (outlived him by 3 years), and Eber (outlived him by 64 years).

Contemporaneous Years

This chart uses the expressions "He lived [number of] years contemporaneously with Adam" for the prediluvian (before the flood) patriarchs and "He lived [number of] years contemporaneously with Noah" for the postdiluvian (after the flood) patriarchs. This suggests that there may have been correspondence between the patriarchs although they may not have lived in the same region or dwelling place.

It is most probable that the first ancestor of the prediluvian patriarchs, Adam, and the first ancestor of the postdiluvian patriarchs, Noah, continuously shared God's love and delivered the gospel to their descendants. It is important to note that Adam, who had experienced the world before and after sin, and Noah, who had lived through the circumstances leading to the flood, the actual judgment, and its consequences, were living in the same time period as their direct descendants. This leaves room for the conclusion that these two ancestors had great influence on the faith of their descendants. Adam lived until Lamech was fifty-six years old, and Noah lived until Abraham was fifty-eight years old.

The Duration of the Ark Construction

In general, commentaries and expositions on the Book of Genesis assert that the construction of Noah's ark took 120 years. The following is a collection of excerpts in support of the view that the duration of the construction of the ark was 120 years.

"120 years were sufficient time for constructing the ark."

The Grand Bible Commentary: With Comprehensive and Synthetic Exegetical Study Methods. Edited by Disciples Publishing House (Seoul: Bible Study Material Publisher, 1991), 1:400

"The fact that the construction period for the ark was 120 years. . . . "

Won Tae Suk, *A Commentary on Genesis* (Seoul: Gyung Hyang, 2002), 95

"Noah built the ark for 120 years according to God's command" [Gen 6:3].

Won Tae Suk, *Complete Sermon Collection*, vol. 2 (Seoul: Gyung Hyang, 1985), 350

"During the long period of 120 years, all eight members of Noah's family (Gen 7:7–13) put their strengths together to complete the ark, the great vessel, according to God's blueprint. . . . They built the ark for 120 years according to God's command."

David Yonggi Cho, *Commentary on the Genesis I* (Seoul: Seoul Logos, 1996), 111

"For about 120 years (Gen 6:3) . . . Noah and his sons followed God's instructions and were building a great ship."

C. H. Kang and Ethel R. Nelson, *Discovery of Genesis: How the Truths of Genesis Were Found Hidden in the Chinese Language* (St. Louis: Concordia, 1998), 113

"A ship is not something that can be built in 1 or 2 years. I would think that it took all 120 years."

Suh Taek Kim, *The Great Flood and the Covenant of the Rainbow* (Seoul: Hong Sung Sa, 1997), 207

"God has always been long-suffering, even under such awful conditions as prevailed in the days of Noah (1 Peter 3:20). Though all had rejected Him, He still granted 120 years to mankind in light of the bare possibility that at least some might 'come to repentance' (2 Peter 3:9). This was more than adequate time even for those who were infants to grow to maturity and have abundant opportunity to accept or reject God."

Henry M. Morris, *The Genesis Record: A Scientific and Devotional Commentary on the Book of Beginnings* (Grand Rapids: Baker, 1976), 171

"We believe that Noah preached for 120 years, and during that time the Spirit of God was striving with men."

J. Vernon McGee, *Genesis: Chapters 1–15* (Nashville: Thomas Nelson, 1991), 119

"Nevertheless both ancient and modern Jewish expositors, e.g. Rashi and Reggio, Abenezra and Heidenheim, explain this 120 years of a respite accorded to men for the purpose of obviating by repentance the judgment of extermination."

Franz Delitzsch, *New Commentary on Genesis*, vol. 2 (Minneapolis: Klock & Klock Christian Publishers, 1978), 230–31

"And the period of 120 years becomes one of probation, in the face of every sign that the doom cannot be averted. All of this accords with the separately established fact that the Flood story in Genesis, unlike its Mesopotamian analogues, was morally motivated."

E. A. Speiser, *Genesis*, Anchor Bible 1 (Garden City, NY: Doubleday, 1979), 7

"Accordingly, we prefer to see in this phrase a reference to a period of time that prefaces the Flood's beginning. It is parallel to Jon. 4:5, 'Yet forty days, and Nineveh shall be overthrown.' God's hand of judgment is put on hold."

Victor P. Hamilton, *The Book of Genesis: Chapters 1–17* (Grand Rapids: Eerdmans, 1990), 269

"It is more likely that 'the period of 120 years becomes one of probation, in the face of every sign that the doom cannot be averted' (Speiser, p. 46)."

Clifton J. Allen, ed., *The Broadman Bible Commentary*, vol. 1, rev. ed. (Nashville: Broadman, 1969), 142–43

Despite arguments presented by many scholars, it is clear that Noah did not spend 120 years building the ark. This is a critical issue, since nothing should be added or taken away from the Word of God recorded in the Bible (Rev 22:18–19). For instance, how erroneous would it be to say that Jesus lived on this earth for thirty-five years when it actually was thirty-three years?

When God mentioned the "one hundred and twenty years" in Genesis 6:3, it was His warning against the fleshliness and corruption of mankind and a warning regarding the impending judgment (Gen 6:7). God did not give a revelation about the ark at this time.

After some time had passed, Noah became the father of three sons (Gen 6:10). After some more time had passed, his sons were married. It was only after all this time had passed that God commanded Noah, "Make for yourself an ark" (Gen 6:14), and gave him detailed instructions for the ark (Gen 6:15–16). Then He declared, "And behold, I, even I am bringing the flood of water upon the earth" (Gen 6:17). Noah was 480 years old 120 years before the flood, and that was twenty-two years before he became the father of Shem, his first son (Gen 5:32; 7:7, 11; 11:10).

Calculation of the duration of the construction:

1. Noah was 600 years old when the judgment of the flood occurred (Gen 7:6, 11). Noah gave birth to his three sons after he was 500 years old (Gen 5:32).

2. By the time Noah received the revelation about the ark, Noah's sons were already born to him and were married.

Genesis 6:10 states, "And Noah became the father of three sons: Shem, Ham, and Japheth." Later, in Genesis 6:14, God instructed Noah to build the ark. God gave him the instructions for building the ark and pronounced destruction upon all the living things on the earth (Gen 6:17).

Thus, the ark was built after Noah's three sons were born (after Noah was 500 years old) until Noah was 600 years old, when the flood occurred. This means that the ark was actually built in less than 100 years.

3. Noah's sons were born to him after he turned 500 years old. They were already grown and married when God commanded Noah to build the ark (Gen 6:14).

The New Revised Standard Version of Genesis 5:32 states, "After Noah was five hundred years old, Noah became the father of Shem, Ham, and Japheth." According to Genesis 11:10, Noah was 502 years old when he became the father of Shem. The Bible states that Noah received the revelation about the flood after his sons grew up and were married (Gen 6:18; 7:13). This is when Noah began to build the ark according to God's instructions (Gen 6:22).

4. Since Noah had Shem at the age of 502, we can conclude that it took Noah less than 98 years to build the ark (Noah's age 600 – 502 = 98). The number of years would significantly decrease when the age of Shem upon marriage is taken into account.

Even if Noah had all three sons consecutively, it would have taken him at least three years from the age of 502. His sons would have had to be at least fifteen years of age in order to be married. Considering this, the period for building the ark can be estimated to have been approximately seventy to eighty years. Therefore, the view that it took Noah 120 years to build the ark is erroneous.

Reference 4

The Meaning of the 120 Years in Genesis 6:3

Genesis 6:3 Then the LORD said, "My Spirit shall not strive with man forever, because he also is flesh; nevertheless his days shall be one hundred and twenty years."

וַיֹּאמֶר יְהוָה לֹא־יָדוֹן רוּחִי בָאָדָם לְעֹלָם
בְּשַׁגַּם הוּא בָשָׂר וְהָיוּ יָמָיו מֵאָה וְעֶשְׂרִים שָׁנָה׃

It is generally believed that it took 120 years to build the ark. Where did this number come from? The assertion that Noah built the ark for 120 years seems to be based on Genesis 6:3. However, as noted in Reference 3, the 120 years mentioned in Genesis 6:3 clearly does not refer to the number of years that it took Noah to build the ark.

What, then, do the 120 years in Genesis 6:3 refer to? There are two differing views among theologians regarding this time period.

I. The View That the 120 Years Refers to the Shortened Life Span

The following is a collection of excerpts from scholars who interpret the 120 years as the maximum life span granted to mankind as a result of sin.

"On the other hand, according to 5:32, Noah was 500 years old when he fathered Ham, Shem, and Japhet, and 600 years old when the Flood began (7:6), so some commentators (e.g., Heil, Konig, Kidner) have suggested that 120 years represents a period of grace before the Flood. It may be, however, that the author thought of the 120 years as the maximum life-span that was only gradually implemented; cf. the slow-acting curses of Eden 3:16–19. In the post-Flood period, the recorded ages steadily decline (chap. 11), and later figures very rarely exceed 120."

Gordon J. Wenham, *Genesis 1–15*, Word Biblical Commentary 1 (Waco, TX: Word, 1987), 142

"Because all the descendants of Seth followed the path of the descendants of Cain, God shortened their lives to 120 years as punishment. Though people lived about 200 years just after the Flood, their lives were to be shortened to 120 years thereafter. The words 'his days' mean that the lives of all mankind would be shortened dramatically as in the case of one man."

Chul Won Suh, *The Book of Genesis* (Seoul: Grisim, 2001), 258–59

"The words '120 years' . . . it seems proper to interpret the meaning as the life span of mankind after the Flood and evidence is found in the fact that the life span of mankind gradually shortened so that it eventually did not exceed 120 years."

Yong Kuk Wone, *A Commentary of Genesis* (Seoul: Se Shin Culture, 1990), 152

" . . . the operation of God's life-giving spirit in man crippled by sin; and in future the normal limit of his life shall not exceed 120 years."

S. R. Driver, *The Book of Genesis* (London: Methuen, 1904), 83–84

"The sense of this passage is apparently this: the earliest generations, which were the strongest on account of their nearness to the Divine source, lived almost to a thousand years, the day of the Almighty; but the span of life was diminishing from generation to generation, and in the end would be stabilized at the point where the healthiest person, if he did not suffer illness or any calamity, would be able to live only a little more than a hundred years—a hundred and twenty years according to the round figure of tradition."

U. Cassuto, *A Commentary on the Book of Genesis: Part 1, From Adam to Noah*, trans. Israel Abrahams (Jerusalem: Magnes, 1961), 297–98

"The limitation of 120 years most likely refers to a reduction of the life span of humans."

John H. Walton, Victor H. Matthews, and Mark W. Chavalas, *The IVP Bible Background Commentary: Old Testament* (Downers Grove, IL: InterVarsity Press, 2000), 36

"The sad reality of the narrative, however, is that such long lives do not belong to mankind as a whole but belonged to another age. . . . Henceforth man's life would be 'a hundred and twenty years' only. Such a short life, in comparison with the long lives of the previous chapter, marks man's fall and separation from his Creator."

John H. Sailhamer, *The Expositor's Bible Commentary with the New International Version*, ed. Frank E. Gaebelein, vol. 2 (Grand Rapids: Zondervan, 1990), 77

II. The View That the 120 Years Was a Respite Period for Repentance before the Judgment

The second view argues that the 120 years was a period of respite granted to men before judgment so that they may repent and return to God.

"This does not mean that life span of man was limited to 120 years, but that there would be the judgment of the Flood after 120 years."

"They were given 120 years of opportunity to repent, but they did not obey."

Yune Sun Park, *A Commentary on Genesis*, vol. 1 (Seoul: Yung Eum Sa, 1991), 132–33

"The word 'days' refers to 120 years. It, however, does not signify the period of man's life. It signifies that God reserved the judgment 120 years."

The Oxford Bible Interpreter. Edited by Disciples Publishing House (Seoul: Bible Study Material Publisher, 1989), 1:391

"It means that God would judge 120 years later. . . . If people do not repent during the period of grace given by God, God's judgment will be upon them so that they perish."

Byung Kyu Lee, *The Commentary on Genesis* (Seoul: Yum Kwang, 1986), 86–87

"More likely, this phrase means that God will extend a (grace period) of 120 years before expending His wrath (in the Flood)."

Earl D. Radmacher, gen. ed., *The Nelson Study Bible: NKJV,* ed. Ronald B. Allen (Nashville: Thomas Nelson, 1997) 16

"God has always been long-suffering, even under such awful conditions as prevailed in the days of Noah (1 Peter 3:20). Though all had rejected Him, He still granted 120 years to mankind in light of the bare possibility that at least some might 'come to repentance' (2 Peter 3:9). This was more than adequate time even for those who were infants to grow to maturity and have abundant opportunity to accept or reject God."

Henry M. Morris, *The Genesis Record: A Scientific and Devotional Commentary on the Book of Beginnings* (Grand Rapids: Baker, 1976), 171

"Early exegesis of this verse prefers to see here a reference to the interval of time remaining before the Flood. The figure would then represent three conventional generations of forty years each."

Nahum M. Sarna, *Genesis: The Traditional Hebrew Text with New JPS Translation,* JPS Torah Commentary (Philadelphia: Jewish Publication Society, 1989), 46

"We believe that Noah preached for 120 years, and during that time the Spirit of God was striving with men."

J. Vernon McGee, *Genesis: Chapters 1–15* (Nashville: Thomas Nelson, 1991), 119

"Nevertheless both ancient and modern Jewish expositors, e.g. Rashi and Reggio, Aben-ezra and Heidenheim, explain this 120 years of a respite accorded to men for the purpose of obviating by repentance the judgment of extermination."

Franz Delitzsch, *New Commentary on Genesis,* vol. 2 (Minneapolis: Klock & Klock Christian Publishers, 1978), 230–31

"And the period of 120 years becomes one of probation, in the face of every sign that the doom cannot be averted. All of this accords with the separately established fact that the Flood story in Genesis, unlike its Mesopotamian analogues, was morally motivated."

E. A. Speiser, *Genesis,* Anchor Bible 1 (Garden City, NY: Doubleday, 1979), 7

"Is this an age limit, or is it a period of grace prior to the Flood (i.e., his [remaining] days shall be 120 years)? The first alternative faces the difficulty that most of the people in the rest of Genesis lived well beyond 120 years. It is possible to interpret the longer life spans of the patriarchs as a mitigation or suspension of the divine penalty, just as an earlier announced divine penalty ('on the day you eat of it you shall surely die') was not immediately implanted.

But the (imminent) withdrawal of the divine Spirit as a means of lowering the life span of humanity does not make a great deal of sense. Rather, it seems to presage some event that is about to occur. Accordingly, we prefer to see in this phrase a reference to a period of time that prefaces the Flood's beginning. It is parallel to Jon. 4:5, 'Yet forty days, and Nineveh shall be overthrown.' God's hand of judgment is put on hold."

Victor P. Hamilton, *The Book of Genesis: Chapters 1–17* (Grand Rapids: Eerdmans, 1990), 269

"It is more likely that 'the period of 120 years becomes one of probation, in the face of every sign that the doom cannot be averted' (Speiser, p. 46)."

Clifton J. Allen, ed., *The Broadman Bible Commentary*, vol. 1, rev. ed. (Nashville: Broadman, 1969), 142–43

"For these words, 'yet shall their days be one hundred and twenty years,' are to be taken in the sense of the traditional interpretation: one last period of grace is fixed by God for the repentance of mankind. . . . Before disposing of the guilty ones a time of grace of no less than one hundred and twenty years is allowed for their repentance."

H. G. Leupold, *Exposition of Genesis*, vol. 1 (Grand Rapids: Baker, 1942), 256

"The 120 years was taken by Luther (also Calvin and The Scofield Bible) to refer to a time of reprieve granted by God to mankind before sending the Flood ('I want to give them yet a reprieve of 120 years,' Luther Bible)."

John H. Sailhamer, *The Expositor's Bible Commentary with the New International Version*, ed. Frank E. Gaebelein, vol. 2 (Grand Rapids: Zondervan, 1990), 77

The two differing arguments presented here on the meaning of the "one hundred and twenty years" in Genesis 6:3 are both valid arguments. It is impossible to conclude which argument is right or wrong, for each person interprets the meaning according to his or her own faith. However, one thing is clear. The "one hundred and twenty years" does not refer to the time it took to build the ark. John H. Walton also views the 120-year period as the grace period before the flood and argues that some have unnecessarily concluded that it took Noah 120 years to build the ark. Walton states, "But even if the 120 does represent the time left until the Flood, there is no hint in the text that all of this period was occupied by Noah's building activity."[1]

1. John H. Walton, *The NIV Application Commentary: Genesis* (Grand Rapids: Zondervan, 2001), 296.

Reference 5

Perspective on Cainan

Noah (10th), Shem (11th), Arphaxad (12th), Cainan, Shelah (13th) (Luke 3:35–36)

Arpachshad (Arphaxad), the twelfth generation from Adam, gave birth to Shelah at the age of thirty-five. Arpachshad lived 403 years after giving birth to Shelah and had other children (Gen 11:12–13). In the biblical genealogies, there are four places that state that Arpachshad gave birth to Shelah (Gen 10:24; 11:12; 1 Chr 1:18, 24). In all four places, however, there is no mention of Cainan (Kenan) between Arpachshad and Shelah. This is because Cainan was not recorded in the original Hebrew text. The only place where Cainan is mentioned between Arpachshad and Shelah is in the Gospel of Luke. How should we view this?

I. Cainan is Missing in the Old Testament

1. The genealogy in Genesis 10 lists the patriarchs in the order of Noah, Shem, Arpachshad, Shelah, Eber, and Peleg (Gen 10:1–25). This shows that Arpachshad was the father of Shelah.

> **Genesis 10:24** And Arpachshad became the father of Shelah; and Shelah became the father of Eber.

2. Genesis 11:10–20 also lists Noah, Shem, Arpachshad, Shelah, Eber, Peleg, Reu, Serug, Nahor, Terah, and Abram.

> **Genesis 11:12–13** And Arpachshad lived thirty-five years, and became the father of Shelah; [13]and Arpachshad lived four hundred and three years after he became the father of Shelah, and he had other sons and daughters.

However, the genealogy in the Gospel of Luke includes Cainan. The genealogy in the Gospel of Luke lists the patriarchs in the order of Noah, Shem, Arphaxad, *Cainan*, Shelah, Heber, Peleg, Reu, Serug, Nahor, Terah, and Abraham (Luke 3:34–36).

II. The Relationship between Arpachshad, Cainan, and Shelah

The Old Testament genealogies in Genesis 10:24 and Genesis 11:12–13 omit Cainan, but Luke 3:36 includes him. Since both the Old and the New Testaments are inerrant, we may speculate as follows:

1. **After Arpachshad, the birthright must have been transferred to Cainan and then to Shelah.**

2. **Therefore, it is possible that Cainan and Shelah were twins.**

Of the two sons of Arpachshad, Cainan was the older and Shelah was the younger. Arpachshad fathered both sons probably at the age of thirty-five.

> **Genesis 11:12** And Arpachshad lived thirty-five years, and became the father of Shelah.

Why the difference between the genealogy in Genesis and the genealogy in Luke? Arpachshad's birthright was transferred from the firstborn, Cainan, to the younger son, Shelah. Although there is no mention of this in the Bible, we may conjecture that Cainan committed some sin that caused him to lose his birthright. As soon as he lost his birthright, it was transferred to his brother, Shelah. Interestingly, the apocryphal book *Jubilees* offers the following explanation for how Cainan sinned:

> **Jubilees 8:2–3** And Cainan grew, and his father taught him writing, and he went to seek for himself a place where he might seize for himself a city. [3]And he found a writing which former (generations) had carved on the rock, and he read what was thereon, and he transcribed it and sinned owing to it; for it contained the teaching of the Watchers in accordance with which they used to observe the omens of the sun and moon and stars in all the signs of heaven.

Although we cannot accept all the apocryphal writings as the truth, we can at least conclude that for some reason Cainan had forsaken God and lost his birthright. This is a plausible reason for the omission of his name from the genealogies of the patriarchs.

3. **It appears that the Gospel of Luke recorded the genealogy according to the order of the possession of the birthright: "the son of Shelah, the son of Cainan, the son of Arphaxad."**

The genealogy in Genesis omits the transference of the birthright from Cainan to Shelah and lists Shelah right after Arpachshad.

There are other similar instances in the Bible. For example, Esau and Jacob, twins born to Isaac and Rebekah, experienced a similar struggle. Isaac's birthright rightly belonged to Esau, for he was the firstborn, but Esau despised it and sold it for a bowl of cooked stew (Gen 25:27–34). Furthermore, Jacob deceived Esau and received the blessing of the firstborn (Gen 27:25–40). Based on the transference of the birthright, the genealogy should read: Abraham, Isaac, Esau, Jacob. However, the genealogy in the Gospel of Matthew reads: Abraham, Isaac, Jacob.

With this perspective on Cainan, the inclusion of Cainan in Luke 3 has no impact on the calculations of the genealogies in Genesis 5 and Genesis 11.

Index

Page numbers relating to the Reference 2 table are in Italics.

Reference 1

Chronology of the Patriarchs

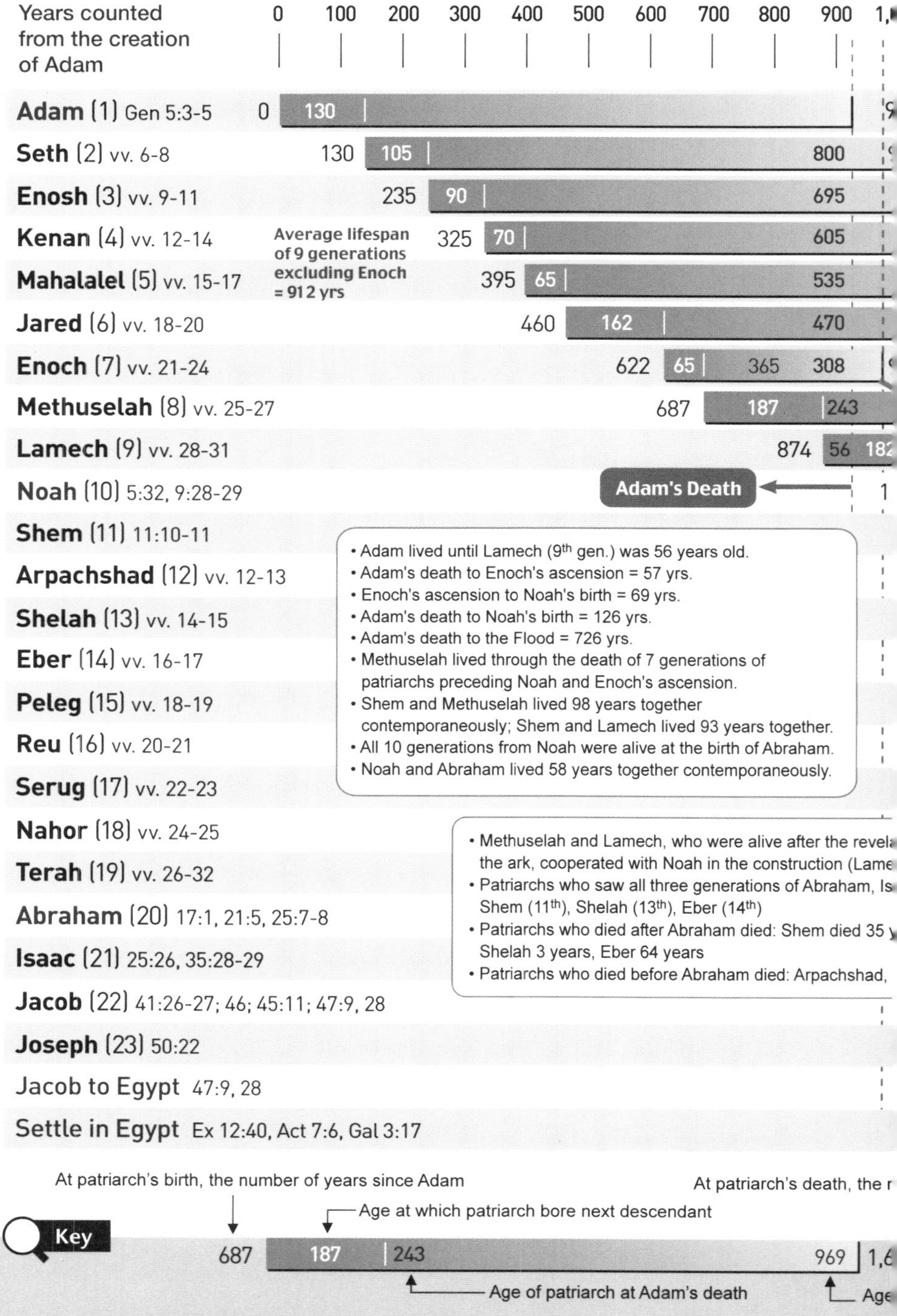

Years counted from the creation of Adam: 0 | 100 | 200 | 300 | 400 | 500 | 600 | 700 | 800 | 900 | 1,

Patriarch	Reference	Birth (years since Adam)	Bar values
Adam (1)	Gen 5:3-5	0	130
Seth (2)	vv. 6-8	130	105 · 800
Enosh (3)	vv. 9-11	235	90 · 695
Kenan (4)	vv. 12-14	325	70 · 605
Mahalalel (5)	vv. 15-17	395	65 · 535
Jared (6)	vv. 18-20	460	162 · 470
Enoch (7)	vv. 21-24	622	65 · 365 · 308
Methuselah (8)	vv. 25-27	687	187 · 243
Lamech (9)	vv. 28-31	874	56 · 182
Noah (10)	5:32, 9:28-29		
Shem (11)	11:10-11		
Arpachshad (12)	vv. 12-13		
Shelah (13)	vv. 14-15		
Eber (14)	vv. 16-17		
Peleg (15)	vv. 18-19		
Reu (16)	vv. 20-21		
Serug (17)	vv. 22-23		
Nahor (18)	vv. 24-25		
Terah (19)	vv. 26-32		
Abraham (20)	17:1, 21:5, 25:7-8		
Isaac (21)	25:26, 35:28-29		
Jacob (22)	41:26-27; 46; 45:11; 47:9, 28		
Joseph (23)	50:22		
Jacob to Egypt	47:9, 28		
Settle in Egypt	Ex 12:40, Act 7:6, Gal 3:17		

Average lifespan of 9 generations excluding Enoch = 912 yrs

Adam's Death

- Adam lived until Lamech (9th gen.) was 56 years old.
- Adam's death to Enoch's ascension = 57 yrs.
- Enoch's ascension to Noah's birth = 69 yrs.
- Adam's death to Noah's birth = 126 yrs.
- Adam's death to the Flood = 726 yrs.
- Methuselah lived through the death of 7 generations of patriarchs preceding Noah and Enoch's ascension.
- Shem and Methuselah lived 98 years together contemporaneously; Shem and Lamech lived 93 years together.
- All 10 generations from Noah were alive at the birth of Abraham.
- Noah and Abraham lived 58 years together contemporaneously.

- Methuselah and Lamech, who were alive after the revel
  the ark, cooperated with Noah in the construction (Lame
- Patriarchs who saw all three generations of Abraham, Is
  Shem (11th), Shelah (13th), Eber (14th)
- Patriarchs who died after Abraham died: Shem died 35
  Shelah 3 years, Eber 64 years
- Patriarchs who died before Abraham died: Arpachshad,

At patriarch's birth, the number of years since Adam

At patriarch's death, the r

Age at which patriarch bore next descendant

Age of patriarch at Adam's death

Age